English Theme Reading

좋은 지문 다 모은

테마영문독해

Living and Health Care

생활과 보건

정연재
중앙대학교 영어영문학과와 같은 학교 대학원 영어영문학과를 졸업하였다.
고등학교 영어교사, 토플·토익 강사로 여러 해 영어를 가르쳤고,
도서출판 고려원 부설 「고려원어학연구원」 원장으로 재직하면서
많은 영어 교재들을 연구하고 개발하였다.
저서로는 《좋은 지문 다 모은 테마영문독해》(전7권)
《좋은 지문 다 모은 주니어 테마영문독해》(전6권)
《TOEFL 초보를 위한 기본독해》《영미문화사전》 등이 있다.

좋은 지문 다 모은 테마영문독해 · 생활과 보건

2009년 5월 15일 발행

편저자 • 정연재
발행인 • 김대현
발행처 • 영어포럼

서울시 영등포구 영등포동 6가 147-7
대표전화 • 02-323-7901 팩스 • 02-323-7902
홈페이지 • www.englishforum.co.kr
등록번호 • 제 318-1999-000125 호
등록일자 • 1999년 2월 2일
English Theme Reading © English Forum 2008
ISBN 978-89-88891-40-7 ISBN 978-89-88891-39-1(전7권)

값 11,000원

좋은 지문 다 모은

테마 영문독해

THEME

English Theme Reading

LIVING AND HEALTH CARE

생활과 보건

정연재 편저

영어포럼

《테마영문독해》를 내면서

지금까지 우리의 읽기 학습은 일부 영역(문화 등)에 치우친 경향이 있었다. 일상어라고 할 때, 그 일상어는 문화 등의 일부 영역의 어휘만을 포함하는 것이 아니라 자연과학, 사회과학, 산업기술, 의학 등 여러 분야의 어휘를 포함한다. 따라서 일부 영역에 치우친 영어 학습은 극히 일상적인 글 예컨대, 간단한 광고문, 인터넷 상의 일반적인 정보, 신문의 가벼운 글 등을 읽는 것조차 부담스럽게 한다. 《**테마영문독해**》는 기존의 독해 학습서들이 가지고 있는 취약점을 극복한 균형 잡힌 독해 학습서이다.

《테마영문독해》는 7권, 26개 영역, 660개 테마로 분류되어 있다.
시험을 준비하는 사람이라면 다양한 영역의 글을 균형 있게 학습해야 하며, 특정 분야의 글을 읽기 위해서 학습하는 사람이라면 어느 한 영역만을 집중적으로 읽을 필요가 있다. 이것이 《**테마영문독해**》가 영역별, 테마별로 분류되어 있는 이유이다.

《테마영문독해》에는 효율적인 독해 방법이 있다.
독해능력을 높이기 위해서는 자기 수준에 맞는, 다양한 글을 많이 읽어야 한다.
초 · 중급 수준의, 영어를 공부하는 사람이라면 한번쯤 읽어야 하는 글을 엄선하여 수록한 것이 《**테마영문독해**》이다.

《테마영문독해》에는 다양한 영역의 지식이 있다.
인류가 축적한 모든 지식을 영역별, 테마별로 골고루 섭취할 수 있어서, 영어 독해력과 함께 다양한 영역의 지식과 교양을 습득할 수 있다. 또한 각 지문에 딸려 있는 〈보너스 상식〉은 영어권 문화를 이해하는 데 좋은 자료가 될 것이다.

한 가지 덧붙이자면, 《**테마영문독해**》에 수록되어 있는 26개 영역의 글들은 결코 전문적인 글이 아니다. 여러분이 토플 · 토익 혹은 수능 등의 시험을 준비하고 있거나 영어로 된 정보를 읽기 위해서 공부하고 있다면, 《**테마영문독해**》는 여러분에게 좋은 교재가 될 것이다. 특히, 토플 · 토익을 처음 준비하는 분에게 《**테마영문독해**》는 유익한 교재가 될 것이다.
《**테마영문독해**》를 공부하면서 중요하다고 생각하는 글을 표시해 두었다가 반복해서 큰소리로 읽고, 테이프를 듣는다면 여러분의 영어 공부에 많은 성과가 있을 것이다.

「정연영어학습법 Jungyun Method」

1. 개념 : 영어의 기본 패턴인 '리듬과 어순을 빨리 효과적으로 습득하는 방법'

2. 영어만의 스타일

① 말 : 음절이나 단어들의 음(sound)이 '강약' (stressed/unstressed), '고저' (high/low), '장단' (long/short)으로 일정하게 조합되는 패턴, 곧 '리듬' (rhythm)에 영어의 특징적인 스타일이 있다.

② 글 : 글의 스타일은 단어의 성격에 따라 나뉘는 '의미어' (meaningful words)와 '기능어' (functional words)가 일정하게 조합되는 패턴 즉, '문장 구조' (sentence structure) 또는 '어순' (word order)이 영어의 특징적인 스타일이다.

▶단어의 분류

1. 의미어(meaningful words)

① 명사, 동사, 형용사, 부사, 의문사 등 의미(뜻)를 가지는 단어이다.

② 문장의 핵심어(key words)가 된다.

③ 강세가 있고(stressed), 고음(high), 장음(long)으로 발음되는 경향이 있어, 뚜렷하게 들린다.

2. 기능어(functional words)

① 관사, 대명사, 전치사, 접속사, 관계사, 조동사, be동사 등이다.

② 스스로 의미를 가지고 있지는 않고, 단어나 문장을 연결해 주거나 의미어를 보조하는 기능적인 단어이다.

③ 강세가 없고(unstressed), 저음(low), 단음(short)으로 발음되는 경향이 있어, 뚜렷하게 들리지 않는다.

3. 문법 학습

① 문법 학습이란 영어의 문장 구조인 어순을 습득하는 과정이다.

② 영어 문장의 어순은 주어가 첫째 자리, 동사가 두 번째 자리를 차지하는 것이 대 원칙이다.
의문문이나 명령문, 도치문 등은 이 어순이 바뀌는 변형문이다.

③ 기능어와 의미어의 조합 과정을 익힌다.

4. 듣기 학습

① 영어를 들을 때 우리말로 옮기려는(통역하려는) 습관을 버린다. 영어를 듣자마자 바로 내용을 연상하는 것이 바른 듣기이다.

② 강세가 있고, 고음, 장음으로 뚜렷하게 잘 들리는 단어가 바로 의미어로, 대화나 말의 내용과 핵심을 이룬다.

③ 기능어와 의미어가 조합된 문장 패턴 속에서 강약, 고저, 장단음으로 이어지는 영어 리듬을 습득한다.

④ 모든 단어의 강세 위치를 반드시 익힌다.

⑤ 녹음된 원어민의 목소리를 반복해서 듣는다.

5. 읽기 학습

① 영문을 읽을 때 우리말로 먼저 번역하는 습관을 버린다. 영문을 읽고 바로 내용을 연상하는 것이 바른 읽기이다.

② 문단의 구조를 습득한다. 문단 내에서 문장들은 논리적 · 시간적으로 일정한 순서로 조합되는데, 이 문장들의 순서(sentence order)를 습득하는 것이다.

③ 습득한 문단 구조를 바탕으로, 의미어 중심으로 훑어 읽는다.(skimming)

④ 6하원칙(when, where, who, what, how, why)을 중심으로 읽는다.

⑤ 필요한 부분만 읽는다.(scanning)

효과적인 영문독해

1. 영문을 읽을 때 우리말로 먼저 번역하는 습관을 버린다. 영문을 읽고 바로 내용을 연상하는 것이 바른 읽기이다.

영어 문장을 눈으로 읽고 우선 우리말을 머리에 떠올린 다음 뜻을 새기는 태도를 고쳐야 한다. 우리는 지금까지 영어를 비롯한 모든 외국어를 우리말로 해석하는 것을 중심으로 학습하는 경향이 있었다. 뜻글자인 한자(또는 한문)를 공부하던 태도와 같이 외국어의 단어나 문장의 뜻을 우리 글로 옮기는 작업을 절대적으로 생각한다. 이것은 말이나 글의 뜻을 새기는 단계를 지나 번역 작업에 치우친 것이다. 우리가 흔히 '해석' 이라고 하는 이 번역 작업은 읽기(독해)와 다르다. 영어 문장을 읽어 나갈 때, 대역되는 우리말 단어를 생각하며 번역 문장을 만들고 나서, 다시 그 의미를 새기는 과정은 '독해' 시간을 오래 걸리게 한다. 눈으로 영문을 보는 즉시 바로바로 의미를 떠올리도록 훈련해야 한다.

'글' 을 읽고 '그림' (의미)을 떠올리는 것이 읽기인데, 중간에 우리말을 끼워넣는 과정을 거치지 말자는 것이다.

2. 문단의 구조를 습득한다.

문단 내에서 문장들은 논리적 · 시간적으로 일정한 순서로 조합되는데, 이 문장들의 순서(sentence order)를 습득하는 것이다. 하나의 주제 아래 통일된 의미를 전달하기 위해 여러 문장들이 일관성 있게 조합된 형식을 '문단' (paragraph)이라고 한다.

이 문단이 구성된 패턴 즉, 문단 구조을 미리 알면 독해를 빨리, 그리고 훨씬 효과적으로 할 수 있다. 다음은 전형적인 문단 구조를 갖고 있는 예이다.

Gold, a precious metal, is prized for two important characteristics. First of all, gold has a lustrous beauty that is resistant to corrosion. Therefore, it is suitable for jewelry, coins, and ornamental purposes. Gold never needs to be polished and will remain beautiful forever. For example, a Macedonian coin remains as untarnished today as the day it was minted twenty-three centuries ago. Another important characteristic of gold is its usefulness to industry and science. For many years, it has been used in hundreds of industrial applications. The most recent use of gold is in astronauts' suits. Astronauts wear gold-plated heat shields for protection outside the spaceship. In conclusion, gold is treasured not only for its beauty, but also for its utility.

— 주제문(subject sentence)

서술문(supporting sentences)

- 논리적 순서(logical order)
- 일관성(coherence)
- 통일성(unity)

— 결론문(concluding sentence)

3. 습득한 문단 구조를 바탕으로, 의미어 중심으로 훑어 읽는다.(skimming)

① 각 단락의 첫 문장과 마지막 문장을 먼저 읽는다. 각 단락의 첫 문장은 그 단락의 주제를 내포하고, 첫 단락의 첫 문장은 글 전체의 주제를, 마지막 단락의 마지막 문장은 대체로 결론을 내포한다. 이때, 자주 등장하는 어구들 (대체로 명사)은 보통 글의 핵심어(key world)이므로 기억해 둔다.

② 초점을 단어 하나하나에 집중하지 않고, 구(phrase) 단위 또는 절(clause) 단위로 훑어 내려가며 시선을 매끄럽게 옮긴다. 중요한 것은 눈에 띄는 어휘를 발견할 때, 되도록 우리 말 단어를 찾지 말고 곧바로 '뜻' (의미)을 연상해야 한다. 머릿속에 떠오르는 그림(내용, 의미)을 붙잡도록 해야 한다. 처음에는 영어 문장들이 무슨 뜻인지 모르지만, 몇 문장을 차분히 그렇게 시선을 옮겨가다 보면 '무엇' (주제 또는 핵심어)에 대해 서술하고 있는지 감이 잡힌다. 즉, 전달받은 어떤 내용이 머릿속에 그림으로 잡힌다.

③ 연결어들을 살펴가면서 읽으면 좀더 정확히 그리고 효과적으로 문맥을 파악할 수 있다.

④ 모르는 단어가 나올 경우, 문장과 문단의 전후 맥락을 통해 그 단어의 뜻을 추측하여 읽는다.

4. 6하원칙(when, where, who, what, how, why)을 중심으로 읽는다.

글을 읽을 때는 늘 6하원칙을 파악한다. 글은 대부분 6하원칙에 의거하여 의사를 전달하므로, 이 6하원칙을 파악하는 것이 곧, 독해의 목적이라 할 수 있다. 독해 문제는 결국 이 여섯 가지 사항을 묻는 문제이다.

5. 필요한 부분만 읽는다.(scanning)

우리는 여러 가지 이유로 글을 읽는다. 영문을 읽을 때도 마찬가지다. 그래서 그 이유에 알맞은 방식으로 글을 읽는 것은 중요하다. 전체를 꼼꼼하게 읽어야 할 필요도 있지만, 필요한 부분만 읽어야 할 경우도 있다. 특히 시험을 준비하는 학습자라면, 문제가 요구하는 답을 찾기 위해 필요한 부분만 읽는 훈련을 많이 해야 한다. 물론 이런 훈련은 시험을 준비하는 학습자에게만 유용한 것은 아니다. 영어 정보를 습득하려는 학습자들에게도 필요한 훈련이다.

Contents

제 1 장 생활 Ways of Living

제 2 장

의약과 식품 Drugs and Foods

제 3 장

보건과 의료 Health and Medicine

제 4 장

환경문제 Environmental Problems

제 1 장

생활 Ways of Living

theme 01 Camping 야영

1 For many people, camping means sleeping in a tent. Some choose to spend the night in a tent in their own backyards. But for most, camping means packing a tent and some food and belongings in a car and driving to a desired camping destination. Tent campers may pitch their tents at state, provincial, or national parks or at privately run campgrounds.

Other people choose to camp using a recreational vehicle (RV). RV's range in size from small trailers to large mobile homes. These vehicles provide living quarters for campers and carry modern conveniences such as sinks, refrigerators, and toilets.

backyárd *n.*뒤뜰 pack *v.* 짐을 꾸리다 belónging *n.* 소지품 desíred *adj.* 바라던 destinátion *n.* 목적지 pitch *v.* (천막을) 치다, 박다, (공을) 던지다 províncial *adj.*지방의 prívately run 사설, 개인이 운영하는 véhicle *n.* 탈 것, 자동차 recreátional véhicle 레저용 자동차(RV) range *v.* (범위가) 미치다 trailer *n.* 트레일러 móbile *adj.* 움직이는, 이동하는 mobile homes 이동 주택 quárters *n.(pl.)* 막사 convénience *n.* 편의 시설

1. Which of the following is <u>not</u> mentioned in the passage as the places where the campers may pitch their tents?

① beach resorts ② national parks
③ privately run campgrounds ④ provincial parks
⑤ state parks

풀이 ① 해수욕장 ② 국립 공원 ③ 사설 야영장 ④ 지방 공원 ⑤ 주립 공원
첫 단락의 마지막 문장에 천막을 칠 수 있는 곳이 열거되어 있다.

보너스 상식!

세계 최장의 캠프 여행

세계에서 가장 오랫동안 캠프 여행을 한 것으로 기록된 사람들은 Harry Coleman과 Peggy Larson으로 2년에 걸쳐 143,716마일을 여행하였다. 1976년 8월 20일에 여행을 떠나 1978년 4월 20일에야 돌아왔다. 두 사람은 113개국을 돌아다녔다.

Cosmetics 화장품

1

Styles in cosmetics are continually changing. Men have often used more perfume, powder, and oils than women. Women painted their cheeks so brightly in the 18th century that the British Parliament passed a law about makeup. The law forbade using cosmetics to catch a husband. In the Victorian period all makeup was frowned upon.

Cosmetics today are used from head to toe and by people of all ages. There are three kinds of cosmetics. One kind can be seen, like lipstick, eye makeup, and nail polish. Another kind is rubbed in or hidden, like hand lotion, perfume, hair dressing, and antiperspirant. A third kind of cosmetic is used during the course of a treatment and is then wiped, rinsed, or rubbed off. Examples are shaving cream, shampoo, mouthwash, and bathing preparations. Soap is not usually considered to be a cosmetic.

cosmétic *n.* 화장품 perfúme *n.* 향수 British Parliament 영국 의회 mákeup *n.* 화장 forbíd *v.* 금지하다(forbid-forbade-forbidden) catch a husband 남편을 유혹하다 frown *v.* 찡그리다, 눈살을 찌푸리다, 불쾌해 하다 nail polish 매니큐어 에나멜 rub *v.* 문지르다, 바르다 hide *v.* 덮다 hair dressing 이발, 미용 antipérspirant *n.* 땀 냄새 억제제 course of treatment 몸 가꾸기 과정 wipe *v.* 닦다 rinse *v.* 헹구다 rub off 문질러 벗겨 내다 shaving cream 면도 크림 móuthwash 양치질 약, 구강 청정제 bathing preparátion 목욕 용품

1. What is the best title for this passage?

① Cosmetics in the Victorian Age
② Men Use Cosmetics, Too!
③ Various Uses of Cosmetics
④ How to Catch a Husband
⑤ Cosmetics, Yesterday and Today

2. Which statement is <u>not</u> true about the passage?

① In Britain there was a law about makeup.
② People care so much for makeup in the Victorian age.
③ Today there are three kinds of cosmetics.
④ Not only women but men use cosmetics, too.
⑤ Shampoo is a kind of cosmetics but soap is not.

theme 02 Cosmetics 화장품

풀이 1. ① 빅토리아시대의 화장품 ② 남자도 화장품을 쓴다. ③ 화장품의 여러 용도
④ 남자를 사로잡는 방법 ⑤ 화장품의 어제와 오늘

2. ① 영국에는 화장에 관한 법률이 있다. ② 빅토리아시대에는 사람들이 화장에 신경을 많이 썼다.
③ 오늘날 화장품에는 3가지 종류가 있다. ④ 여자 뿐 아니라 남자도 화장품을 쓴다.
⑤ 샴푸는 화장품의 일종이지만, 비누는 아니다.

보너스 상식

클레오파트라와 화장

이집트의 클레오파트라는 피부를 아름답게 하려고 우유로 목욕을 하고 이상한 향수를 사용하였다고 한다. 그녀는 눈썹과 속눈썹을 검게 칠하였다. 눈꺼풀은 검은 청색으로, 아래쪽은 초록색으로 화장을 하였다.

Dreaming 꿈 03 theme

1 Nightmares are experienced by almost everyone. They are long, frightening dreams that appear to be very lifelike. The dreamer may dream, for example, of monsters, wild animals, dangerous people, running from danger, or falling from a cliff or out of a tree. Sometimes normal, everyday objects become frightening parts of such dreams.

Nightmares usually occur during the last several hours of nighttime sleep. They are usually more frequent when a person is under stress and may also occur during traumatic events such as war. Nightmares are also more common during childhood. At least half of all children experience them.

níghtmare *n.* 악몽 fríghtening *adj.* 무서운, 끔찍한 lífelike *adj.* 실제 같은 mónster *n.* 괴물 cliff *n.* 벼랑 be under stress 스트레스를 받다 traumátic *adj.* 정신적 쇼크의, 잊지 못할

1. According to the passage, nightmares usually occur **except** which of the following?

① During childhood
② During the last several hours of nighttime sleep
③ During traumatic events such as war
④ When a person is under stress
⑤ When a person takes a nap

2. According to the passage, nightmares are more likely to be dreamed by ____________.

① housewives
② travelers
③ children
④ comedians
⑤ mountaineers

theme 03 Dreaming 꿈

풀이 1. ① 어린 시절 ② 밤잠의 후반 몇 시간 동안 ③ 전쟁 같은 잊지 못할 사건 동안 ④ 스트레스를 받을 때 ⑤ 낮잠을 잘 때
둘째 단락의 모든 문장들이 답지로 옮겨졌다. 하나씩 대조한다.
2. ① 가정주부 ② 여행자 ③ 어린이 ④ 코미디언 ⑤ 등반가

보너스 상식

꿈(dream)

잠을 자고 있을 때 눈동자가 이리저리 빨리 움직이는 것은 바로 그 사람이 꿈을 꾸고 있는 것이라고 한다. 신체는 잠을 들었지만, 뇌가 잠들지 않고 사고 활동을 계속 하는 것이 꿈이다. 어떤 사람들은 꿈을 꾸지 않는다고도 한다. 보통 사람들은 하루 8시간의 수면중에 1~2시간 정도 꿈을 꾼다.

1 The first clothes were probably made just to protect people from the cold. But men and women soon wanted their clothes to be more than practical: they wanted them to be beautiful, too. The more advanced a society became, the more attention was paid to the manner of dress. By the time the Egyptians had built the great pyramids, grooming was as important as it is today.

Until recently, beautiful clothes were made by hand. They were usually elaborate and always expensive. Fashion was for the royal, the rich, and the famous. Now mass production has made stylish clothes available to almost everyone. The modern fashion business—from the design room to the store window—is one of the busiest, most imaginative, and most glamorous activities in the world.

advánce *v.* 발전하다 pay attention to ― ~에 관심을 주다 manner of dress 의상 양식 groom *v.* 가꾸다, 단장하다, (옷을) 차려입다 eláborate *adj.* 정교한 the royal 왕족들 the rich 부자들 the famous 유명 인사들 mass production 대량생산 stylish *adj.* 멋진 glámorous *adj.* 매력적인

1. According to the passage, which of the following might probably be the main purpose of the first clothes?

① beauty ② business
③ manner ④ practicality
⑤ royalty

풀이 ① 아름다움 ② 산업 ③ 태도 ④ 실용성 ⑤ 왕권
'초기 의복'의 목적은 첫 문장과 둘째 문장에 제시되어 있다.

보너스 상식

모직(wool)의 역사

양이 처음 가축으로 길러진 석기 시대 후반에 모(毛)를 이용한 흔적이 있다. 5,000년 전 고대 바빌로니아인들은 모를 직조하여 옷을 만들어 입었다고 한다.

theme 04

Fashion 패션

2 One basic element of good fashion is good grooming. The most stylish clothes will not look good on someone who does not have good posture. Another important element is individuality. The clothes of a well-dressed person reflect that individual's personality. To be fashionable it is essential to know what is becoming—which silhouette, fabrics, and colors are most flattering. For instance, short people often choose clothes that make them look taller, while some tall people want to draw attention away from their height.

grooming *n.* 차림새 pósture *n.* 자세 individuálity *n.* 개성 refléct *v.* 반영하다 personálity *n.* 인격 what is becoming 어울리는 것 silhouétte *n.* 실루엣, 옷의 모양 fábric *n.* 섬유 fláttering *adj.* 돋보이는 draw – away from – ~에서 ~을 돌리다 height *n.* 키

1. Which is <u>not</u> mentioned in the passage as the elements of good fashion?

① colors ② grooming
③ height ④ individuality
⑤ silhouette

풀이 ① 색상 ② 차림새 ③ 키 ④ 개성 ⑤ 옷의 모양
패션의 3요소는 silhouette, fabrics, colors 이다.

보너스 상식!

패션 디자인의 3요소

① 실루엣(silhouette) : 옷의 모양(shape)
② 직물(fabric) : 옷감의 종류
③ 색상(color)

Fire Prevention 화재 예방

05 theme

1 Few things are more frightening than catching on fire. Reacting in fear, however, can kill or leave scars that last a lifetime. When a person catches on fire, a normal reaction is to run. But this will only make the fire worse. There are three things to remember: stop, drop, and roll. If your clothing catches fire, immediately stop moving, drop to the ground, and roll over and over to extinguish the flames. Cover your nose and mouth with your hands. A bystander who knows what to do could help roll and cover a person on fire with coats or blankets until the fire is out. The fire must be completely out before stopping because flames might be smoldering beneath the clothing. If injury results, emergency care should be sought immediately.

fríghtening *adj.* 무서운 catch on fire 불붙다 reácting *n.* 반작용, 반응 in fear 겁에 질려 scar *n.* 상처, 흉터 roll *v.* 구르다 over and over 계속해서 extínguish *v.* (화재를) 끄다 flame *n.* 화염 bystander *n.* 구경꾼(= looker-on) smólder *v.* 연기가 나다 ínjury results 다치다 seek *v.* 찾다(seek-sought-sought)

1. When a person catches on fire, you should <u>not</u> do which of the following?

① cover with coats ② drop
③ stop ④ roll
⑤ run

풀이 ① 코트로 덮는다 ② 눕는다 ③ 멈춰 선다 ④ 구른다 ⑤ 달린다
이 글에는 3가지 동작과 함께 담요나 코트로 덮어주라는 설명이 있다.

보너스 상식

화재에 관한 진실

1. 화염은 보기보다 매우 뜨겁다. 실제로 1000°F (538℃)까지 쉽게 올라가 모든 것을 순식간에 태운다.
2. 화재 시에 사람을 죽게 하는 것은 화염이 아니라 연기와 독가스이다.
3. 화재는 영화처럼 밝고 환하지 않다. 실제로는 너무 어두워서 아무 것도 보이지 않는다. 그래서 출구를 찾지 못하고 죽는 경우가 많다.
4. 화재가 번지는 것은 순식간이므로 탈출할 시간은 매우 적다.

theme 05

Fire Prevention 화재 예방

2 Cooking fires can be avoided by watching food while it cooks and by using timers that alert the cook or that automatically turn off ovens or electric skillets. A large lid and an appropriate fire extinguisher kept near the stove can be used to put out grease fires by a person who knows how to use them. Keep the exhaust fan over the stove free of excess grease and dirt. __________ loose clothing should not be worn near cooking sources, and curtains or dishcloths should not be placed close to open flames or electric burners. Outdoor grills should never be used indoors or in carports or garages.

cooking fire 요리 화재 avóid *v.* 피하다 alért *v.* 경보하다 turn off (스위치를) 끄다 skíllet *n.* 프라이팬 lid *n.* 뚜껑, 덮개 apprópriate *adj.* 적당한 fire extínguisher 소화기 put out (화재를) 끄다(= extínguish) gréase *n.* 기름, 유성 물질, 윤활유 gréase fire 유성(油性) 화재 exháust *n.* 배기, 배출 excéss *adj.* 지나친, 초과하는 loose clothing 헐렁한 옷 cooking source 조리대 díshcloth *n.* 행주, 접시 닦는 천 cárport *n.* 간이 차고 garáge *n.* 차고, 창고

1. Which of the following is the best title for the passage?

① Appropriate Fire Extinguishers ② Cooking Sources
③ Kinds of Cooking Fires ④ Prevention of Cooking Fires
⑤ Watching Food

2. Which way is <u>not</u> proper for preventing cooking fires?

① Using timers
② Keeping a large lid near
③ Keeping the exhaust fan clean
④ Wearing loose clothing
⑤ Watching food carefully

3. What is suitable for the blank?

① In addition,
② Ultimately,
③ Namely,
④ Hence,
⑤ Nevertheless,

풀이 1. ① 적당한 소화기 ② 조리대 ③ 요리 화재의 종류 ④ 요리 화재의 예방 ⑤ 음식을 지켜보기
첫 문장에서 유추할 수 있다. 'Cooking fires can be avoided by ...'와 같은 뜻의 제목을 찾는다.
2. ① 타이머 사용 ② 커다란 덮개를 근처에 둘 것 ③ 환기팬을 깨끗이 보관할 것
④ 헐렁한 옷 입기 ⑤ 음식을 잘 살필 것
3. ① 게다가 ② 결국 ③ 즉 ④ 그러므로 ⑤ 그럼에도 불구하고

보너스 상식

화재의 등급(미국)

① A급 화재 : 나무나 쓰레기, 종이 등 일반적인 연소 물질의 화재
② B급 화재 : 석유, 타르, 그리스(greases), 휘발성 페인트, 라커(lacquers), 플라스틱 등 인화성 액체의 화재
③ C급 화재 : 가전제품, 전선, 퓨즈 박스, 라디오, 텔레비전 등 전기제품의 화재
④ D급 화재 : 칼륨(potassium), 나트륨(sodium) 등 주로 연소 가능한 금속에 불이 나는 산업 설비의 화재

theme 06 Fishing 낚시

1

Most spin-casting reels mount on top of the rod like bait-casting reels, although a few mount underneath. Below the rod handle is a small protrusion called a trigger. Grasp the handle with your index finger on the trigger and your thumb resting on the line-release button at the back of the reel. As in bait-casting, the rod and reel should be at a comfortable angle, about 45 degrees.

The execution of the cast is similar to that of bait-casting and spinning. The difference is in how the line is controlled. In spin-casting, the line is released by depressing the line-release button with your thumb. To stop it, release the button by raising your thumb.

spin casting 제물 낚시(로 하는 던질 낚시)질 reel *n.* 얼레, (낚싯대의) 감개, 릴 mount *v.* (미끼가) 달리다, 달다 bait *n.* 미끼 bait-casting 미끼 낚시 rod *n.* 낚싯대 rod handle 낚싯대 손잡이 protrúsion *n.* 돌출부 trígger *n.* 방아쇠 grasp *v.* 움켜쥐다, 잡다 índex finger 검지 thumb *n.* 엄지 rest on — ~에 두다, 자리잡다 line-release button 낚싯줄을 풀어 주는 버튼 execútion *n.* 실행 depréss *v.* 내리누르다

1. Which of the following does the passage mainly discuss?

① boating ② fishing
③ hang gliding ④ hunting
⑤ swimming

풀이 ① 보트 타기 ② 낚시 ③ 행글라이딩 ④ 사냥 ⑤ 수영
이 글에 등장하는 spin casting, bait casting, reels, rods 등의 도구들을 통해서 유추할 수 있다.

보너스 상식 낚시 미끼의 종류

① 농어(bass) 낚시 : 지렁이(worms), 피라미, 메뚜기(grasshoppers), 새우, 개구리
② 송어(trout) 낚시 : 지렁이, 연어알, 애벌레 새우, 피라미, 메뚜기
③ 메기(catfish) 낚시 : 지렁이, 물고기 살, 냄새나는 미끼

Hair and Hairstyling 모발과 헤어스타일

07 theme

1 Clean hair feels better, looks better, and even smells better. Perspiration mixed with hair oil can make hair look greasy and stringy. To keep your hair fresh and shiny, shampoo often. If you use a mild shampoo, a daily sudsing will not hurt your hair. Be sure to rinse well. Shampoo left in can dry out the hair.

If you are active in sports, protect your hair with a hat. Most outdoor sports tend to dry out hair. Always rinse your hair thoroughly after swimming. The sun, wind, chlorine, and saltwater can also dry your hair.

Always treat hair gently, especially when it is wet. That is when it is the most breakable. Remove tangles with a wide-toothed comb. Do not brush wet hair. Do make sure your comb and brush are as clean as your hair.

How your hair looks depends a great deal on your diet, getting enough rest, and lots of exercise. Remember, hair is nourished from the inside out. A well-balanced, nutritious diet will mean a healthier head of hair.

perspirátion *n.* 땀(= sweating) greasy *adj.* 기름기 있는, 미끈한 stringy *adj.* 실오리 같은 shiny *adj.* 윤기 있는 shampóo *n.* 샴푸 *v.* 머리감다 suds *n.* 비눗물, 비누 거품 *v.* 거품이 일다, 비누로 씻다 rinse *v.* 헹구다, 린스하다 dry out 건조시키다 chlórine *n.* 염소 tangle *n.* 엉김 wide-toothed comb 빗살이 성긴 빗 nutrítious *adj.* 영양이 좋은 inside out 철저히, 완전히

1. What is the best title for the passage?

① How to Care Your Hair ② How to Keep Your Comb Clean
③ How to Keep Your Hair Fresh ④ How to Nourish Your Hair
⑤ How to Shampoo Your Hair

풀이 ① 모발을 보호하는 방법 ② 빗을 깨끗이 유지하는 방법 ③ 모발을 신선하게 유지하는 방법 ④ 모발에 영양을 주는 방법 ⑤ 머리감는 방법
이 글은 따로 주제문이 제시되어 있지는 않고, 문장 전체가 '모발을 보호하는 방법'을 설명하고 있다.

보너스 상식

모발을 자를 때 아프지 않은 까닭은?

통증을 뇌에 전달하는 것은 신경이다. 신경이 없으면 통증을 느끼지 못한다. 모발은 신경세포를 가지고 있지 않은, 생명이 없는 세포로 구성되어 있다. 그래서 통증을 못 느낀다. 손발톱 역시 신경세포가 없어서 깎을 때 아무런 감각이 없다.

theme **07**

Hair and Hairstyling 모발과 헤어스타일

2 There are a variety of ways to change hair color. Temporary coloring shampoos in and washes out. It contains no bleach, so it will not lighten hair, but it can add warm highlights. Semipermanent coloring shampoos in and lasts for three or four washings. Because it is left on for a few minutes, the color sinks into the hair shaft. It does not contain peroxide, so it cannot lighten hair. But it can brighten its natural shade. Permanent hair coloring contains peroxide that can lighten hair by several shades. It can also darken hair. Because permanent hair coloring penetrates the hair shaft, it will not wash out. Instead it must grow out.

Highlighting, streaking, and painting add highlights to hair. This is done by bleaching only a few strands rather than the whole head. If done well, it looks as if the sun did the work.

témporary *adj.* 일시적인 bleach *n/v.* 표백/하다, 표백제 líghten *v.* 바래다 warm highlight 강한 강조 semipérmanent *adj.* 반영구적인 shaft *n.* 줄기, 대 hair shaft 머리카락 peróxide *n.* 과산화수소 shade *n.* 명암, 색조 natural shade 자연 색조 pénetrate *v.* 침투하다, 투과하다 streaking *n.* 탈색 strand *n.* 가닥, (머리카락의) 숱

1. According to the passage, which of the following does <u>not</u> add highlights to hair?

① bleaching ② highlighting
③ painting ④ streaking
⑤ washing

풀이 ① 표백 ② 강조 ③ 염색 ④ 탈색 ⑤ 세척
둘째 단락에 여러 가지 'highlights'의 종류가 열거되어 있다.

보너스 상식

모발 관련 용어

① hairdresser : 미장원
② curly hair : 곱슬머리
③ wavy hair : 물결 모양 모발 *cf.* permanent wave (퍼머) : 2~3개월 지속
④ straight hair : 곱슬하지 않은 직상 모발
⑤ baldness : 대머리
⑥ hair weaving : 부분 가발을 엮어 넣는 일
⑦ hair implanting/transplanting : 모발 이식

Heating Systems 난방 시스템

1 Modern heating systems are equipped with automatic controls to provide comfort, safety, and economy of fuel. Boilers and furnaces have devices to keep them from getting too hot. Electric heaters usually have an internal fuse to prevent overheating. Hydronic heating systems can be 'zoned' to provide different temperatures in different parts of the building. Electric heating systems can have thermostats in every room.

Recent control innovations include the two-stage room thermostat, which keeps the burner shut off completely until heating is needed. Also, indoor-outdoor devices adjust the operation of the heating system according to changes in the outdoor temperature. Another popular control is the clock thermostat, which automatically reduces or increases the indoor temperature at different times of the day.

In the home there are many other ways to conserve heat and reduce fuel bills. The proper insulation, tightly sealed windows and doors, turning down the heat in unused rooms, and the use of space heaters or stoves are just some of the steps that can be taken.

equíp *v.* 장비를 갖추다, 장치하다 cómfort *n.* 편안함 fúrnace *n.* 난로 devíce *n.* (기계)장치 keep/prevent – from – ing ~가 ~하지 못하게 막다 fuse *n.* 퓨즈, 신관(= fuze) thérmostat *n.* 온도조절 장치 innovátion *n.* 혁신 shut off 끄다, 차단하다 operátion *n.* 작동 clock thermostat 온도 조절 시계 장치 consérve *v.* 보존하다 fuel bill 연료비 insulátion *n.* 절연, 단열 seal *v.* 밀봉하다 turn down 줄이다 space heater 실내 난방기

1. Which of the following is <u>not</u> stated in the passage as the ways to conserve heat and reduce fuel bills in the home?

① Hydronic heating systems
② Tight sealing of windows and doors
③ The proper insulation
④ The use of space heaters or stoves
⑤ Turning down of the heat in unused rooms

풀이 ① 물 순환 난방 시스템 ② 적절한 단열 ③ 창과 문의 단단한 밀봉 ④ 쓰지 않는 방의 난방 줄이기 ⑤ 실내 난방기와 난로의 사용
'가정에서(In the home ...)'의 난방 관리 방법은 마지막 단락에 열거되어 있다.

theme 08 Heating Systems 난방 시스템

보너스 상식!

온돌의 가치

지구상에서 '온돌'을 사용한 민족은 우리 민족이다. 온돌은 방바닥을 데워서 난방을 하는 방식이다. 우리는 수 천 년 간 따뜻한 바닥에 익숙해져 있다. 주택 구조가 서구화되고 난방 설비 기술이 발달한 오늘날도 우리 나라 주택이나 아파트의 난방은 여전히 바닥을 따뜻하게 하는 온돌 방식이다. 전통적으로 난방을 하지 않고 다다미라는 장판을 깔고 생활해 온 일본인들 가운데 한국에서 생활해 본 사람들은 한국식 난방에 대해 감탄을 하고 일본에 돌아가서도 주택의 난방 구조를 온돌식으로 개조하는 사람들이 많다.

High-Fidelity System 하이파이(Hi-Fi) 시스템

09 theme

1

High-fidelity (hi-fi) systems consist of electronic equipment designed to reproduce sound. They do so with the highest possible degree of fidelity, or faithfulness, to the original sound. They are often called stereos because they usually deliver stereophonic (two-channel) sound.

Even the very best high-fidelity system does not sound the same as a live performance. This is because no mechanical or electrical part, no matter how sophisticated, can do its job perfectly; each adds distortion and noise. The level of fidelity is determined by how accurately the system re-creates the sound of the original performance.

All high-fidelity systems are composed of three types of audio components, or parts. Source components, such as the compact disc player, tape recorder, and tuner, generate weak electrical signals. These are then sent to amplifiers, which strengthen the signals and send them to loudspeakers. There the signals are converted into sound waves, which move through the air to our ears.

Sound may be stored on a material substance, such as magnetic tape, or it may come from airwaves, as in a radio broadcast.

high-fidelity system 하이파이 시스템, 고충실도 시스템 reprodúce *v.* 재생하다 fidélity *n.* 충실, 성실(= faithfulness) stéreo *n.* 스테레오, 입체 음향 전축 delíver *v.* 전달하다 stereophónic *n.* 입체 음향의 (= two channel) live perfórmance 실황 공연 mechánical *adj.* 기계적인 no matter how – 아무리 ~일지라도 sophísticated *adj.* 정교한 distórtion *n.* 뒤틀림 source compónent 공급원 요소, 소스 요소 ámplifier *n.* 증폭기, 앰프 stréngthen *v.* 증폭시키다, 강화하다 lóudspeaker *n.* 확성기, 스피커 convért *v.* 변환하다 store *v.* 저장하다 magnétic tape 자기테이프 áirwave *n.* 공중파

1. What is the correct process which we listen to music through hi-fi system?

① amplifier → loudspeaker → turner → human ears
② loudspeaker → amplifier → turner → human ears
③ loudspeaker → turner → amplifier → human ears
④ tuner → amplifier → loudspeaker → human ears
⑤ tuner → loudspeaker → amplifier → human ears

풀이 ① 앰프 → 스피커 → 튜너 → 귀 ② 스피커 → 앰프 → 튜너 → 귀 ③ 스피커 → 튜너 → 앰프 → 귀 ④ 튜너 → 앰프 → 스피커 → 귀 ⑤ 튜너 → 스피커 → 앰프 → 귀
셋째 단락에 차례로 설명하고 있다.

보너스 상식

홈 시어터(Home theater)

가정에서 텔레비전과 오디오시스템을 결합한 것을 'home theater'라고 한다. 1980년대 들어 비디오테이프의 화질과 음질이 향상되고, 텔레비전과 훌륭한 음질의 오디오시스템을 결합하는 경우가 생겼다. 이것이 '홈 시어터'의 시작이다. 기본적으로 'Stereo video-cassette recorder'와 'Surround-sound processor'가 필요하고, 양질의 화면을 위해서 'Laserdisc player'나 'Digital video disc plaer'(DVD player)가 있으면 좋다.

theme 10 Hiking and Backpacking 도보여행과 배낭여행

1 There are thousands of hiking trails in North America. Beginners can choose from any number of local, provincial, and state parks, forests, and wildlife refuges, as well as the many national parks and forests. And then there are the famous long trails, such as the Appalachian Trail, which runs between Georgia and Maine, or the magnificent Pacific Crest Trail, which runs from the Mexico-California border all the way north to the Washington-British Columbia border. The best sources of information on hiking trails are your local sporting goods store, outing clubs, and the library.

Hiking and backpacking are similar to other sports in that once you have tried them and liked them, you cannot get enough of them. With repeated experiences in the backcountry, you will learn many skills—how to pack a backpack, how to build a fire, how to choose a campsite, and more. Learning these skills will greatly add to your enjoyment of hiking and backpacking.

híking *n.* 도보여행 trail *n.* 행로, 발자취, 길 wíldlife réfuge 야생동물 보호구역 magnífìcent *adj.* 장대한 crest *n.* 꼭대기, 정상 all the way north 계속 북쪽으로 British-Columbia 브리티시-컬럼비아, 캐나다 남서부의 주 outing *n.* 소풍, 여행, 행락 báckpacking *n.* 배낭여행 símilar to – ~와 비슷한 get/have enough of – ~은 이제 질색이다, 싫증나다 báckcountry *n.* 산간 오지, 두메 build a fire 불을 피우다 cámpsite *n.* 야영지

1. Which of the following does the passage mainly discuss?

① Appalachian Trail
② Hiking and backpacking
③ Hiking trails
④ North America
⑤ Pacific Crest Trail

풀이 ① 애팔래치아 행로 ② 도보여행과 배낭여행 ③ 도보 여행길 ④ 북미 ⑤ 태평양 정상 행로
주제문인 첫 문장에서 핵심어를 찾으면 된다.

보너스 상식!

배낭여행의 준비물

1. 옷 : 두꺼운 옷보다는 얇은 옷을 여러 벌 껴입도록 준비한다. 소매 긴 셔츠, 긴 바지, 파카와 판초 우의 등은 필수.
2. 신발 : 운동화, 하이킹 부츠, 양말 등
3. 침구 : 침낭, 텐트 등 비싼 것은 빌리는 것이 좋다.
4. 배낭 꾸리기 : 일반적으로 10㎏을 넘지 않아야 한다. (당일 여행은 5㎏)
5. 기타 : 손전등, 방수 성냥, 칼, 물병, 구급함, 지도, 로션, 화장지 등

Hobbies 취미

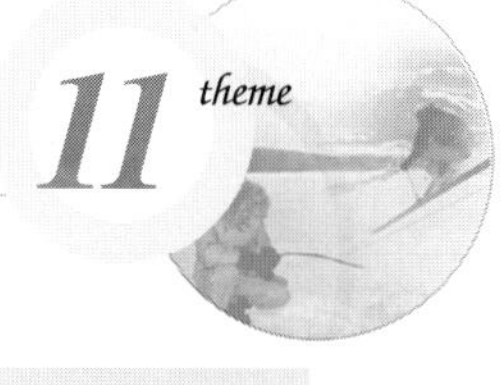

1 If you've ever had a hobby you enjoyed, you know the interest and pleasure it can give you. But hobbies have other advantages, too. A hobby can give you the satisfaction of starting and carrying through a project all on your own. Seeing a completed piece of your own work—a bench you've made or a scarf you've knitted—gives you a special feeling of pride. You'll discover, too, that when you have an absorbing hobby, you're able to spend time alone quite happily.

Often a hobby teaches you a great deal without your even being aware of it. When you put stamps in your album, for instance, you're learning something about the geography and history of the particular country. And when you classify the rocks in your collection, you're also learning something about geology and earth history.

satisfáction *n.* 만족 on your own 혼자서, 스스로 knit *v.* 뜨개질하다 absórb *v.* 몰입하다 be awáre of – ～을 의식하다 geógraphy *n.* 지리 clássify *v.* 분류하다

1. Which of the following is <u>not</u> stated in the passage as the advantages that a hobby gives us?

① feeling of pride ② satisfaction
③ spending time alone happily ④ learning
⑤ works

풀이 ① 긍지 ② 만족 ③ 홀로 즐겁게 시간 보내기 ④ 배움 ⑤ 작품
이 글은 취미의 이점을 설명하고 있으므로, 'It(a hobby) gives you ...'로 표현된 문장을 찾아 보라.

보너스 상식

취미의 종류

① 수집(collecting) : 골동품(antique), 서명(autograph), 단추(button), 동전(coin), 인형(doll), 나뭇잎(leaf), 음반(record), 조개껍질(shell), 우표(stamp) 등의 수집
② 미술과 공예 : 진흙 공예(clay modeling), 콜라주(collage), 그림(drawing or painting), 꽃꽂이(flowerarranging), 뜨개질(knitting), 바느질(needlecraft) 목공(woodworking) 등
③ 모형 제작(making models) : 비행기, 자동차, 기차 등의 모형 제작
④ 동식물 기르기(raising plants and animals) : 수족관(aquariums), 새 · 고양이 · 개 기르기, 정원 가꾸기(gardening), 실내 식물(houseplants), 테라리움(terrariums) 등
⑤ 야외 활동(outdoor activities) : 사이클, 보트, 캠핑, 낚시, 하이킹, 승마(horseback riding), 스케이트(ice-skating), 연날리기(kite flying), 등산, 스키 등
⑥ 특기(special skills) : 아마추어 무선, 포크댄스, 마술, 사진, 비디오 제작 등

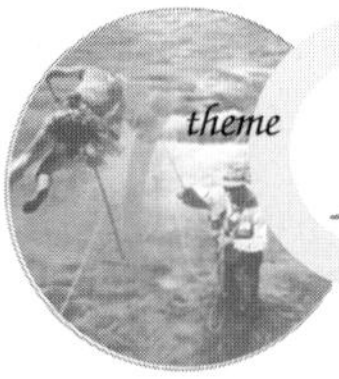

theme 12 Homes 집

1 A home is a place where people cook, eat, sleep, and care for their children. It protects people from harsh weather—cold, rain, wind, the burning rays of the sun—as well as from insects, wild animals, and other dangers.

Some people live in grass huts perched high in trees or on stilts. Others live in towering apartment buildings. Home for some people means a tent made of animal skins, a cottage with a thatched roof, or a cave in the side of a cliff. People live on houseboats and in trailers, in simple farmhouses and in stately mansions. There are homes of steel, glass, concrete, wood, stone, brick, mud, snow, grass, earth, and leaves.

The kinds of homes people built long ago depended almost completely upon the kind of climate in which they lived, the building materials that were close at hand, and the dangers they faced in their daily lives. These are still important, but modern machinery and new building methods have lessened their importance. Houses are still built to resist the effects of climate, but heating and air conditioning can make a house comfortable in any climate. It is cheaper and easier to build a house with materials that are close at hand. But today it is possible to transport building materials from faraway places.

protéct *v.* 보호하다 harsh *adj.* 거친 grass hut 초가 perch *v.* (새들처럼 나무나 기둥 위에) 둥지나 집을 짓다, 자리잡다 stilt *n.* 나무기둥 tówering *adj.* 높이 솟은 thatch *v.* (지붕을) 짚(풀)으로 이다 houseboat *n.* 집배, 숙박을 하는 배 stately *adj.* 장중한 mánsion *n.* 대저택 be close at hand 가까이 있는 léssen *v.* 줄이다 transpórt *v.* 수송하다

1. According to the passage, the kinds of homes depend on all the following **except**

① building materials. ② building methods.
③ dangers. ④ kinds of climate.
⑤ people.

풀이 ① 건축 재료 ② 건축 방법 ③ 위험 ④ 기후의 종류 ⑤ 사람들
마지막 단락에 '집의 종류에 영향을 주는' 요소들이 설명되어 있다. 문장 'The kinds of homes ... depended ... upon ...'이하에 그 요소들이 나열되어 있다.

보너스 상식

주택의 분류

① 건축 재료에 따른 분류 : 목조 주택(house of wood) 초가(house of grass) 눈 집(house of snow) 에스키모(Igloo) 진흙 주택 (house of mud) 벽돌 주택(house of bricks) 석조 주택(house of stone) 철재 주택(still house)
② 새로운 가옥 종류 : 아파트(apartment house) 옥상 주택(penthouse) 콘도(condominium) 태양열 주택(solar house)

Home Economics 가정학

1 <u>Home economics</u> is a field of knowledge and a profession. The aim of the field is to improve the quality of day-to-day living for individuals and families. The subjects are those that people, especially families, must deal with every day—food, shelter, clothing, management, how people grow and develop, and how they relate to one another. Home economics may deal with these areas separately. But it also emphasized how they fit together to improve daily life.

Home economics is the title used to describe most programs in this field of study. But other titles are sometimes used. Some of them are consumer and homemaking education, consumer studies, family sciences, human development, human ecology, and human resources. Usually people working in the field are called home economists, but they are sometimes known by other titles.

home ecónomics 가정학, 가정경제학(미국에서 가정학을 가리키는 명칭) proféssion *n.* 직업 deal with – ~을 다루다 mánagement *n.* 관리, 경영 séparately *adv.* 따로따로 émphasize *v.* 강조하다 fit together 어우러지다 consúmer *n.* 소비자 ecólogy *n.* 생태학 resóurce *n.* 자원

1. The underlined expression <u>home economics</u> refer to all of the following **except**

① consumer studies. ② family sciences.
③ human ecology. ④ human resources.
⑤ home development.

풀이 ① 소비자학 ② 가족학 ③ 인간 생태학 ④ 인간 자원 ⑤ 가정 발달
둘째 단락이 가정학의 여러 명칭들을 열거하고 있다.

보너스 상식

가정학

가정에서 이루어지는 인간의 활동을 분석하는 학문이다. 예전에는 주로 요리나 재봉 등의 가사 작업을 연구하는 정도였으나, 점차 영양학, 위생학 등이 편입되었고, 에너지, 시간, 자재, 금융, 소비 등을 관리하는 학문이 되었다. 최근에는 가정 생활과 인간 자체에 대해서도 연구하는 가정관리와 의사결정 등이 관심사가 되었다. 영국에서는 '가정학'(domestic science)이라 하고, 미국에서는 '가정경제학'(home economics)이라고 한다.

theme 14 Interior Decorating 실내장식

1 Decorators work in many areas. Real-estate developers work with decorators. Many furniture stores have decorators on their staffs to advise their customers. And decorators help design offices, restaurants, schools, and hospitals, as well as homes. In fact, commercial interiors account for more than half of all interior decorating work.

Most successful decorators have had some formal study in preparation for their profession. There are six-month courses that teach the basics of using colors, fabrics, and wall coverings. But if you are thinking seriously about a career in interior design, there are a number of schools that offer a full four-year curriculum. These schools teach you how to draw, how to measure rooms and make scale drawings, how to decide what furnishings are appropriate for what space, and how to design structural changes. The course covers design for homes and businesses, as well as the history of interior decoration.

décorator *n.* 장식가 real estate 부동산 staff *n.* 중역 commércial intérior 상업 인테리어 account for – ~을 설명하다 intérior décorating 실내장식 in preparation for – ~을 준비하여, 대비하여 wall coverings 벽지 currículum *n.* 교육과정 curricula scale drawing 축적 도면 fúrnishing *n.* 장식 apprópriate *adj.* 적절한

1. Which of the following is <u>not</u> stated as the full four year curriculums in interior design?

① History of interior decoration
② How to decide what furnishings are appropriate for what space
③ How to design structural changes
④ How to make wall coverings
⑤ How to measure rooms and make scale drawings

풀이 ① 실내장식의 역사 ② 어떤 공간에 어떤 장식이 적당할지 결정하는 방법 ③ 구조 변경을 설계하는 방법 ④ 벽지를 만드는 방법 ⑤ 실내를 측량하고 축적 도면을 작성하는 방법
둘째 단락의 후반부에 4년제 대학의 실내장식 교육과정이 열거되어 있다.

보너스 상식

실내 디자인의 요소

①Style 스타일	②Balance 균형	③Scale 크기
④Color 색상	⑤Light 밝기	⑥Pattern 구조
⑦Texture 구성		

2 Study your room. What shape is it? How high, wide, and long is it? Measure your room accurately, then make a scale drawing of it on graph paper. Remember to include the location of the windows, doors, and radiators. You want to use the natural light from the windows. Doors should not hit anything, and no furniture should block a radiator. On another piece of paper, draw the shape of your bed and other furniture to scale, and cut them out. Place the furniture shapes on the drawing so that they represent the way your furniture is arranged now. By moving the paper pieces, you can experiment with arrangements until you get a look that you like.

Think again about the activities you do in your room and think about what furniture accommodates those activities. A sturdy chair and a practical desk with a good light are important for doing homework. Could you use a work table for projects? If you have enough space, you may want to separate your room into sleeping and work or play areas. Some furniture can do double duty. A bed placed along a wall can be used as a couch if you add the right cushions.

Now, with someone's help, try to arrange the actual furniture. Is the arrangement practical and appealing to you? Does it work? If it does, you have done an excellent job. If it does not, rearrange it on paper and try again.

scale drawing 축적 도면 scale *v.* 축적으로 그리다, 줄이다 graph paper 그래프용지 block *v.* 막다, 차단하다 cut out 오려 내다 arránge *v.* 정돈하다 arrangement *n.* 정돈 accómmodate *v.* 수용하다, 융통하다, 조정하다 sturdy *adj.* 튼튼한 work table 작업 테이블 appéaling *adj.* 매력적인 do an éxcellent job 훌륭히 해내다

1. What does this passage mainly discuss?

① Activities in the Room
② Arrangement of a Room
③ Furnitures in a Room
④ Scale Drawings
⑤ Study of a Room

theme 14 Interior Decorating 실내장식

2. What kind of paragraphs are these?

① persuasive paragraphs
② contradictory paragraphs
③ conclusive paragraphs
④ descrptive paragraphs
⑤ explanatory paragraphs

3. What is the suggested order of arrangement of a room?

① measuring your room — placing the shapes — drawing the shape of furniture — making a scale drawing — arranging the actual furniture
② measuring your room — drawing the shape of furniture — making a scale drawing — placing the shapes — arranging the actual furniture
③ measuring your room — making a scale drawing — placing the shapes — drawing the sae of furniture — arranging the actual furniture
④ measuring your room — drawing the shape of furniture — placing the shapes — making a seale drawing — arranging the actual furniture
⑤ measuring your room — making a scale drawing — drawing the shape of furniture — placing the shapes — arranging the actual furniture

풀이 1. ① 방에서의 활동 ② 방의 정돈 ③ 방의 가구 ④ 축적 도면 ⑤ 방의 연구
마지막 단락이 결론이 있는 핵심 단락이다. 'arrangement'라는 말이 핵심어이다.

2. ① 설득 ② 반박 ③ 결론 ④ 묘사 ⑤ 설명

3. ① 방의 측정—모양으로 위치 선정—가구모양 그리기—축적도면 작성—실제 가구 배치
② 방의 측정—가구모양 그리기—축적도면 작성—모양으로 위치 선정—실제 가구 배치
③ 방의 측정—축적도면 작성—모양으로 위치 선정—가구모양 그리기—실제 가구 배치
④ 방의 측정—가구모양 그리기—모양으로 위치 선정—축적도면 작성—실제 가구 배치
⑤ 방의 측정—축적도면 작성—가구모양 그리기—모양으로 위치 선정—실제 가구 배치

보너스 상식

방 꾸미기

1. 벽면과 가구의 일관된 색상을 고른다.
2. 용도에 따라 방의 공간을 설정한다.
3. 각종 수납 공간을 마련하여 정리한다.
4. 자신이 소유하고 있거나 좋아하는 액세서리를 장식한다.

Jewelry 귀금속

15 theme

1 Jewelry is made in a great variety of types and from many different kinds of materials. Precious jewelry is made of the rarest and most beautiful metals and gemstones. Non-precious jewelry is made of materials that are easier to find and less expensive.

Early men adorned themselves with pebbles, shells, berries, and feathers. They made necklaces of pieces of stone, horn, or the teeth of animals. Indians of early America wore necklaces of wampum (beads of polished shells), bone, and metal. Primitive peoples in many parts of the world still wear similar decorations.

jéwelry *n.* 귀금속 précious *adj.* 귀중한 gémstone *n.* 보석(의 원석) adórn *v.* 장식하다, 꾸미다 pébble *n.* 조약돌, 자갈 bérry *n.* 열매 feather *n.* 새의 깃털 nécklace *n.* 목걸이 wámpum *n.* 조가비 염주 bead *n.* 염주, 목걸이 prímitive people 원시인들

1. Which is <u>not</u> stated in the passage as the things which early men adorned themselves?

① berries ② feathers
③ glass ④ pebbles
⑤ shells

풀이 ① 열매 ② 새의 깃털 ③ 유리 ④ 조약돌 ⑤ 조개껍질
둘째 단락에 원시인들(early men)이 장식(adorn)으로 쓴 사물들이 나와 있다.

보너스 상식

캐럿(carat)과 캐럿(karat)

1. 'Carat'은 보석의 표준 무게 단위. 국제적으로 합의된 바, 1 carat은 200㎎ 또는 1/142 ounce(온스)이다.
2. 'Karat'은 황금의 순도를 나타내는 단위로서 미국에서 사용된다. 순수한 황금은 24 karat이다. 합금된 황금은 24 karat(24K)보다 순도가 떨어진다. 합금 6개에 순금 18개를 섞은 것을 18K, 합금 10가지에 순금 14개이면 14K라고 한다.

theme 16 Kites 연

1

Two opposing forces act on a kite. One is the lifting force of the air. The other is the pull of the kite string back to the earth. When these two forces are balanced or nearly equal, a kite remains in the air.

The lifting force of the air also makes it possible for an airplane to fly. When you hold a kite in launching position, the air meeting it is divided into two streams. One stream passes over the upper surface of the kite, and one passes along the undersurface.

The stream of air passing over the upper surface of the kite has a longer path to travel than the stream of air passing along the undersurface. This is because of the shape of the kite and the angle at which it is held. But the upper airstream must travel the longer path in the same time as the lower airstream. This means that the upper airstream travels faster than the lower airstream. As a result, the air in the upper stream is thinner. The pressure of the air on the undersurface is greater and so the kite rises.

oppósing *adj.* 반대되는 lifting force 상승하는 힘 kite string 연줄 launching position 출발 위치 stream *n.* 흐름, 기류(= airstream) path *n.* 경로, 행로, 길 pressure of the air 기압

1. Which of the following is the best title for the passage?

① How Is a Kite Made?
② When Does Men fly Kites?
③ Who Made a Kite at First?
④ Why Does a Kite Fly?
⑤ What Does Men Fly Kites for?

풀이 ① 연은 어떻게 만들어지는가? ② 사람들은 언제 연을 날리는가? ③ 연을 최초로 만든 사람은?
④ 연이 날게 되는 까닭은? ⑤ 사람은 왜 연을 날렸을까?
이 글은 연이 나는 과정을 설명하고 있으며, 마지막 문장에 연이 날게 되는 원인이 결론으로 나와 있다.

보너스 상식

연의 발명

누가 연을 발명하였는지는 확실히 알려지지 않으나, B.C.400년에 그리스인 'Archytas'가 만들었다는 설도 있고, 200년 후에 중국의 '한신'(韓信)이 만들었다는 설도 있다. 전통적으로 중국, 한국, 일본에서 연을 많이 날렸다. 중국은 구구절(9월 9일)이 연을 날리는 날이라고 한다.

Knitting 뜨개질

1 Knitting needles come in many different sizes and styles. They are most often made from metal, plastic, or wood. In the United States, size is indicated by numbering needles from 0 to 50. The higher the number, the fatter the needle. There are three different styles of knitting needles—double-pointed, circular, and straight. Double-pointed needles come in sets of four and are used mainly for knitting small tube-shaped items such as socks or mittens. Circular needles are flexible with a metal or plastic point at each end. They are primarily used for large tubular items such as skirts or sweater bodies. The most common type of needles are straight needles. They always come in pairs, usually in lengths of 10 or 14 inches. A beginner will find 10-inch metal needles easiest to use because they are a comfortable length and are not likely to bend.

knitting needles 뜨개질 바늘 índicate *v.* 표시하다, 가리키다 double-pointed 쌍침의, 침이 두 개인 círcular *adj.* 원형의 straight *adj.* 직선형의, 곧은 tube-shaped 튜브형의 sock *n.* 양말 mítten *n.* 장갑(= gloves) fléxible *adj.* 유연한 túbular *adj.* 튜브형의(= tube-shaped) cómfortable *adj.* 편안한 bend *v.* 구부리다

1. Which of the following is the best title for the passage?

① How to Make Needles
② Kinds of Knitted Items
③ Sizes of Knitting Needles
④ Skills of Knitting
⑤ Types of Knitting Needles

풀이 ① 바늘을 만드는 방법 ② 뜨개질 제품의 종류 ③ 뜨개질 바늘의 크기 ④ 뜨개질의 기술 ⑤ 뜨개질 바늘의 형태
첫 문장에서도 핵심어로 나와 있어 제목을 쉽게 만들 수 있다. 'style of ..., type of ...'등의 말이 글 가운데 자주 등장하고 있다.

보너스 상식

뜨개질의 기술(Skills of Knitting)

① Casting on 코 만들기
② Knitting stitch 바로 뜨기
③ Purling stitch 뒤집어 뜨기
④ Binding off 코 마무리
⑤ Decreasing 코 수를 줄여 좁히기
⑥ Increasing 코 수를 늘려 확대하기

theme 18 Ocean Liners 해양 여객선

1 A modern cruise ship is like a floating hotel. Besides the many cabins and staterooms where passengers sleep, there are lounges, dining rooms, kitchens, recreation rooms, shops, swimming pools, gymnasiums, a movie theater, a hospital, a garage, and even a kennel for pets. Elevators carry the passengers from one deck to another.

Feeding several thousand people for a number of days requires huge quantities of food. Large liners carry tons of meat, poultry, fish, vegetables, eggs, and other foods.

A large ship needs hundreds of crew members to run it and take care of the passengers. Room stewards clean the cabins and perform personal services for the passengers. Diningroom stewards wait on tables. Deck stewards set up deck chairs and serve food and drink to passengers on deck.

The ship's officers are in charge of running the ship and are responsible for the safety of all. The chief officer is the captain. He is the master of the ship, with authority over officers, crew, and passengers. In an emergency such as a storm or serious accident it is the captain who decides what action must be taken.

Soon after a liner sails, all passengers are required to attend a lifeboat drill. The liner provides a life jacket for each passenger. During the drill passengers must put on their life jackets and report to their assigned lifeboat station.

cruise *n.* 유람선 float *v.* (물위에) 뜨다 cábin *n.* 객실 státeroom *n.* 접견실 díning room 식당 kénnel *n.* 개집 feed *v.* (식사를) 먹이다 liner *n.* 여객선 póultry *n.* 닭고기, 가금 crew *n.* 승무원, 선원 stéward *n.* 승무원 wait on 시중들다 set up 설치하다 deck *n.* 갑판 ófficer *n.* 선원 be in charge of – ~을 책임지다, 맡다 authórity *n.* 권한, 권위 take an action 조치를 취하다 lifeboat drill 구명정 훈련 life jacket 구명조끼 assígn *v.* 맡기다, 배정하다, 할당하다 lifeboat station 구명정 보관소

1. According to the passage, what are all passengers needed to do soon after a liner sails?

① Attending a lifeboat drill
② Checking lifeboats and life jackets
③ Going to their cabins
④ Meeting the crew members
⑤ Reporting to the captain

풀이 ① 구명정 훈련에 참가한다. ② 구명정과 구명 조끼를 점검한다. ③ 자기들의 객실로 간다. ④ 선원들을 만난다. ⑤ 선장에게 보고한다.
'유람선이 출항한 직후' (Soon after a liner sails ...)의 일은 마지막 단락에 설명되어 있다.

보너스 상식! 20세기 세계의 여객선

①Titanic (영) 1912년 침몰
②Queen Elizabeth (영) 1930년대 진수
③Queen Mary (영) 1930년대 진수
④Normandie (프) 1930년대 진수
⑤United States (미) 1950년대 진수
⑥Queen Elizabeth 2 (영) 1967년 진수

theme 19 Park 공원

1 Amusement parks, sometimes called theme parks, specialize in rides, games, and entertainment. Unlike public parks these parks are owned by private businesses or individuals. They charge admission, and they usually also charge for all goods and services inside the park.

The oldest amusement park still operating is Bakken Amusement Park, in Copenhagen, Denmark. It was started more than 400 years ago. But Copenhagen has a more famous park—Tivoli Gardens, which is right in the middle of the city. This park combines rides and games with theaters, concert halls, restaurants, and beautiful gardens.

The first American amusement parks were built by streetcar companies in the mid-1850's. There were no automobiles then, and only wealthy people owned carriages. If average people wanted to go somewhere, they had to walk or ride the streetcars.

amúsement *n.* 즐거움, 오락, 놀이 amusement park 놀이 공원 theme park 테마 공원 spécialize in – ~을 특화하다, 전공하다 ride *n.* 탈것 entertáinment *n.* 오락, 연예 charge *v.* 부과하다, 물리다 admíssion *n.* 입장 óperate *v.* 운영하다 stréetcar *n.* 전차 áutomobile *n.* 자동차 cárriage *n.* 마차 áverage *adj.* 평균의

1. Which of the following is the oldest amusement park still operating?

① Bakken Amusement Park ② Copenhagen Park
③ Denmark Amusement Park ④ Disney World
⑤ Tivoli Gardens

풀이 ① 바켄 놀이 공원 ② 코펜하겐 공원 ③ 덴마크 놀이 공원 ④ 디즈니 월드 ⑤ 티볼리 가든
'지금도 운영되는 가장 오래된 놀이 공원'(The oldest amusement park still operating ...)은 둘째 단락에 서술되어 있다.

보너스 상식

디즈니랜드(Disneyland)

월트디즈니가 1955년 캘리포니아주 'Anaheim'에 미국 최초의 테마 공원을 개장한 이후, 1971년에 플로리다주 'Orlando'에 두 번째 디즈니 테마 공원 '디즈니 월드'(Disney World)를 개장한다. 1983년에는 일본 도쿄에, 1992년에는 프랑스 파리에도 '디즈니랜드'(Disneyland)를 개장하였다.

Perfumes 향수

1 Perfume is a delightful fragrance. It may come from a woodland after rain, an apple tree in bloom, a freshly cut orange, or a liquid in a pretty bottle.

The fragrance of natural materials are caused by oils within them. These oils are used to make perfumes in either a liquid or a solid form. The liquid perfumes are those usually found in bottles, aerosol sprays, and bath oils. Liquid perfumes are also used to add a pleasant scent to soap, hand cream, and other toilet preparations. Perfume sticks, incense, and perfumed candles are examples of perfume in solid form.

Usually we think of perfumes as flowery or fruit-scented substances used to make a person or a room smell pleasant. But it is also possible to make scents that smell like popcorn, new cars, or a seashore.

perfúme *n.* 향수 frágrance *n.* 향기 delíghtful *adj.* 즐거운 wóodland *n.* 숲, 삼림 in bloom 꽃이 핀 pretty bottle 예쁜 병, 향수병 áerosol *adj.* 연무의, 에어로졸 scent *n.* 향 tóilet preparátion 화장실 탈취제, 냄새 제거제 incénse *n.* 분향, 연기로 피우는 향 perfumed candle 향 넣은 양초 flówery *adj.* 꽃의 fruit-scented 과일 향이 나는

1. Which of the following is <u>not</u> mentioned in the passage as the perfumes in solid form?

① aerosol sprays ② incense
③ perfumed candles ④ perfume sticks

풀이 ① 에어로졸 스프레이 ② 분향 ③ 향 양초 ④ 향 지팡이
'고체 향'(... perfume in solid form)의 예들은 둘째 단락의 후반부에 나와 있다.

보너스 상식! 향수의 원료로 쓰이는 식물

① 꽃(Blossoms) : Jasmine(자스민), Orange(오렌지), Carnation(카네이션), Rose(장미)
② 잎(Leaves) : Violet(제비꽃), Peppermint(박하), Rosemary(로즈메리), Lavender(라벤더)
③ 열매나 씨(Fruits or Seeds) : Lemon(레몬), Orange, Nutmeg(너트메그 열매 씨), Grapefruit(자몽)

theme 20 Perfumes 향수

2 Cologne is a perfumed liquid that is used in or after a bath and for a skin freshener. It is largely alcohol. Traditionally, cologne has been based on the fragrance of citrus, and this fragrance has distinguished cologne from toilet water. But few companies today make toilet water and cologne in the traditional way. Now the words 'cologne' and 'toilet water' refer to different concentrations of perfumed oils. Toilet water is usually the stronger of the two. Both are intended to be splashed freely over the body or sprayed in the hair. Because they contain a great deal of alcohol, toilet water and cologne are much less expensive than perfume. Because they are more diluted, their fragrance does not last nearly so long as the fragrance of perfume.

cologne *n.* 콜로뉴. 프랑스 콜로뉴가 원산인 화장수 이름 cítrus *n.* 밀감류, 감귤류 toilet water 화장수 concentrátion *n.* 농도 be inténded to do ~하기로 되어 있다 splásh *v.* (물을) 튀기다, 뿌리다 dilúte *v.* (농도를) 묽게 하다

1. According to the passage, which is <u>not</u> true about 'cologne'?

① It is a perfumed liquid.
② It is a skin freshener.
③ It is largely alcohol.
④ It is stronger than toilet water.
⑤ It is much cheaper than perfume.

풀이 ① 향수 액이다. ② 피부 청결제이다. ③ 대체로 알코올이다. ④ 화장수보다 더 강하다. ⑤ 향수보다 훨씬 싸다. 이 글은 전체가 'cologne'와 'toilet water'에 대한 설명이므로, 답지를 먼저 읽은 다음, 글을 읽으며 확인하는 것이 효과적이다.

보너스 상식!

향수의 사용

고대 이집트 사람들은 목욕할 때 향유와 향 연고를 발랐다고 한다. 클레오파트라의 향수 사용은 유명하다. 그녀는 자신만 사용한 게 아니라 자기 배의 선원들에게도 향수를 쓰게 하였다고 한다. 꽃향기는 그리스 사람들이 사용하였다고 한다.

Postal Service 우편

1

The postal service is the government agency that handles the mail. The job of the postal service is to deliver letters and packages to people and businesses all over the world. Its goal is to see that your mail gets to its destination as quickly as possible. People rely on the postal service to deliver important letters and even valuables, on time and to the right person.

Much of the world's business depends on the postal service. That is why most countries co-operate closely on postal matters. The mail always 'goes through.' A flood in South America or an earthquake in Asia may cause a delay, but new routes are quickly found and mail is delivered. A letter mailed from Alaska, in North America, may travel to Kenya, in Africa, by boat, plane, train, truck, and even horseback.

postal service 미국의 우정 공사. 종래의 'post office'를 통합하였음. delíver *v.* 전달하다 get to – ~에 도착하다 destinátion *n.* 목적지 rely on – ~에 의존하다(= depend on) on time 정확한 시간에 right person 임자 co-operate *v.* 협조하다 go through 통과하다 flood *n.* 범람, 홍수 éarthquake *n.* 지진

1. Which of the following is the main goal of postal service?

① Delivering packages to businesses all over the country
② Delivering letters to people all over the world
③ Delivering a mail to its destination as quickly as possible
④ Delivering important letters on time
⑤ Delivering valuables to the right person

풀이 ① 온 나라의 기업들에 소포를 전달하는 것 ② 전세계의 사람들에게 편지를 전달하는 것 ③ 우편물을 목적지까지 가능한 빨리 전달하는 것 ④ 중요한 편지를 제시간에 전달하는 것 ⑤ 귀중품을 임자에게 전달하는 것
'postal service'의 목표(goal)는 첫 단락에 기술되어 있다.

보너스 상식

우편 용어

1. Post Office Box (P.O. Box) : 사서함. 개인이나 단체에게 전용으로 빌려준 우체국 내의 우편함이다.
2. ZIP Code(Zoning Improvement Plan) : 우편번호. 1940년대에 처음 등장하였다.
3. Special Delivery : 특급 우편(= Express Mail)

theme 22 Rollerskating 롤러스케이팅

1 Rollerskating requires a flat, fairly smooth surface. The area must be rather large and uncrowded because the ease of rolling makes a skater travel far. Outdoor rinks usually have a skating surface of smooth concrete. Indoor rinks have floors of flake board, which is a pressed wood that is coated with plastic.

In skating, you control your balance differently from the way you do in walking. Rollerskating differs from walking in that you place your foot flat, rather than your heel followed by your toe. To maintain good balance, you bend your knees whenever you take a step and try to keep your body in between your head and the foot that is off the floor.

Rollerskating provides good muscular exercise. Since no strenuous movements are required, roller-skating is suited for people of all ages and physical conditions.

flat *adj.* 평평한 rink *n.* 링크, 스케이트장 flake board 얇은 나뭇조각을 합성하여 수지로 붙인 나무판, 합판 pressed wood 압착된 목재 place *v.* 두다, 위치시키다 heel *n.* 발뒤꿈치 tow *n.* 발끝 muscúlar éxercise 근육 운동 strénuous *adj.* 격렬한, 분투하는, 열심히 하는

1. According to the passage, with which of the following is the floors of indoor rinks covered?

① flake board ② coated plastic
③ lawn ground ④ marbled
⑤ smooth concrete

풀이 ① 합판 마루 ② 코팅된 플라스틱 ③ 잔디 구장 ④ 대리석 바닥 ⑤ 매끄러운 콘크리트
'실내 스케이트장'(Indoor rinks ...)은 첫 단락에 기술되어 있다.

보너스 상식

롤러스케이트의 기원

1. 1760년에 영국인 '조셉 멀린'(Joseph Merlin)이 롤러스케이트를 처음 만들었다.
2. 1819년 프랑스인 '페티블레'(Petitbled)가 직선의 한쪽 스케이트 날에 바퀴를 2~4개씩 단 롤러스케이트를 고안하였다.
3. 1863년 미국인 '제임스 플림프턴'(James Plimpton)이 4바퀴 롤러스케이트를 만들어 유행시켰다.

Skateboarding 스케이트보드

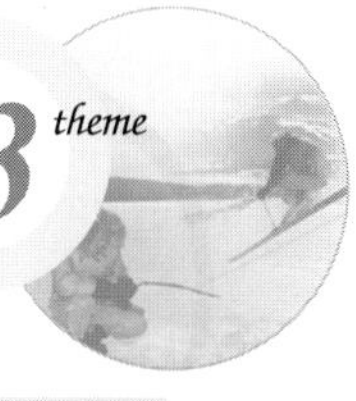

1

Skateboarding began in the United States in the early 1960's, when California teenagers attached roller skates to wood boards so that they could practice 'surfing' on the sidewalk. The ride was far from perfect. Bumpy roads and stones often stopped the small skate wheels and this sent the sidewalk surfers sprawling.

In the 1970's, manufacturers responded to this fad by using improved wheels and boards. Newer plastic wheels made out of polyurethane were larger and softer than skate wheels. These plastic wheels provided a smoother ride and excellent traction. The wheels were mounted on special shock absorbers called trucks that made boards easier to maneuver. Improved boards came in different models and were made of different woods as well as plastic, fiberglass, and aluminum. With the new equipment, the sport caught on quickly, and today more than 20 million people all over the world are skateboarding. Some of them even use custom-made skateboards.

attách *v.* 붙이다, 대다 sídewalk *n.* 보도, 인도 far from 결코 ~아닌 bumpy *adj.* 울퉁불퉁한 send someone sprawling 누구를 넘어뜨리다, 굴복시키다 manufácturer *n.* 제작자 respónd *v.* 반응하다, 대응하다 fad *n.* 일시적 유행, 열광 traction *n.* 마찰, 접착력 mount *v.* 붙박다, 놓다 truck *n.* (완충용)차대, 트럭 manéuver *v.* 기동하다, 연습하다 fíberglass *n.* 유리섬유 catch on 인기를 얻다, 붙잡다 custom-made 주문한, 맞춤의

1. According to the passage, the improved skateboards are made of all the following **except**

① aluminum. ② fiberglass.
③ plastic. ④ steel.
⑤ woods.

풀이 ① 알루미늄 ② 유리섬유 ③ 플라스틱 ④ 강철 ⑤ 목재
글 가운데서 재료의 이름을 찾으면 빠르다. 둘째 단락의 후반부에 최근의 재질을 열거하고 있다.

보너스 상식

스케이트보드 안전 수칙

1. 항상 운동화를 신고, 헬멧, 장갑, 팔꿈치와 무릎 패드, 손목 밴드 등 보호 장비를 착용하고 탄다.
2. 스케이트보드 장비를 잘 관리한다. 타기 전에는 이음새나 바퀴 등이 이상이 없는지 반드시 살피고 탄다.
3. 스케이트보드를 탈 수 있도록 허용된 지역에서만 탄다.
4. 보도에서 탈 때는 보행인을 잘 살피고, 도로에서 탈 때는 교통 신호, 교통 표지, 교통 규칙들을 준수한다.
5. 교통이 복잡한 지역에서는 절대로 스케이트보드를 타지 않는다.
6. 밤에는 절대로 타지 않는다. 어두워서 장애물들이 잘 안보이므로 위험하다.
7. 자전거, 자동차 등에 매달아 끌도록 하지 않는다.

theme 24 Sleep 잠

1 The depth of sleep does remain the same throughout the period of sleep. The depth of sleep can be measured by the amount of sound needed to awaken the sleeper. The first cycle of sleep lasts about $1\frac{1}{2}$ hours. During this cycle, deep sleep alternates with lighter sleep. These $1\frac{1}{2}$-hour cycles continue throughout the night. Toward the end of the night there is less deep sleep and more lighter sleep.

Recent research has proven that there are two types of sleep—dreaming and nondreaming sleep. Everyone dreams while asleep, although a person may not remember the dreams when awake. The ability to dream appears to play a part in making the person feel refreshed and rested upon awakening.

The amount of sleep a person requires varies with each individual. Most adults need from 7 to 9 hours daily. The average 2-year-old needs 12 hours of sleep at night and 1 to 2 hours of nap. Between the ages of 6 and 9 the night's sleep may be shortened to about 11 hours. A 12-year-old may do well with 10 hours of sleep each night. These are average figures, however.

last *v.* 지속하다 álternate *v.* 대체하다, 교체하다 play a part in – ing ~에 어떤 역할을 하다 refréshed *adj.* 상쾌한 rested *adj.* 편안한 upon awakening 깨어나자마자 nap *n.* 낮잠 shórten *v.* 줄이다 do well with – ~로도 잘하다 fígure *n.* 통계, 수치

1. According to the passage, how many hours of sleep do 2-year-old babies need every day?

① 7 to 9 hours
② 9 to 10 hours
③ 10 to 11 hours
④ 11 to 12 hours
⑤ 13 to 14 hours

풀이 마지막 단락에 수면이 시간이 적혀 있다. 밤잠 12시간, 낮잠 1~2시간이다.

보너스 상식

잠과 체온

사람이 잠을 잘 때는 반드시 체온이 내려간다. 우리가 잠을 잘 때 이불을 덮고 자는 이유가 바로 이 때문이다. 낮에 깨어 있고 밤에 잠을 자는 것이 습관이 된 사람은 밤에 잠을 자지 않아도 체온이 내려간다. 밤에 일하고 낮에 잠을 자는 사람 역시 낮에 잠을 자건 자지 않건 체온이 내려간다.

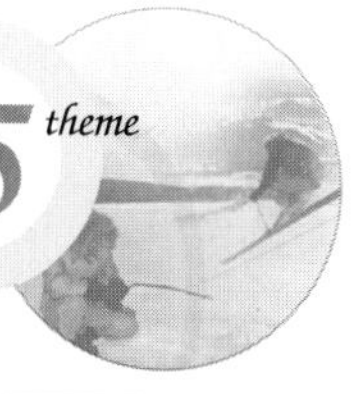

Tapestry 태피스트리

1

A tapestry is a handwoven textile. It is usually made with heavy threads of several colors. Most tapestries are hung on walls or suspended from ceilings.

The weaving of textile by hand requires much time and a great deal of skill. The weaver is limited by problems that other artists seldom face. He has no canvas to paint, no clay to model, no wood or stone to carve. Given only colored threads, he must manufacture and decorate his textile at the same time. Artists with patience, ability to plan, and skill to weave have always been rare, and tapestries traditionally are very expensive and precious.

In the days when the church and great royal houses ruled the world, tapestries were symbols of wealth. Whenever plays, official ceremonies, or public celebrations were held, tapestries lent beauty and richness to the events. Religious processions followed routes marked with tapestries.

tápestry *n.* 태피스트리. 색색의 실로 수놓은 벽걸이나 실내 장식용 비단 hándwoven *adj.* 손으로 짠 téxtile *n.* 직물 thread *n.* 실 suspénd *v.* 걸다, 매달다 céiling *n.* 천장 weave *v.* (직물을) 짜다, 뜨다(weave-wove-woven) clay *n.* 점토 carve *v.* 조각하다 pátience *n.* 인내 précious *adj.* 고귀한 celebrátion *n.* 축전 cárpet *n.* 융단 procéssion *n.* 행렬, 행진

1. According to the passage, a tapestry is usually made with which of the following?

① clay ② crayon
③ stone ④ threads
⑤ wood

풀이 ① 점토 ② 크레용 ③ 석재 ④ 실 ⑤ 나무
첫 문장에도 나타나 있지만, 글 곳곳에 있는 textile, thread, weave, handwoven 등의표현들로 실로 짜는 것임을 알 수 있다.

보너스 상식

'태피스트리'의 황금기

'Tapestry'란 벽걸이나 실내장식용으로 색색의 실로 수를 놓은 비단(융단)을 말한다. 이 태피스트리의 황금기는 13~15세기 중세 고딕 시대(the Gothic Era)이다. 이 시대를 상징하는 것이 바로 성경 이야기의 장면을 그린 벽화, 아름다운 스테인드 글래스로 된 유리창, 벽걸이 태피스트리가 걸린 교회이다. 큰 교회에서 행해지는 각종 의식에서 태피스트리는 매우 중요한 역할을 하였다.

theme 26 Time management 시간 관리

1

Ask a busy person who gets things done how he or she can possibly take on other jobs with such a full schedule. Chances are the answer will be, "By making lists of what needs to be done and crossing jobs off as I do them."

Making a list of jobs to be done is one of the best ways to organize your time. List items in order of priority—that is, decide how important a job is and when it must be completed. For example, if your science project is due this Friday and your reading assignment is due next week, list the science project first. List both these jobs ahead of something less important, like re-arranging your room.

Make a new list at the beginning of each week, or each day if you have a very busy schedule. Try to work steadily at each job until it is completed, and move promptly to the next one on your list. Putting things off or wasting time only prolongs an unpleasant job, leaving you with less free time. After you have crossed off the last job on your list, reward yourself by doing something you really enjoy.

get things done 일을 해치우다 take on (일을) 수행하다, 떠맡다 cross off (가위 표시로) 지우다 priórity *n.* 우선권, 우선 사항 órder of priórity 우선 순위 compléte *v.* 마치다, 완성하다 science project 과학 과제 reading assígnment 독서 숙제 due *n.* 예정, 만기 ahead of − ~의 앞에 steadily *adv.* 착착, 착실하게, 성실하게 prómptly *adv.* 즉시, 당장 put off 미루다, 연기하다 prolóng *v.* 연장하다 rewárd *v.* 보상하다, 보답하다

1. What is the main idea of the passage?

① Make lists of what needs to be done and cross jobs off as I do them.
② Decide how important a job is and when it must be completed.
③ Make a new list at the beginning of each week or each day if you are very busy.
④ Making a list of jobs to be done is one of the best ways to organize your time.
⑤ Putting things off or wasting time only prolongs an unpleasant job.

풀이 ① 해야 할 일의 목록을 작성하고, 그 일들을 할 때마다 지운다. ② 어떤 일이 얼마나 중요하고 언제 마쳐야 하는지를 결정한다. ③ 매우 바쁘면, 일주일 또는 하루를 시작할 때 새로운 목록을 작성한다. ④ 할 일들의 목록을 작성하는 것이 자신의 시간을 관리하는 최선의 길이다. ⑤ 일들을 미루거나 시간을 낭비하는 것은 유쾌하지 않은 일을 연장하는 것이다. 주제문은 첫 단락의 마지막 문장을 정리한, 바로 둘째 단락의 첫 문장이다.

보너스 상식

시간의 단위

second(초), minute(분, 60초), hour(시, 60분), day(일, 24시간), week(주, 7일), fortnight(2주, 영국), month(월, 30일), year(년, 12월), decade(10년), century(100년), millenium(1,000년)

Video Games 비디오 게임

1

Many advancements in game technology are being studied and perfected. Players of video games may one day be able to control the action by use of brain waves. In the more immediate future are games in which players use voice commands to control the course of events. In such games the computer recognizes certain words and reacts to them.

Most video games display images of cartoon characters or computer figures acting out a story or a sequence of events. But new video technology allows people to play games displaying real actors. These games are a combination of computer instructions and filmed images recorded on videodiscs. Depending on what the player does, the computer goes to different parts of the videodisc, and the action on the screen changes.

Multi-user games are also being developed. These will use telephone lines to transmit information so that many people—50 players in 50 different towns, for example—can play in the same game at the same time. Some of these games might require the players to cooperate with one another to achieve certain goals. Other games might pit the players against one another in mass contests.

Video games are still in the early stages of development. In the future they are certain to become more complex and therefore more challenging.

one day (미래에) 언젠가 brain wave 뇌파 récognize *v.* 인식하다 reáct *v.* 반응하다 cháracter *n.* 주인공, 캐릭터 fígure *n.* 인물 act out 연기하다 séquence *n.* 연속 a sequence of – 일련의 displáy *v.* 기용하다, 전시하다 filmed image 영상 이미지 depend on – ~에 달려 있다 go to 이용하다 multi-user game 다중 이용자 게임 transmít *v.* 전송하다 coóperate *v.* 협조하다 pit – against ~를 맞붙이다, 경쟁시키다 mass contest 대규모 경연 chállenging *adj.* 도전적인, 해볼 만한

1. Which of the following is the best statement about the multi-user game in the passage?

① It allows people to play games displaying real actors.
② The computer goes to different parts of the videodisc.
③ It may be able to control the action by use of brain waves.
④ Many people can play in the same game at the same time.
⑤ Players use voice commands to control the course of events in games.

theme 27

Video Games 비디오 게임

풀이 ① 사람들에게 실제 연기자를 등장시키는 게임을 하게 한다. ② 컴퓨터가 비디오 디스크의 여러 부분들을 이용한다. ③ 뇌파를 이용하여 작동을 통제할 수 있을 것이다. ④ 많은 사람들이 같은 게임을 동시에 할 수 있다. ⑤ 플레이어들이 음성 명령을 사용해 게임 과정을 통제한다.
글 가운데 'multi-user games'가 있는 곳을 찾아보면 그 개념이 있을 것이다.

보너스 상식

비디오게임의 분류

1. Player에 따른 분류 : ① 혼자서 하는 게임(playing by yourself) ② 둘이서 하는 게임(playing against another person) ③ 컴퓨터와 하는 게임(playing against a computer)
2. 운영자에 따른 분류 : ①Home games : 'video game machine'이나 'computer'를 이용 ②Arcade games(Game shop 에서) : 동전으로 작동 ③Pocket/wrist game machines : 주머니에 가지고 다닐 수 있는 게임기

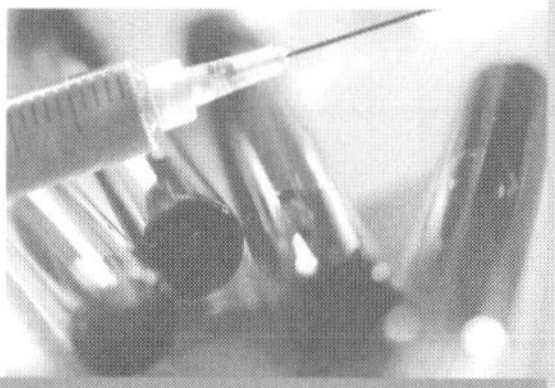

제 2 장

의약과 식품 Drugs and Foods

theme 01

Antibiotics 항생제

1 Scientists are actively working to find new antibiotics and to understand how bacteria fight off these drugs. Using computers, scientists can work with models to see whether a drug is likely to work on a microbe. New natural products are being found in plants and animals. Sharks and frogs contain small protein molecules, called defensins, that scientists hope to develop into antibiotics.

Some scientists are testing new molecules that stop the spread of bacteria rather than kill them. These molecules keep the bacteria from attaching to cells and starting an infection. But whether antibiotics stop the spread of bacteria or kill them, the goal of antibiotic research is to eliminate microbial disease. The lives of many people depend on it.

antibiótic *n.* 항생제 fight off 퇴치하다 mícrobe *n.* 세균, 미생물 shark *n.* 상어 mólecule *n.* 분자 defensin 디펜신(신조어) attách *v.* 달라붙다 inféction *n.* 감염 antibiótic reséarch 항생제 연구 elíminate *v.* 제거하다 micróbial *adj.* 세균성의, 세균에 의한

1. What does the passage mainly discuss?

① antibiotics ② bacteria
③ defensins ④ drugs
⑤ microbes

풀이 ① 항생제 ② 박테리아 ③ 디펜신 ④ 약 ⑤ 세균
이 글에서 가장 많이 등장하는 단어를 찾는다. 첫 문장과 마지막 문장에서 핵심어를 찾으면 그것이 바로 정답이다.

보너스 상식

항히스타민제(Antihistamine)

알레르기나 감기약에 쓰이는 물질이다. 천식이나 두드러기 등을 알레르기 질환이라고 한다. 어떤 물질이 체내에 들어가 항체가 만들어진 사람은 다음에 같은 물질이 들어오면 항원항체 반응이 일어나 알레르기 증상이 나타난다. 의학계에서는 항원항체 반응이 일어날 때 히스타민이나 아세틸콜린 같은 물질이 생기는 것으로 추정한다. 그래서 히스타민 등에 대항하는 약을 쓰면 증상이 가라앉을 것으로 본 데서 항히스타민제가 생기게 되었다.

Beer and Brewing 맥주와 양조

1

Beer is an alcoholic beverage that has been drunk for thousands of years. The making, or brewing, of beer appears to have begun very early in many parts of the world. A beerlike beverage was made in Mesopotamia as early as 6,000 B.C. Beer was also brewed in ancient Egypt, Greece, and Rome.

During the Middle Ages most beer was brewed by monks, and almost every monastery had a brew house. Eventually others took over this task and brewing grew into an industry with organizations, or guilds, of brewers. Beer in the Middle Ages was a thick, heavy beverage with a much higher alcohol content than today's beer. This thick, nourishing beer, almost as much a food as a drink, was an important item in people's daily diet.

In medieval England, beer, or ale, was often the chief drink at festivals and celebrations. It was such an important part of these revels that the word 'ale' was sometimes used to mean a festival. Lamb-ales were celebrations held at lamb-shearing time. College-ales were parties at which students drank the ale they had brewed. The word 'bridal' comes from 'bride-ale,' which was a wedding feast.

The knowledge of brewing beer was brought to the New World by the early colonists. At first, beer was made in small home breweries. However, as the colonies grew, brewing was established as an industry. One of the first breweries was built in 1683 at Pennsbury, Pennsylvania. Within a hundred years, the brewing industry had become an important part of the nation's economic life.

béverage *n.* 음료 brew *v.* (술을) 양조하다 brewer *n.* 양조자 bréwery *n.* 양조장 monk *n.* 수사(修士) mónastery *n.* 수도원 take over 인수하다 guild *n.* 길드 thick and heavy (술이) 진하고 독한 cóntent *n.* 함유량 nóurishing *adj.* 영양가 있는 diet *n.* 식사, 식단 médieval *adj.* 중세의 ale *n.* 에일, 맥주의 일종 또는 축제 rével *n.* 주연, 술잔치 lamb-ale 램에일, 양(羊)축제 lamb-shearing 양털 깎기 college-ale 대학 축제 feast *n.* 잔치, 축연 cólonist *n.* 식민지인 estáblish *v.* 수립하다, 형성하다

1. What is the best fitle for this passage?

① How to Brew Beer
② Beer and Ale
③ The Beer Industry
④ The History of Beer
⑤ The Ancient Beer

Beer and Brewing 맥주와 양조

2. The underlined word it refers to

① medieval England. ② festival.
③ ale. ④ diet.
⑤ alcchol content.

3. The underlined word <u>revels</u> is closest in meaning to

① beer. ② feast.
③ lamb-shearing time. ④ brewery.
⑤ heavy beverage.

4. Which statement is <u>not</u> true about the passage?

① Brewing grew into an industry with guilds of brewers.
② Beer has been brewed for over 8000 years.
③ The early colonists brought beer to the American continent.
④ Religious people couldn't brew alcoholic beverages.
⑤ In the Middle Ages, people regarded beer as a part of their diet.

풀이 1. ① 맥주 양조법 ② 비어와 에일 ③ 맥주산업 ④ 맥주의 역사 ⑤ 고대 맥주
2. It는 앞 문장의 주어를 다시 받고 있다.
3. revel = feast
4. ① 양조는 양조자들의 길드를 갖춘 산업으로 성장했다. ② 맥주는 8000년 동안 양조되어 왔다. ③ 초기 식민지인들이 맥주를 미국 대륙으로 가져왔다. ④ 종교인들은 술을 양조하지 못했다. ⑤ 중세 사람들은 맥주를 식품의 일부로 여겼다.

보너스 상식!

맥주의 종류

1. Lager beer : 저온에서 몇 달 저장한 맥주, 연노랑 색에 알코올 함유 3~4%로 약하다.
   ①bock beer (라거 맥주 가운데 가장 진하고 어두운 색이다)
   ②light beer (탄수화물과 칼로리를 줄인 것)
   ③dry beer (다른 라거 맥주에 비해 단맛이 덜하다)
2. Ale beer : 알코올 함유 4~5%로 lager보다 독하고 색깔도 더 연한 맥주
3. Porter beer: 약간 단맛이 있는 진한 갈색의 맥주이다.
4. Stout beer : 알코올 함유 5~6.5%로 가장 독하고, 색깔도 가장 진한 맥주이다.

Chocolate 초콜릿

1 Chocolate in the form of candy has about 145 calories an ounce (30 milliliters), or about 220 calories in the average chocolate bar. A $1\frac{1}{2}$-ounce (43-gram) chocolate bar has more than 5 percent of the U.S. Recommended Daily Allowance for protein, riboflavin, and calcium. Milk chocolate is about 35 percent fat and 50 percent carbohydrate. Although chocolate contains caffeine, it would take more than a pound of chocolate to equal the caffeine in one cup of coffee.

When chocolate was first introduced in Europe, it was thought to have many health benefits that have never been proved. In recent times it was thought to cause acne and dental cavities. Studies have shown that chocolate does not cause acne and that it is less likely to cause cavities than many other candies.

Chocolate is the favorite flavor for candy, cookies, ice cream, and other sweets in the United States, where consumption averages about 10 pounds (4.5 kilograms) per person per year. But the United States is only eleventh in worldwide consumption of chocolate. The leader is Switzerland, where average consumption per person is as high as 22 pounds (9.5 kilograms) per year.

áverage *adj.* 평균의 recomménded *adj.* 권장되는 allówance *n.* 허용, 허용 기준 prótein *n.* 단백질 riboflávin *n.* 리보플라빈, 비타민 B2 또는 G fat *n.* 지방 carbohydrate *n.* 탄수화물 contáin *v.* 함유하다 cáffeine *n.* 카페인 health bénefits 건강에 유익한 것들 ácne *n.* 여드름 cávity *n.* 충치 flávor *n.* 향, 맛 sweet *n.* 과자 consúmption *n.* 소비 áverage *v.* 평균이 되다

1. 이 글에 나타난 미국의 초콜릿 소비 순위를 다음에서 찾으시오.

① 1　　② 3　　③ 7　　④ 9　　⑤ 11

풀이 미국의 초콜릿 소비는 마지막 문단에 설명되어 있다.

보너스 상식

주요 Cacao **생산국**

① Ivory Coast (30%) ② 브라질 (20%) ③ 가나 ④ 나이지리아 ⑤ 말레이시아

주요 Chocolate **생산국**

① 미국 (20%) ② 독일 ③ 네덜란드 ④ 영국 ⑤ 스위스

theme 04 Cooking 요리

1 No one knows how long ago people began to cook. There is evidence that Stone Age people cooked food over open fires. Cooking advanced as people learned to grow grain and make clay pots. The ancient Egyptians are thought to have been the first to make leavened bread, which they baked in clay ovens heated by fire. The ancient Romans were fond of huge banquets, at which elaborately prepared dishes were served.

Fire was the basic source of heat for cooking right into the 1800's, when coal stoves were invented. Today most home kitchens in developed countries have electric or gas ranges and other modern conveniences, such as microwave ovens. Cooking is easier and faster. But many of the basic steps in preparing and cooking food have not changed for centuries.

évidence *n.* 증거 advánce *v.* 발전하다 grain *n.* 곡식 clay pot 토기 léaven *v.* 발효시키다 clay oven 토기 솥 be fond of – ~을 좋아하다 bánquet *n.* 연회, 잔치 eláborately *adv.* 정교하게, 정성 들여 dish *n.* 음식, 요리 coal stove 석탄 난로 convénience *n.* 편리한 도구 mícrowave óven 전자 오븐

1. According to the passage, who are thought to be the first to make bread?

① The ancient Egyptians ② The ancient Greeks
③ The ancient Romans ④ Stone Age people
⑤ The Mesopotamians

풀이 ① 고대 이집트인들 ② 고대 그리스인들 ③ 고대 로마인들 ④ 석기 시대 사람들 ⑤ 메소포타미아인들
첫 단락에 최초(the first)와 빵(bread)이라는 표현이 있다.

보너스 상식 요리법의 종류

①Baking (빵) 굽기 ②Roasting 로스 요리 ③Broiling (고기) 굽기
④Grilling 그릴에 굽기 ⑤Frying 튀김 ⑥Simmering 끓이기
⑦Boiling 삶기 ⑧Steaming 찜 ⑨Microwave cooking 전자 렌지 요리

Dairy Products 낙농 제품

05 theme

1 Most butter today is made in mechanical churns. The cream is shaken back and forth until the fat collects and separates from the rest of the cream. The part left after butter has been made is called buttermilk. It has about the same makeup as skim milk.

Buttermilk from buttermaking is used chiefly in making other food products. The buttermilk sold for drinking is cultured buttermilk, produced by the action of special bacteria.

The butter is washed with water and then kneaded until it becomes smooth. Salt is often added. Sometimes air is whipped into butter to make the lighter whipped butter. Butter is called the 'golden gift' because of its color and because it comes from cream, the richest, most expensive part of milk.

churn *n.* 교유기(攪乳器), 버터를 만드는 큰 양철통 shake *v.* 흔들다 back and forth 앞뒤로 fat *n.* 지방 makeup *n.* 구성, 성분, 조직 skim *v.* 우유의 기름기를 걷어내다 skim milk *v.* 탈지우유 culture *v.* (세균 등이) 배양하다 knead *v.* 반죽하다 whip *v.* (바람을) 훽 불어넣다

1. The butter is made of which of the following part of milk?

① calcium ② cream
③ fat ④ minerals
⑤ protein

풀이 ① 칼슘 ② 크림 ③ 지방 ④ 무기물 ⑤ 단백질
마지막 문장에 정답이 있다. 또 첫 단락에서 알 수 있다.

보너스 상식

저온 살균법(Pasteurization)

우유에 열을 가하여 박테리아를 죽이는 과정이다. 마시기에 안전한 우유를 만드는 법을 발견한 유명한 과학자 파스퇴르(Louis Pasteur)의 이름을 따서 붙인 말이다. 파스퇴르는 본래 포도주가 시어지지 않도록 이 살균법을 개발하였으나 우유의 살균 효과도 있음을 알았다. 현재까지 ① 63℃에서 30분 ② 72℃에서 15초 ③ 138℃에서 2초 살균하는 세 가지 방법이 있다.

Dairy Products 낙농 제품

2 Yogurt is a food of many uses. It is a good source of protein, calcium, certain B vitamins, and minerals. Because of its nutritional value, many people eat yogurt as a supplement to their regular diet or as a snack between meals. Yogurt can be enjoyed by itself or combined with other foods, such as apple sauce, peanut butter, or dry cereal. Many cooks use yogurt in recipes for salad dressings, sauces, soups, main dishes, and desserts.

Yogurt is a popular food in many parts of the world. In India, the Balkans, and the Middle East, yogurt is used as an ingredient in many dishes,

nutrítional *adj.* 영양의, 영양학적인 **súpplement** *n.* 보조 식품 **régular díet** 일상적인 식사 **snack** *n.* 간식 **by itself** 그 자체로 **céreal** *n.* 곡물, 시리얼 **récipe** *n.* 조리(법) **main dish** 주식, 주된 요리 **ingrédient** *n.* 성분, 재료

1. Which of the following is <u>not</u> mentioned in the passage as the nutritions of yogurt?

① calcium ② certain B vitamins
③ fat ④ minerals
⑤ protein

풀이 ① 칼슘 ② 비타민 B군 ③ 지방 ④ 무기물 ⑤ 단백질
둘째 문장에 요구르트의 각종 영양소들이 열거되어 있다.

보너스 상식

요구르트의 종류

① Sundae-style yogurt(선디식 요구르트) : 바닥에 과일을 까는 방식
② Swiss-style yogurt(스위스식 요구르트) : 전체를 과일로 만드는 방식
③ Western-style yogurt(서구식 요구르트) : 바닥에 과일을 깔고, 겉에 과일 시럽이나 과자를 입히는 방식

3 To make cheese, the milk first must be curdled. For hundreds of years rennet was put in milk to make it curdle. Rennet is a digestive juice, or enzyme, found in the stomachs of some plant-eating mammals. Nowadays rennet is obtained from young calves' stomachs. But most commercial cheese makers today also add special cultures of beneficial, harmless bacteria to sour the milk. Sometimes milk is curdled by acids.

In the second stage of cheese making, most of the whey is removed from the curdled milk. Whey can taken out more quickly by cutting the coagulated milk, or curd, into smaller pieces. This is done with a harplike instrument called a curd knife.

curdle *v.* 응결하다, 응고하다 rénnet *n.* 응유(凝乳)효소, 송아지의 4번째 위 속에 있는 응유(凝乳). 치즈 제조에 쓴다. digéstive *adj.* 소화의 énzyme *n.* 효소 obtáin *v.* 얻다, 채취하다 calf *n.* 송아지 cúlture *n.* 배양 benefícial *adj.* 유익한 sour *v.* 시게 하다 acid *n.* 산(酸) whey *n.* 유장(乳漿) remóve *v.* 제거하다(= take out) coágulate *v.* 응고시키다 curd *n.* 응유(凝乳) hárplike 하프같이 생긴

1. Which of the following is the first stage of cheese making?

① culturing ② curdling
③ cutting ④ shaking
⑤ souring

풀이 ① 배양하기 ② 응결하기 ③ 자르기 ④ 흔들기 ⑤ 시게 하기
둘째 단락의 시작 부분이 'the second stage'이므로 첫 단락을 살핀다. 첫 문장에 바로 정답이 나와 있다.

보너스 상식

세계에서 가장 큰 치즈

1995년 9월 7일 캐나다 퀘벡주 Granby의 로브로스(Loblaws) 수퍼마켓과 아그로퍼(Agropur) 목장이 함께 만든 치즈가 세계에서 제일 큰 것으로, 26.06톤이나 되었다.

theme **06**

Drugs 약품

1 One of the most basic ways to classify drugs has to do with their method of purchase. Some drugs can be purchased without a doctor's order, or prescription. These are called over-the-counter drugs. Pharmacies, grocery stores, and even gas stations sell over-the-counter drug products. Common over-the-counter drugs include antacids for stomach upset, aspirin for fever and headaches, and calamine lotion for poison ivy. Millions of dollars are spent every year to advertise over-the-counter drugs.

Drugs that are considered safe and effective for a particular person only after a doctor diagnoses a disease or ailment are called prescription drugs. They are usually obtained from a pharmacy. A physician writes out and signs a piece of paper, called a prescription, which is then taken to a pharmacist, a person who has been trained and licensed to give people the drugs requested by the doctor. The prescription indicates what and how much drug is to be dispensed, or given, to the patient. It also includes directions for taking it properly. In the United States, the drug container must have a label that states: "Caution: Federal Law Prohibits Dispensing Without Prescription."

clássify *v.* 분류하다 have to do with – ～와 관계가 있다 púrchase *n/v.* 구매/하다 prescríption *n.* 처방 over-the-counter drugs 약국이나 일반 상점에서 계산대 위에 놓고 파는 약품이란 뜻으로 의사의 처방 없이도 살 수 있는 약품(= non-prescription drugs) phármacy *n.* 약국 pharmacist *n.* 약사 gas station 주유소 antácid *n.* 제산제, 산을 중화하는 약품 stómach upsét 복통 cálamine *n.* 피부 염증 치료제 칼라민 poison ivy 옻독 ádvertise *v.* 광고하다 efféctive *adj.* 효과적인 díagnose *v.* 진단하다 áilment *n.* 질환 prescription drugs 처방약 physícian *n.* 의사, 내과 의사 requést *v.* 요청하다 dispénse *v.* (약을) 조제하다 contáiner *n.* 용기, 봉지 caution *n.* 주의 féderal law 연방 법률 prohíbit *v.* 금지하다

1. Which of the following is the best title for this passage?

① Common Over-the-counter Drugs ② Dispensing Without Prescription
③ The Methods of Drug Purchase ④ The Most Basic Ways to Classify Drugs
⑤ Over-the-counter and Prescription Drugs

풀이 ① 일반적인 계산대 약품 ② 처방 없는 약품 조제 ③ 약품 구매의 방법 ④ 약을 분류하는 가장 기본적인 방법
⑤ 계산대 약품과 처방약
첫 단락은 계산대 약품을, 둘째 단락은 처방 약품을 설명하고 있다.

보너스 상식!

1. 의약분업

진료와 치료는 의사가, 약의 조제는 의사의 처방전으로 약사가 담당하는 제도이다. 의약 분업의 장점은 ① 약이 필요한 의료가 개선된다 ② 전문 기술의 분리로 의료가 충실해진다 ③ 처방 내용이 밝혀지므로 환자의 치료에 대한 자가이 높아진다 ④ 약의 조제 시간이 단축된다는 점 들이다. 반면에 환자는 진료를 받은 다음 약국을 다시 찾아가야 하는 불편이 있다. 최근에는 슈퍼에서도 간단한 두통약이나 드링크류를 팔 수 있다.

2. 가장 흔한 질병

세상에서 가장 흔한 질병은 감기로 종류가 180종이나 된다. 공기나 직접 접촉으로 발병시키는 바이러스만도 40여 가지가 있다. 재채기나 기침이 나고, 목이 아프고, 눈물이나 콧물이 나고, 두통과 열이 나는 것이 일반적인 증상이다.

theme **06** Drugs 약품

2 Pharmacology is the science dealing with properties of drugs and the way in which they act on particular organs or cells of the body.

Drugs can enter the body and go to work in a variety of ways. Tablets, liquids, and capsules are all swallowed. They enter the bloodstream after being absorbed through the stomach or small intestines. Some drugs are given by injection directly into muscle tissue or body cavities. Creams, ointments, and some liquids such as eye drops are applied directly to the body's surface. Other drugs, such as anesthetic gas, are inhaled. The ways in which drugs produce their effects on the body is termed their mechanism of action. The mechanism of action of many drugs is to change the speed of chemical reactions in the cells. Drugs can correct these imbalances and either cure the disease or ailment or prevent it from spreading throughout the body.

Because drugs usually cannot distinguish between healthy cells and diseased cells, no drug is totally safe. Drugs sometimes produce undesirable side effects when they affect healthy cells or organs. For this reason it is important that drugs be used only according to a doctor's direction. You should tell your doctor if any drug is producing side effects so that an adjustment in the dose can be made or a different drug prescribed.

pharmacólogy *n.* 약리학 deal with – ~을 다루다, 연구하다 própertу *n.* 특성 órgan *n.* (인체의) 기관 táblet *n.* 알약 cápsule *n.* 당의정 swállow *v.* 삼키다 absórb *v.* 흡수하다 small intéstine 소장 injéction *n.* 주사 muscle tíssue 근육질 cávity *n.* 구멍, 공동 óintment *n.* 연고 eye drop 안약 apply *v.* 바르다 anesthétic *adj.* 마취제의 inhále *v.* 흡입하다, 들이마시다 (*opp.* exhále 내쉬다) méchanism *n.* 메커니즘 imbálance *n.* 불균형 áilment *n.* 질환 distínguish *v.* 구별하다 undesírable *adj.* 바람직하지 않은 side effect 부작용 adjústment *n.* 조정 dose *n.* 약의 1회분, 약의 첩 prescríbe *v.* 처방하다

1. Which of the following is <u>not</u> included in the ways which you have drugs?

① applying ② inhaling
③ injection ④ prescribing
⑤ swallow

풀이 ① 바름 ② 흡입 ③ 주사 ④ 처방 ⑤ 삼킴
둘째 단락의 첫 문장부터 복용 방식이 하나씩 열거되어 있다.

3 The oldest sources of drugs are plants and animals. The foxglove plant, for example, was the original source of digoxen, a drug used to treat a failing heart. The poppy plant provided morphine to alleviate pain. Animal glands still provide insulin for the treatment of diabetes and growth hormones for dwarfism.

Bacteria and molds, which are also living organisms, are the source of antibiotics. Each bacteria and mold cell secretes tiny amounts of a chemical that can kill other bacteria or fungi. Billions of these cells are grown by drug manufacturers in large tanks called fermentors.

Though many drugs originally came from plants or animals, most drugs today are created synthetically in the laboratories of pharmaceutical chemists. Synthetic drugs are those made by combining simple molecules in a series of chemical reactions to produce larger, more complex molecules. The great number of possible molecule combinations makes synthetic drugs an important source for new drug products.

fóxglove *n.* 디기탈리스, 심장마비 치료제의 원료 dígoxen *n.* 디고센, 심장마비 치료제 failing heart 심장마비(= heart failure) poppy *n.* 양귀비 alléviate *v.* 완화시키다, 줄이다 gland *n.* 선(腺), 내분비샘, 땀샘 diabétes *n.* 당뇨병 dwárfism *n.* 왜소 발육증 mold *n.* 곰팡이 sécrete *v.* 보유하다, 간직하다 fúngus *n.* 버섯, 균 (*pl.* fungi) férmentor *n.* 발효조 synthétically *adv.* 합성으로, 인공적으로 láboratory *n.* 실험실 pharmacéutical *adj.* 약제의, 약품 조제의 mólecule *n.* 분자 chemical reaction 화학반응

1. Which of the following is not mentioned in the passage as the sources of drugs?

① animal glands ② bacteria
③ fossils ④ molds
⑤ poppy

풀이 ① 동물 내분비샘 ② 박테리아 ③ 화석 ④ 곰팡이 ⑤ 양귀비
첫 단락과 둘째 단락에 있다.

보너스 상식

본초(本草)

생명체에 대한 양생, 치료, 예방에 제공되는 천연 약물을 말한다. 초근목피(草根木皮)를 위주로 하고 동물, 광물을 포함하는 약품으로 한방 약물을 대표하는 말이다. 중국 명나라 때의 본초학자 이시진(李時珍)이 엮은 약학서인 《본초강목》에는 약용으로 쓰이는 대부분의 약재가 분류되어 있다.

theme 07 Fast Food 패스트푸드

1 Fast food is inexpensive food items available at restaurants offering a limited menu and quick service. Most fast foods are at least partially prepared at a central facility and then distributed to individual restaurants. Fryers, grills, microwave ovens, and other machinery—some of it computerized—are used to finish cooking the food before sale. Popular items in fast-food restaurants include hamburgers, fried chicken, milk shakes, french-fried potatoes, and salads. Since the first McDonald's restaurant opened in the 1950's, fast-food chains have grown into a multibillion-dollar industry.

inexpénsive *adj.* 값싼 céntral fac lity 중앙 공장 distríbute *v.* 배달하다, 배포하다 fryer *n.* 프라이팬, 프라이 기구
a multibillion-dollar industry 수 십억 달러짜리 산업

1. Which of the following is <u>not</u> included in the characteristics of fast food?

① chain restaurants ② cheap
③ expensive ④ limited menu
⑤ quick service

풀이 ① 체인 식당 ② 싸다 ③ 비싸다 ④ 한정된 메뉴 ⑤ 신속한 서비스
주제문인 첫 문장에 특징이 나와 있다.

보너스 상식

단식(Fasting)

일정한 기간 동안 음식을 먹지 않는 것이다. 때로는 물까지도 마시지 않을 수 있다. 주로 종교적인 행사로, 죄를 회개하거나, 죽은 가족을 애도하기 위해서 단식을 한다. 항의의 형태로 단식을 하기도 한다. 몇 날에서 몇 주일 계속하기도 하며, 단식을 끝낸 뒤에 보식을 조심해서 해야 한다. 영어 'break-fast'는 밤 사이의 단식(?)을 끝낸다는 뜻을 가지고 있다.

1 Few countries have added as much to the art of cooking as France. Leading restaurants throughout the world feature the traditional French style of cooking called haute cuisine, which means 'high, or artful, style of cooking.' Nouvelle (new) cuisine also originated in France. It is a lighter way of cooking, avoiding heavy sauces and the abuse of butter in food preparation.

French cooks are famous for mixing together herbs, seasonings, and wines with a touch of imagination. Fine sauces for meat, poultry, and fish are the result. France is known for its pastries and breads. French wines and cheeses are among the world's best.

Thomas Jefferson learned to make ice cream while he was living in Paris as America's minister to France. He brought the recipe, written in his own hand, back to the United States. He was among the first to serve ice cream as a desert at a state dinner.

féature *v.* 특징짓다 oríginate *v.* 기원하다, 비롯되다 avóid *v.* 회피하다 abúse *n.* 남용 séasoning *n.* 양념 póultry *n.* 가금, 닭고기 pástry *n.* (구워서 만드는) 과자 mínister *n.* 공사 récipe *n.* 조리법 state dinner 공식 만찬

1. France is famous for all of the following foods **except**

① cheese. ② pastries.
③ sauces. ④ steaks.
⑤ wines.

풀이 ① 치즈 ② 과자 ③ 소스 ④ 스테이크 ⑤ 와인
둘째 단락에 프랑스의 유명한 식품들이 열거되어 있다.

보너스 상식

레스토랑에서 포도주 마시기

고급 레스토랑에서 포도주를 시키면 주문자가 시음을 하는 것이 격식처럼 되어 있다. 웨이터는 코르크 마개를 따기 전에 상표를 보여준다. 이의가 없으면 따서 주문자의 잔에 맛보기로 조금 따라준다. 맛을 본 주문자는 솔직하게 느낀 대로 말하면 된다. 할 말이 없으면 고개를 끄덕여 주어도 좋다. 이런 과정이 번거롭게 느껴지는 사람도 있겠지만, 손님에게 좋은 포도주를 맛보게 하려는 배려이니 당황하거나 귀찮게 여길 필요는 없다.

theme 08 Food 식품

2 Almost everyone enjoys eating the Italian pastas—dried dough in the form of spaghetti, noodles, macaroni, or ravioli, served with different sauces. Small restaurants called pizzerias feature the traditional Italian pizza. This is a circle of dough that may be covered with tomato sauce, melted cheese, mushrooms, anchovies, or bits of meat or sausage and then baked.

Italy's limited meat and dairy supply has not kept good Italian cooks from making many fine dishes. They 'stretch' small portions of meat with pastas, rice, cornmeal, sauces, and cheese and enliven their dishes with herbs. Scaloppine, thin slices of veal cooked in butter or olive oil and bathed in sauce, is a popular dish. Italian wines, cheeses, and pastries are shipped to many parts of the world.

pásta *n.* 파스타. 달걀을 섞은 가루 반죽을 재료로 한 이탈리아 요리 dough *n.* 가루 반죽, 굽지 않은 빵 noodle *n.* 국수 ravióli *n.* 라비올리. 저며서 양념한 고기를 얇은 가루 반죽에 싼 요리 sauce *n.* 양념 múshroom *n.* 버섯 ánchovy *n.* 안초비(멸치류) dish *n.* 음식메뉴 stretch *v.* 넓히다, 뻗치다 pórtion *n.* 부분, 영역 enlíven *v.* 생기를 돋우다, 활기를 주다 scaloppíne *n.* 스캘러피니. 얇게 썬 송아지 고기를 기름에 튀긴 이탈리아 요리 slice *n.* (얇게 썬) 조각 veal *n.* 송아지 고기 pástry *n.* 가루 반죽을 구워서 만든 과자

1. Which of the following is <u>not</u> included in the kinds of Italian Pastas?

① macaroni ② noodles
③ pizza ④ ravioli
⑤ spaghetti

풀이 ① 마카로니 ② 국수 ③ 피자 ④ 라비올리 ⑤ 스파게티
'pastas'라는 요리의 종류는 첫 문장에 열거되어 있다.

보너스 상식 세계에서 가장 큰 피자(Pizza)

세계에서 제일 큰 피자는 1990년 12월 8일, 남아프리카의 Norwood의 'Norwood 수퍼마켓'에서 만든 것으로 직경이 37.4m나 되었다.

3 Some foods spoil less easily than others. An orange resists spoiling because its tough skin helps keep out micro-organisms. The high acidity, or sourness, of its pulpy interior also slows down spoilage. Few bacteria can grow in surroundings as strongly acidic as those inside an orange.

On the other hand, fresh milk and meat spoil easily. With no protective coverings like oranges have, they can be contaminated by airborne bacteria during processing. They also may contain bacteria that lived in the animal from which they were obtained.

Many processes have been developed to control or destroy those agents responsible for food spoilage. These processes include drying, refrigeration and freezing, heat processing, and preserving with chemicals.

spoil *v.* 상하게 하다, 부패시키다 spóilage *n.* 부패 keep out 쫓아내다 micro-organism 미생물 acídity *n.* 산성도 sóurness *n.* 신맛 contáminate *v.* 오염시키다, 감염시키다 áirborne bactéria 공중 박테리아 prócess *n.* 처리과정 refrigerátion *n.* 냉장 presérve *v.* 보존하다 chémical *n.* 화학약품

1. Which of the following is the process that was developed to prevent the food spoilage?

① drying ② freezing
③ heating ④ protecting
⑤ refrigeration

풀이 ① 건조 ② 냉동 ③ 가열 ④ 보호 ⑤ 냉장
마지막 단락에 부패 방지 처리과정들이 열거되어 있다.

보너스 상식

식품을 상하게 하는 것들

① Pests(해충) : 곤충, 기생충, 쥐 등
② Chemicals(화학 물질) : 효소(enzymes)
③ Micro-organisms(미생물) : 곰팡이(molds), 박테리아 등

theme

08 Food 식품

4 In 1804, Nicolas Appert, a French candy maker and chef, discovered how to preserve food by heating precooked food in a glass container and then sealing it tightly. Cooking alone will not preserve food, because when the food cools, micro-organisms in the air will touch the food and in time cause spoilage.

Appert's process actually sterilized the food, killing all micro-organisms. It also kept air—and new micro-organisms—from entering the container. Food treated in this way will keep for years and be good to eat when the container is opened. Glass bottles, cans, molded plastic containers, plastic bags, and foil-lined cartons are all used to package sterilized foods.

chef *n.* 요리사, 주방장 seal *v.* 밀봉하다 stérilize *v.* 살균하다, 황폐시키다 mold *v.* 형성하다 cárton *n.* 상자, 용기

1. Which of the following is Nicolas Appert' s way of preserving food?

① drying ② freezing
③ heating ④ packing
⑤ refrigeration

풀이 ① 건조 ② 냉동 ③ 가열 ④ 포장 ⑤ 냉장
주제문인 첫 문장에 바로 등장하고 있다.

보너스 상식

식품 보존 방식

① 건조(drying) : 가장 오래된 식품 보존 방식
② 냉장(refrigerating)과 냉동(freezing)
③ 열처리(heat processing) : 통조림, 저온 처리법(pasteurization)
④ 화학적 처리(chemical preservatives)
⑤ 발효(fermentation)
⑥ 설탕(sugar)과 소금(salt)에 절임
⑦ 훈제(smoking)
⑧ 자외선(ultraviolet light) 보존법
⑨ 냉동건조(freeze-drying)

Food 식품 08 theme

5 The new U.S. food-labeling regulations also help protect consumers from false claims made about food products. Precise definitions are now given to descriptive words used on food labels.

In addition, health claims are permitted on a food label for only seven food-disease relationships. These relationships are calcium and osteoporosis; sodium and high blood pressure; fat and cancer; fat and heart disease; fiber and cancer; fiber and heart disease; and fruits and vegetables and cancer. A food product must meet specific requirements regarding its nutrient content to make claims related to these health issues.

food-labeling 식품 상표 regulátion *n.* 규정 consúmer *n.* 소비자 precíse *adj.* 정확한 definítion *n.* 규정, 정의 descríptive *adj.* 설명적인, 구체적인 health claim 건강 문구 permít *v.* 허용하다 osteoporósis *n.* 골다공증 sódium *n.* 나트륨 high préssure 고혈압 fíber *n.* 섬유질 specífic requírement 특정한 조건 regárding – ~을 고려하여 nútrient contént 영양 함유

1. Which of the following is the main purpose of the new U.S. food-labeling regulations?

① Issuing health claims of consumers
② Labeling food-disease relationships
③ Precise definitions on food label
④ Protecting the food consumers
⑤ Regarding foods' nutrient content

풀이 ① 소비자들의 건강 요구를 부각하기 위해 ② 식품과 질병의 관계를 표시하기 위해 ③ 식품 설명서에 정확한 설명 ④ 식품 소비자들을 보호하기 위해 ⑤ 식품의 영양 함유를 고려하기 위해
첫 문장에 주제로 나온 문제이다.

보너스 상식

식품 보관 상식

1. 채소 : 요리하지 않은 육류와 가까이 두지 않는다. 육류의 기름기가 채소를 상하게 한다.
2. 마요네즈 : 일단 뚜껑을 딴 마요네즈도 냉장고에 보관할 경우 6개월은 안전하다.
3. 쇠고기 : 요리하지 않은 육류는 냉장고에서 5일까지는 안전하다. 그러나, 일단 저민 고기는 냉장고에서도 이틀을 넘기면 안 된다.
4. 닭고기 : 냉장고에서 이틀 정도 보관할 수 있다.

theme 08

Food 식품

6 About 15 percent of an average American family's income is spent on food. Planning ahead will help to make sure that you will get the most for your money. The first step is to prepare a menu of meals for several days or even for a week or two. Next, make a grocery list of foods you will need to prepare the meals on the menu. Follow this list closely when you shop. It is a good idea to avoid grocery shopping when you are hungry. Otherwise, you will be tempted to buy appealing-looking items that are not on your grocery list.

íncome *n.* 수입 ahéad *adv.* 미리 get the most for — ~을 최대한 활용하다 tempt to do ~하도록 유혹하다
appéaling-looking ítems 맛있어 보이는 품목

1. What is the best title for this passage?

① American Family's Food Shopping
② Making a Grocery List of Foods
③ Planning for Food Shopping
④ Preparing a Menu of Meals
⑤ Steps for Grocery Shopping

풀이 ① 미국인 가정의 식품 구매 ② 식품 리스트 작성 ③ 식품 구매의 계획 ④ 식단의 준비 ⑤ 식품 구매의 단계
둘째 문장이 이 글의 주제문이다. 핵심어가 'planning'이다.

보너스 상식

알뜰한 식품 구매 방법

1. 세일 때 구입한다.
2. 조리된 편의 식품은 피한다.
3. 브랜드 식품보다는 일반 식품이 저렴하다.
4. 포장이 많은 것은 비싸다.
5. 식품에 붙은 라벨을 꼼꼼히 읽는다.
6. 영수증을 챙긴다.

7 In any one year, the world's food supply consists mainly of what is produced that year. Some food is carried over into the next year. To build up such reserves, more food must be produced than is needed. But only a few countries, such as the United States, are able to do this. Other countries must import additional supplies because, for a variety of reasons, they cannot produce enough for their needs.

Some countries are too poor to import enough food or to grow it for themselves. These countries need economic development and a fairer distribution of the benefits of a growing economy to the people.

consíst of – ~로 구성되다 carry over 넘기다, 이월하다 resérve *n.* 준비, 비축 addítional supplíes 추가 공급량
distribútion *n.* 분배

1. What does this passage mainly discuss?

① Economic development ② Fair distribution
③ Food import ④ Food production
⑤ Food supply

풀이 ① 경제 개발 ② 공정한 분배 ③ 식량 수입 ④ 식량 생산 ⑤ 식량 공급
주제문인 첫 문장의 핵심어이다.

보너스 상식!

식량 공급에 영향을 미치는 요인

1. land(토지) : 우선 농토가 많아야 한다.
2. water(물) : 물이 풍부해야 한다.
3. climate / weather(기후/날씨) : 가뭄과 홍수는 작황에 큰 영향을 미친다.
4. energy(에너지) : 현대 농업에는 에너지가 필요하다.
5. transportation(교통) : 식량의 반입과 배포에 매우 중요하다.

Food 식품

8 New technology and improved methods of distribution may help feed the world in the future. New foods are being made from soybeans and other protein-rich oil seeds, for example. Genetic engineering may help to develop new plants more resistant to disease and drought. More food may one day be harvested from the sea.

But what is most needed now is increased development in the food-short countries. Although basic decisions for the future must be made by those countries themselves, a greater international effort to support them will also be needed.

méthod of distribútion 유통 방법 feed *v.* 먹이다 sóybean *n.* 콩 genétic enginéering 유전 공학 resístant to – ~에 저항하는 drought *n.* 가뭄 hárvest *v.* 수확하다, 추수하다

1. Which of the following is the best topic of the passage?

① Genetic Engineering
② Food for the Future
③ Improved Methods of Food Distribution
④ New Foods
⑤ New technology for Food Production

풀이 ① 유전 공학 ② 미래의 식량 ③ 향상된 식량 유통 방법 ④ 새로운 식량 ⑤ 식량 생산을 위한 새로운 기술
첫 단락에서 유추해야 한다. 각 문장의 동사들의 시제를 참고할 것.

보너스 상식

식량조기경보시스템(Global information and early warning on food and agriculture)

각국이 자기 나라의 식량 생산이나 수요의 동향, 식량 수출과 수입의 전망 등을 '유엔식량농업기구'(FAO)에 적어도 매월 1회 보고하고 FAO가 그것을 집계, 분석한 것을 세계의 식량 정보로서 일괄하여 각국에 되돌려 주는 체제이다. 식량 수급이 어려운 가운데 세계의 식량 동향을 조기에 파악, 각국이 적절한 대응책을 세우게 하자는 것이 목적이다. 1974년 11월에 로마에서 열린 세계 식량 회의에서 이 체제를 수립하였다. FAO가 각국에 배포하는 보고서는 분기별 보고, 월례 보고, 월례 보고서의 해설, 부정기적인 새로운 뉴스 등이 있다.

Ice Cream 아이스크림

1

The history of ice cream is a mystery. No one knows exactly where or when people began to eat it. One story tells how the Roman emperor Nero sent slaves to the mountains to bring back snow, which was served to him sweetened with honey and fruit pulp. We do know that Marco Polo tasted flavored ices during his famous travels in Asia because he brought back the recipes when he returned to Italy in 1295.

Recipes for flavored ices spread from Italy to the rest of Europe in the 1500's. The chefs of kings constantly experimented with new combinations to please their masters. At some point, cream and butter were added to the recipes, and the new dish was called 'cream ice.'

It is not known exactly when ice cream was first made in the United States. One of the earliest-known American references to ice cream was in a tavern's advertisement in a New York newspaper in 1786. Dolley Madison, wife of President James Madison, was the first to serve ice cream in the White House in the early 1800's. Throughout the 1800's, 'ice cream socials' became a popular way to entertain friends. Today people can still have fun making ice cream at home with electric or hand-cranked ice cream machines.

fruit pulp 과육, 과일 말린 것 flávor *v.* 맛을 내다 récipe *n.* 조리법 cónstantly *adv.* 꾸준히 réference *n.* 참고문헌 távern *n.* 선술집 ice cream socials 아이스크림 친목회

1. Who was the first to serve ice cream in the White House?

① A New York newspaper ② Doly Madison
③ John F. Kennedy ④ A tavern owner
⑤ Thomas Jefferson

풀이 ① 뉴욕의 어느 신문 ② 돌리 매디슨 ③ 존 케네디 ④ 어느 선술집 주인 ⑤ 토마스 제퍼슨
셋째 단락에 있는 백악관을 찾아 아이스크림을 접대한 사람을 찾으면 된다.

보너스 상식

'아이스크림 콘'을 만든 사람

시리아의 Damascus에서 미국으로 이민을 온 '함위'(Ernest A. Hamwi)라는 사람은 1904년 미주리주 St. Louis에서 가게를 열어, 와플(Waffle)을 구워 팔았다. 그 가게 옆에 아이스크림 행상이 한 사람 있었다. 당시에는 아이스크림을 접시에 담았는데, 더운 여름날 아이스크림이 금방 녹아 버리는 것이었다. Hamwi는 재빨리 자신의 '와플'을 콘(corn, 원뿔) 모양으로 싸서 아이스크림을 담았다. 다음부터는 자신의 와플에 아이스크림을 담아서 이웃들과 단골들에게 나누어주었다고 한다.

theme 10

Meat 육류

1

Before refrigerators came into widespread use, meat was eaten fresh or preserved by curing and smoking processes. Cured meats were heavily salted to keep them ____ ______. Today the curing process, which involves injecting a solution of salt, water, and sometimes sugar into the meat, is used mostly to enhance flavor. Smoking, a curing process that exposes meat to the smoke of burning hardwood, also gives meat a distinctive flavor and aroma. Smoked meats include most ham, bacon, and sausages.

Two other common methods of preserving meat are canning and freezing. Canned goods containing meats, such as sandwich spreads, chile con carne, beef stew, and corned-beef hash, may be stored unopened for several years. Meat can also be frozen, but for a more limited period of time. Uncooked beef and lamb may be kept up to 6 months in the freezer (3 months if cooked); uncooked pork and veal can be kept frozen for 4 months (2 months if cooked).

refrígerator *n.* 냉장고 cure *v.* 소금에 절이다 smoking *n.* 훈제 injéct *v.* 주사하다 solution *n.* 용액 enhánce *v.* 향상시키다 flávor *n.* 맛 expóse *v.* 노출시키다 hárdwood *n.* 단단한 나무, 장작 distínctive *adj.* 뚜렷한 aróma *n.* 향기 canning *n.* 통조림 freezing *n.* 냉동 spreads *n.* 빵에 발라먹는 것 (버터와 잼 등) chile con carne 칠레 고추 corned-beef hash 소금 절이 쇠고기 해시 요리 lamb *n.* 양고기 pork *n.* 돼지고기 veal *n.* 송아지 고기

1. According to the passage, which of the following is <u>not</u> stated as the methods of preserving meat?

① canning ② curing
③ freezing ④ injecting
⑤ smoking

2. What is the suitable words for the blanks?

① apart — spoiled ② away — spoiling
③ from — spoiled ④ frow — spoiling
⑤ of — spoiling

풀이 1. ① 통조림 ② 소금절이 ③ 냉동 ④ 주사 ⑤ 훈제
첫 단락은 curing과 smoking, 둘째 단락은 canning과 freezing을 설명하고 있다.
2. keep from -ing

보너스 상식!

1. 육류의 종류

①Beef(쇠고기)
②Veal(송아지 고기, 수놈)
③Pork(돼지고기)
④Mutton(양고기)
⑤Lamb(어린 양고기, 생후 1년 미만)

2. 육류의 부위별 이름

① Beef(쇠고기) : chuck(어깨목 살) rib(갈비) loin(허리 고기) rump(엉덩이 살) round(스테이크용 고기) flank(다진 고기) plate(갈비 살) shank(스튜용 고기)
② Pork(돼지고기) : shoulder butt(소시지용 고기) loin(허리 고기) ham(햄) ribs(갈비) bacon(베이컨) foot(족발) picnic(어깨 살)

theme 10 Meat 육류

2 Meat has many nutrients. It contains fats, proteins, and some carbohydrates and is a good source of minerals, such as iron, copper, potassium, and phosphorus. Meat also contains vitamins B1, B2, B6, pantothenic acid, and B12.

Much of an animal slaughtered for meat is not edible. Not more than half the weight of a typical steer, for example, is actually beef. But the rest of the animal does not go to waste. Almost every part of it can be used for some purpose.

The glands of meat animals are used to make medicines, such as pepsin, cortisone, and insulin. Steer hides and pigskins are made into leather products, including wearing apparel and athletic equipment. Hog hair is used to make brushes and upholstery. Animal fats make soaps, cosmetics, and animal feed. Bones, horns, and hooves are made into buttons, bone china, gelatin, and glue. Lamb's wool is turned into yarn and clothing. Other inedible parts are used as fertilizers.

nútrient *n.* 영양소 carbohydrate *n.* 탄수화물 potássium *n.* 칼륨 phósphorus *n.* 인산 pantothénic *n.* 판토텐산, 비타민 B군 slaughter *v.* 도살하다, 살해하다 édible *adj.* 먹을 수 있는, 식용의 (*opp.* inedible 못 먹는) steer *n.* 수송아지 gland *n.* 분비샘 pépsin *n.* 펩신, 위액 속의 단백질 분해효소 córtisone *n.* 코티손, 부신피질 호르몬의 일종, 류머티즘이나 관절염 치료제 ínsulin *n.* 인슐린, 췌장에서 분비되는 단백질 호르몬, 당뇨병 치료제 hide *n.* (큰 동물의) 가죽 appárel *n.* 의복(= clothing) athlétic *adj.* 운동의, 체육의 equípment *n.* 장비 hog *n.* 돼지 uphólstery *n.* 실내 가구 cosmétics *n.* 화장품 animal feed 동물사료 hoof *n.* 발굽 bone china 본 차이나, 동물의 뼈를 섞어 만든 자기 gélatin *n.* 젤라틴, 정제된 아교 glue *n.* 풀 turn into ― ～로 변하다 yarn *n.* 털실 fértilizer *n.* 비료, 거름

1. According to the passage, animal' s bones, horns, and hooves are made into all the following **except**

① bone china. ② button.
③ gelatin. ④ glue.
⑤ yarn.

풀이 ① 본 차이나 ② 단추 ③ 젤라틴 ④ 풀 ⑤ 털실
뼈와 뿔, 발굽은 마지막 단락에 나온다. 그 문장에 답들이 나와 있다.

Nutrition 영양 11 *theme*

1 Though food contains many different chemicals, there are certain essential elements called nutrients that we must obtain from food to function normally. Our bodies use these nutrients for energy and growth and to repair damaged tissues.

There are six main groups of nutrients that are vital to the health of the human body: proteins, carbohydrates, fats, vitamins, minerals, and water. While all the essential nutrients help cells function normally, proteins, carbohydrates, and fats are the nutrients that supply the body with energy, which is measured in kilocalories. One calorie equals the amount of heat energy required to raise the temperature of 1 gram of water by 1 degree Celsius. Although food energy is technically described in kilocalories, it is most often expressed simply as 'calories.'

chémical *n.* 화학 요소 function *v.* 기능을 하다, 작용하다 dámaged tíssue 손상된 조직 vítal *adj.* 활력이 있는 carbohydrate *n.* 탄수화물 fat *n.* 지방 méasure *v.* 측정하다 descríbe *v.* 묘사하다, 설명하다

1. According to the passage, how many are the nutritions that supply the human body with energy?

① 2 ② 3 ③ 4 ④ 5 ⑤ 6

풀이 둘째 단락에서 인체에 에너지를 공급하는 영양소들을 찾는다.

보너스 상식

채식이 육식보다 좋다(?)

채식 식단도 치즈나 달걀 같은 지방과 콜레스테롤이 높은 단백질 식품을 포함할 수 있다. 적당한 양의 달걀과 함께 두부를 포함한 콩 제품, 저지방 치즈 등을 섭취하여야 한다. 채소의 영양을 잘 모르고 채식만 할 경우, 단백질이나 칼슘, 철분, 비타민 B12 등의 영양소가 결핍될 수 있다.

theme **11**

Nutrition 영양

2 Unlike some of the other nutrients, water does not supply the body with energy. Nevertheless, it has several important functions that make it, perhaps, the most important nutrient of all. Water provides the environment for all of the body's chemical processes to take place. As a component of blood, it transports nutrients to all the cells of the body and carries waste away from them. This tasteless liquid is crucial for cooling the body. It also carries waste out of the body as urine.

The human body needs about $2\frac{1}{2}$ quarts (2.5 liters) of water a day to function. An individual can live without other nutrients for up to several weeks but would not survive for much longer than a week without water. Luckily, water is readily available. Along with the water we drink, we also get water from beverages and fruits and vegetables. Other solid foods also contain water, but in much smaller quantities than in fruits and vegetables.

envíronment *n.* 환경 chémical prócess 화학적 과정 take place 발생하다 compénent *n.* 요소, 성분 transpórt *v.* 운송하다, 나르다 carry – away from/out of – ~에서 ~을 배출시키다 tásteless *adj.* 무미건조한 crúcial *adj.* 결정적인, 중요한 úrine *n.* 오줌 béverage *n.* 음료

1. Which is the best title for the passage?

① The Environment and Water ② The Function of Water
③ The Human Body and Water ④ The Importance of Water
⑤ The Sources of Water

풀이 ① 환경과 물 ② 물의 기능 ③ 인체와 물 ④ 물의 중요성 ⑤ 물의 원천
이 글은 인체에서 물이 하는 기능의 중요함을 설명하고 있다

보너스 상식

모든 필수 영양소를 얻는 가장 확실한 방법은 복합비타민 같은 영양제를 먹는 것이다(?)

비타민이나 무기물 같은 필수 영양은 영양제보다 음식에서 섭취하는 것이 최선이라고 한다. 식품은 다양한 영양소를 포함하고 있는 데 반해, 영양제는 한 가지씩만을 함유하고 있다. 또 식품에는 섬유소 같은 영양제에는 없는 유익한 물질들이 포함되어 있다.

Poisons and Antidotes 독약과 해독제

12 theme

1

There are some first aid measures that will help the poisoning victim. If the victim is conscious and is not having convulsions, he or she should be given half a glass of milk or water to drink. Next, the kind of poison taken should be determined. If the poison is a drug, a pesticide, or a poisonous plant, the victim should be made to vomit. Giving syrup of ipecac will make the person vomit. Salt water or mustard should not be used to induce vomiting.

But the person who has swallowed a petroleum product or a caustic product should not be made to vomit. These two kinds of poisons will cause more problems as they are vomited. Petroleum products may get into the lungs and cause chemical pneumonia. Caustic poisons that burn the throat and stomach as they go down may cause more burning as they come back up during vomiting.

A person who has inhaled a poison such as the cleaning fluid carbon tetrachloride should be taken to an open window immediately. This enables the person to inhale fresh air and exhale to carbon tetrachloride. If a person has spilled a liquid poison such as cleaning fluid or insecticide on the skin, it should be washed away with water.

first aid measure 응급조치 póisoning víctim 중독 환자 cónscious *adj.* 의식이 있는 convúlsion *n.* 경련 pésticide *n.* 농약 póisonous plant 유독 식물 vómit *v.* 토하다 ípecac *n.* 토제(吐劑), 토하게 하는 약 mústard *n.* 겨자 indúce *v.* 유도하다 swállow *v.* 삼키다 petróleum *n.* 석유 caustic *adj.* 가성(苛性)의, 부식성의 lung *n.* 폐 pneumónia *n.* 폐렴 throat *n.* 목구멍, 식도 stómach *n.* 위 inhále *v.* 흡입하다 cleaning fluid 세제 액 carbon tetrachloride 4염화탄소, 드라이클리닝 약품 spill *v.* 쏟다, 엎지르다 insécticide *n.* 살충제

1. Which of the following is the suggested first aid measure that will help the victim who had a drug or a pesticide?

① burning ② inhaling fresh air ③ spilling
④ vomiting ⑤ washing

풀이 ① 화상 ② 신선한 공기 흡입 ③ 쏟기 ④ 토하기 ⑤ 씻어 내기
'drug, pesticide'는 첫 단락에 나와 있다. 첫 단락에서 응급 처방을 찾아볼 것.

보너스 상식

가정에서 의약품을 보관할 때 주의할 사항

1. 의약품 같은 유독성 물질은 착오를 일으키지 않도록 본래의 포장 용기에 담아 두어야 한다.
2. 의약품이나 가정용 화학제품들, 표백제(bleaches) 분말 세제(detergents) 양잿물(lye) 액체 세제(cleaning fluids) 가구 광택제(furniture polishes) 살충제(insect killers) 화장품(cosmetics) 수면제(sleeping pills) 진정제(tranquilizers) 기침약(cough medicines) 비타민(vitamins) 등은 어린이들의 손이 닿지 않는곳에 둔다.

theme

13 Rice 쌀

1

Rice is used in many ways. It supplies abundant food energy, but other foods are needed to provide a well-balanced diet. In North America, there are three classes of rice—long grain, medium grain, and short grain. All have the same food value. But long-grain rice tends to cook dry. Medium- and short-grain rice cook moist, yet firm.

Rice may be eaten boiled or baked or in the form of a breakfast cereal. Rice flour, a byproduct of milling, is used to make bread, sugar, starch, face powder, and glue. Wine can be made by fermenting rice. Such wine is called sake in Japan, samshu in China, and arrack in India. Rice also can be used to make malt—an ingredient of beer.

Hulls and bran from milled rice can be fed to farm animals. The hulls also are used as bedding for farm and laboratory animals, as packaging around fragile items, and as a fuel. In Asia, rice straw is used to make paper and for mats, hats, baskets, and roof thatching.

abúndant *adj.* 풍부한 well-balanced diet 균형 있는 식사 long/medium/short grain 장/중/단곡 moist *adj.* 촉촉한, 습기 있는 firm *adj.* 굳은 boil *v.* 삶다, 끓이다 bake *v.* 찌다, 굽다 byproduct *n.* 부산물 milling *n.* 제분 starch *n.* 전분, 녹말 face powder 얼굴 화장용 분 fermént *v.* 발효시키다 malt *n.* 맥아, 엿기름 ingrédient *n.* 성분 hull *n.* 껍질, 외피 bran *n.* 겨 bedding 바닥 깔개 frágile *adj.* 깨지기 쉬운 rice straw 볏짚 roof thatching 지붕 이는 재료

1. Which of the following is the best title for the passage?

① Kind of Rice ② Milling of Rice
③ Rice Farming ④ Rice Foods
⑤ Uses of Rice

풀이 ① 쌀의 종류 ② 쌀의 제분 ③ 쌀 농사 ④ 쌀 식품 ⑤ 쌀의 이용
이 글은 쌀의 용도를 설명하고 있다. 모든 문장에 'be used to do'라는 표현이 가장 많이 등장하고 있다.

보너스 상식!

쌀의 영어 명칭

① 나락(paddy rice or rough rice) : 도정하지 않아 겨에 덮여 있는 낟알 상태
② 현미(brown rice)
③ 백미(white rice)
④ 개량종 쌀(converted rice)

Tea 차(茶) 14 theme

1 To make a good pot of tea, use fresh water and bring it to a full boil. Use a preheated pot for the tea. For each cup of water place one full teaspoon of loose tea into the pot or into a tea strainer in the pot. Pour the boiling water over the tea. Let the tea steep (soak) for 3 to 5 minutes. If the tea is steeped too long, it will have a bitter taste.

To make a cup of tea with a tea bag, use fresh water and bring it to a full boil. Preheat the cup before you put the tea bag in, and fill it with the boiling water. Steep for 3 to 5 minutes, then remove the tea bag.

Iced tea is made with 50 percent more tea leaves, to allow for the melting ice. The tea is poured into tall glasses that are two-thirds full of ice. Sliced lemons are served with it, and sugar may be added, according to individual taste. Flavorings of cloves, grated orange peel, or mint are sometimes added.

bring it to a full boil 완전히 끓이다 prehéat *v.* 미리 데우다 loose tea (일반적으로 병에 담긴) 분말 차 tea strainer 차 여과기 steep *v.* 담그다, 적시다(= soak) bitter taste 쓴맛 tea bag 차 봉지 remóve *v.* 제거하다, 꺼내다 sliced lemons 얇게 썬 레몬 flávorings 향료 clove *n.* 클로브, 정향(丁香) grate *v.* 빻다, 갈다 peel *n.* 껍질

1. Which of the following is the best title for the passage?

① Flavorings for Tea ② Growing of Tea
③ How to Make Tea ④ Kinds of Tea
⑤ Tastes of Tea

2. According to the passage, which of the following is <u>not</u> stated as things that may be added to ice tea?

① Flavorings for Tea ② Growing of Tea
③ How to Make Tea ④ Kinds of Tea
⑤ Tastes of Tea

풀이 1. ① 차를 위한 향료 ② 차의 재배 ③ 차를 만드는 법 ④ 차의 종류 ⑤ 차의 맛
이 글은 차를 끓여 만드는 방법을 적고 있다. 각 단락의 첫 문장에 'To make a ... tea'라고 시작하고 있다.
2. 아이스티에 타서 먹을 수 있는 것들은 마지막 단락에 설명되어 있다.

theme 14 Tea 차(茶)

보너스 상식!

차의 종류

1. 홍차(Black Tea) : 전 세계 차의 95%가 홍차이다. 차 잎이 발효 과정을 거쳐서 만들어지므로 향이 풍부하다. 주로 인도, 스리랑카, 중국, 대만에서 생산된다. 일설에는, 이들 아시아 국가들에서 생산된 녹차 잎이 배에 실려 영국으로 수송되던 중 썩어서 발효되었고, 이것을 차로 만들어 마신 것이 홍차가 되었다고 한다. 녹차가 발효되어 흑갈색의 홍차가 되었다는 이야기다.
2. 녹차(Green Tea) : 차 잎을 발효시키지 않은 동아시아의 전통차이다. 중국과 일본, 한국에서 주로 생산된다.
3. 우롱차(Oolong Tea) : 홍차와 녹차의 중간 상태인 차. 발효 과정에서 차 잎이 완전히 발효되기 전에 중지한 상태이다. 중국과 대만에서 많이 생산된다.

1

Vegetables differ in the length of time they last after harvesting. The stage of development at which a vegetable is harvested has much to do with its quality after shipping, processing, or storing. Tomatoes, for instance, commonly are harvested while still green if they are to be shipped long distances. Vine-ripened tomatoes, which are usually far superior in taste, are available only from local sources or home gardens. Peas and lima beans keep for a fairly long period if they are left in the pod and not shelled.

Many kinds of vegetables, such as white potatoes, sweet potatoes, onions, and carrots, can be stored for months at cool temperatures. Dry storage has been used since the days of primitive man. In early days vegetables were stored in caves. Today specially constructed buildings keep vegetables stored at the temperature and humidity that is best for each kind. The buildings are often cooled by refrigeration.

For many years most cities were surrounded by small truck farms, which sent produce to market daily. Later, vegetables were shipped long distances in refrigerated railroad cars. Recently, however, many large specialized farms have been set up in the best growing areas for a specific crop. Field packaging and long-distance refrigerated trucking have made it possible to deliver the fresh vegetables to market quickly. In some cases vegetables are transported by air, so that they will arrive at far-distant markets in prime condition.

last *v.* 지속하다 hárvesting *n.* 수확 have to do with — ~와 관련이 있다 shipping *n.* 선적 storing *n.* 저장 vine-ripened 줄기가 마른 supérior *adj.* 뛰어난, 우수한 home garden 텃밭 pea *n.* 완두콩 lima *n.* 리마콩, 강낭콩 종류 pod *n.* (콩의) 꼬투리 shell *v.* 껍질을 벗기다 dry storage 건조 저장 constrúct *v.* 건설하다 humídity *n.* 습도 refrigerátion *n.* 냉장 surróund *v.* 에워싸다 truck farm 트럭 농장 próduce *n.* 농산물, 상품 spécialized farm 특화된 농장 field páckaging 들에서 바로 포장하기 delíver *v.* 배달하다

1. Which of the following is the best title for the passage?

① Dry Storage and Refrigeration
② Growing and Harvesting of Vegetables
③ Packaging and Transporting of Vegetables
④ Storing Methods of Vegetables
⑤ Storing and Shipping of Vegetables

Vegetables 채소

풀이 ① 건조 저장과 냉장 ② 채소의 재배와 수확 ③ 채소의 저장 방법 ④ 채소의 저장과 운반
이 글의 핵심어는 두 가지이다. 채소의 storing(저장)과 shipping(운반)이다.

보너스 상식!

먹는 부위에 따른 채소의 분류

① 뿌리(root) : 감자(potato) 고구마(sweet potato) 무(radish) 당근(carrot) 양파(onion)
② 줄기(stem) : 아스파라거스(asparagus) 샐러리(celery)
③ 잎(leaves) : 시금치(spinach) 양배추(cabbage) 양상추(lettuce)
④ 열매(fruit) : 옥수수(corn) 오이(cucumber) 가지(eggplant) 참외(melon) 고추(pepper) 토마토(tomato) 수박(watermelon) *cf.* 참외, 수박, 토마토 등은 곳에 따라서 과일로 분류하기도 한다.
⑤ 씨(seed) : 콩(bean) 완두콩(pea)

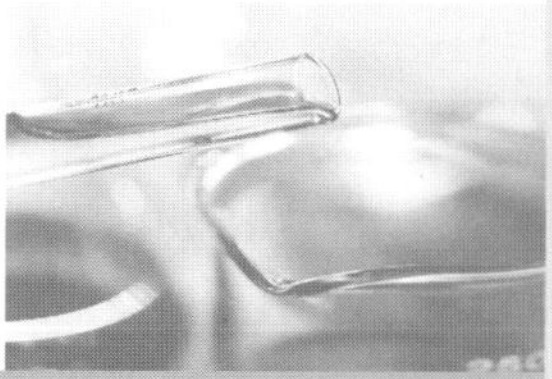

제 3 장

보건과 의료 Health and Medicine

theme **01**

Abortion 낙태

1 Abortion is the early ending of a pregnancy before the fetus (unborn child) has developed and grown enough to live outside the mother. If abortion happens naturally, before the 20th week of pregnancy, it is called a spontaneous abortion, or miscarriage. If abortion is caused by artificial means such as a medical procedure, it is called an induced abortion. In the United States, a debate rages over the ethical and legal aspects of induced abortion. Members of the right-to-life movement believe that abortion is morally wrong and should be restricted or prohibited. Other people, who refer to themselves as pro-choice, believe that women should have the right to choose for themselves whether or not to have an abortion. In 1973, in the Roe v. Wade case, the U.S. Supreme Court ruled that a woman could not be prevented from having an abortion during the first three months of pregnancy. Since then, the Court has allowed some restrictions on abortions; for example, states may require parental notification or a 24-hour waiting period.

abórtion *n.* 낙태 prégnancy *n.* 임신 fétus *n.* 태아(= unborn child) spontáneous *adj.* 자연적인, 자발적인 miscárriage *n.* 유산, 조산 indúce *v.* 유도하다 indúced abórtion 유도낙태, 임신중절 right-to-life *adj.* 낙태를 반대하는(= pro-life) mórally *adv.* 도덕적으로 restríct *v.* 규제하다 prohíbit *v.* 금지하다 pro-choice *adj.* 낙태 합법을 지지하는 (*opp.* pro-life) have an abortion 낙태하다 prevent from −ing ∼을 막다, 방지하다 paréntal notificátion 부모가 알아야 권리, 부모 고지 24-hour waiting period 24시간 대기 기간

1. The subject of this passage is

① A Debate over Induced Abortion
② The Definition of Abortion
③ The Right-to-life Movement
④ The Roe v. Wade Case
⑤ Some Restrictions on Abortions

풀이 ① 인공 낙태에 대한 논쟁 ② 낙태의 개념 ③ 낙태 반대 운동 ④ 로우-웨이드 사건 ⑤ 낙태에 대한 몇 가지 규제
이 글은 인공 낙태의 찬반 논쟁을 설명하고 있다.

보너스 상식

체외 수정

보통 여성의 난관 속에서 일어나는 수정을 연구실의 시험관에서 인공적으로 이루어지게 하여 증식하기 시작한 수정관을 자궁에 이식하는 것을 말한다. 시험관 수태라고도 하는데, 영국의 에드워드(Edward) 박사에 의해 최초로 성공하여 1978년 7월에 세계 최초의 시험관 아기가 태어났다.

1

Another type of research on aging involves the collection of facts about ages and growth rates in animals. It is very hard to study the force of mortality in animals by keeping them for life and recording when they die. The reason is that many live half as long as we do ourselves.

What we needed to find out is the force of mortality at different ages in a mixed population of animals. This means we must know the age of each one—but wild creatures do not have birth certificates. For the most part we must rely on research records, though the records are far from complete. In a few cases, however, we can tell the ages of animals by some structure on the animal's body that grows regularly. The shells, bones, or teeth of certain animals lay down a fixed number of marks or rings every year. We can tell the ages of these animals just as we can tell the age of a tree by counting its rings.

reséarch *n.* 연구 aging *n.* 늙음, 나이 먹음 mortálity *n.* 사망, 유한성 the force of mortality 사망의 원인(힘) mixed populátion of ánimals 혼합된 동물 집단 wild créature 야생 동물 birth certíficate 출생증명서 for the most part 대부분 rely on – ~에 의존하다 far from – 결코 ~아닌 régularly *adv.* 규칙적으로 lay down 적다, 그리다

1. Which is <u>not</u> mentioned in the passage as the things which show some animals' age?

① bones ② feet ③ shells ④ teeth

풀이 ① 뼈 ② 발 ③ 껍질 ④ 이빨
둘째 단락 후반에 나이를 표시하는 동물의 신체 조직이 나와 있다.

보너스 상식

파킨슨병(Parkinson's disease)

영국의 의사 파킨슨이 1817년에 처음으로 보고한 질환이다. 주로 50세 전후에 발병하는데, 손발이 떨리고 근육이 경직되는 것이 특징이다. 떨리는 것은 대개 손발부터 시작되어 점차 전신을 마음대로 움직이지 못한다. 그래서 보행은 종종걸음이 되고, 몸이 앞으로 구부러지며, 얼굴 표정이 없고, 대화나 눈을 깜박이는 것조차도 어려워진다.

theme **03**

AIDS 에이즈

1 Great progress has been made in understanding AIDS. The virus that causes the disease was identified in 1983; it is called HIV, or human immuno-deficiency virus. Scientists have developed blood tests to find out if people have been infected. These tests look for AIDS antibodies, substances that the body produces in an effort to fight the virus.

But researchers are still a long way from finding a cure for AIDS. Drugs have been found to slow the progress of the disease. But they are not a cure and can cause serious side effects. Nor is there yet a vaccine that will protect people from AIDS. Until one is found, the best defense lies in teaching people to avoid those behaviors that spread the disease.

prógress *n.* 진전 idéntify *v.* 확인하다 human immuno-deficiency virus 인체 면역결핍 바이러스 blood test 혈액검사 inféct *v.* 감염시키다 look for － ～을 찾다 antibódy *n.* 항체, 항생물질 súbstance *n.* 물질 cure *n.* 치료제 side effect 부작용 defénse *n.* 방어 lie in － ～에 있다 spread *v.* 확산시키다

1. Which of the following is <u>not</u> a correct statement about researches in AIDS?

① The virus that causes the disease was identified in 1983.
② Scientists look for AIDS antibodies through blood tests.
③ Drugs have been found to slow the progress of the disease.
④ Through blood tests, scientists find out if people have been infected.
⑤ There is a vaccine that will protect people from AIDS.

풀이 ① 병을 일으키는 바이러스가 1983년에 확인되었다. ② 혈액검사를 통해서 에이즈 항체를 찾고 있다. ③ 병의 진전을 늦추는 약품이 발견되었다. ④ 사람들이 감염되었는지 혈액검사를 통해서 확인하고 있다. ⑤ 에이즈로부터 사람들을 보호할 백신은 있다.
먼저 답지를 읽고 한 문장씩 확인한다.

보너스 상식!

AIDS(Acquired Immunity Deficiency Syndrome **후천성면역결핍증**)

면역력이 극도로 저하되어 신체가 무방비 상태에 이르기 때문에 흔히 무해한 세균이나 곰팡이에도 생명을 잃게 된다. 감염력은 강하지 않으나 적절한 치료법이 없어 치사율이 높다. 당초 남성 동성연애자들(Homosexuals)이나 약물 중독자에게 특유한 병으로 보았으나, 감염자와의 성관계, 수혈에 의한 감염률이 높아졌다. 성관계 시 반드시 콘돔을 사용할 것과 보건 당국의 철저한 혈액 관리가 요구되고 있다.

Alcoholism 알코올 중독

1 Even though the exact cause of alcoholism is not known, the problems associated with this illness can be treated. For the alcoholic, the use of alcohol in any form must be forever avoided.

To achieve this aim, organizations like Alcoholics Anonymous give patients guidance, support, and hope. Doctors, psychologists, and trained counselors can help motivate the patient to enter into a plan for recovery. Private rehabilitation centers have been established to help the alcoholic recover. Many large businesses have also set up programs to help their employees who are alcoholics.

Several programs were established to help the families of alcoholics better understand their problems. Al-Anon is for the family and friends of alcoholics. Alateen, a division of Al-Anon, is for young people 12 to 20 years of age who live in an alcoholic family situation. Adult Children of Alcoholics (ACOA) helps adults who have problems because they grew up with an alcoholic parent. Research into methods of treatment and even prevention also will help to deal with this major health problem.

exáct *adj.* 정확한 álcoholism *n.* 알코올 중독 alcohólic *n.* 알코올 중독자 assóciate with – ~와 관련하다 achíeve *v.* 성취하다 organizátion *n.* 조직, 단체 anónymous *adj.* 익명의 Alcohólics Anónymous 알코올중독자 자주(自主) 치료 협회(= Al-Anon) mótivate *v.* 동기를 부여하다, 고무하다 plan for recovery 회복 계획 recóver *v.* 회복하다 rehabilitátion *n.* 재활, 사회 복귀 divísion *n.* 부서 prevéntion *n.* 예방 deal with – ~을 치료하다, 다루다

1. Which is the organization for the young people who live in an alcoholic family situation?

① AAA ② ACOA
③ Al-Anon ④ Alateen
⑤ APEC

풀이 마지막 단락의 청소년 연령을 찾으면 쉽게 알 수 있다.

보너스 상식

환각제(hallucinogens)

정상인이 환각제를 복용했을 때 나타나는 증상으로는 대체로 혈압이 오르고, 오줌이 자주 마렵고, 시력이 약화되는 등 자율 신경계에 장애가 있고, 쾌감, 과대망상 등의 감정 변화, 집중력 장애, 엉뚱한 생각 등, 사고 과정에도 변화가 일어나며 심하면 환각을 일으키기도 한다. 환각제의 종류로는 '아마니타 무스카리아'(Amanita Muscaria)라는 멕시코 산 '버섯'과 '대마', 합성된 리세르긴산(lysergic acid) 유도체로 대표적인 'LSD', 'DMT'(Dimethyltryptamine), '마리화나' 등이 있다.

Anesthesia 마취

1 Every anesthetic has both advantages and disadvantages. There is no single all-purpose anesthetic. Doctors choose what seems best for the patient and the kind of operation. They may choose one particular anesthetic. Or they may use several together.

Any good anesthetic must free the patient from pain, be safe and dependable. In most cases the muscles must be relaxed in order for an operation to be performed successfully.

Ideally, an anesthetic should also be pleasant to take, put the patient to sleep rapidly, have the smallest possible effect on the heart and lungs, and wear off quickly, leaving no unpleasant aftereffects.

A preanesthetic (before the anesthetic) drug is given to help prepare the patient for the anesthetic. It makes sure that the anesthetic will work smoothly and reduces anxiety, especially in children. The drugs most frequently used as preanesthetics are Demerol or Seconal, which make the patient drowsy, and Valium, which relaxes the patient. These drugs also help to reduce the aftereffects of anesthesia, such as nausea.

anesthétic *adj.* 마취의 *n.* 마취제 advántage *n.* 이점 (*opp.* disadvantage 해) all-purpose 다목적의 operátion *n.* 수술 free – from – ~에게서 ~을 없애다, 자유롭게 하다 depéndable *adj.* 믿을 만한 múscle *n.* 근육 reláx *v.* 이완시키다 idéally *adv.* 이상적으로 wear off 사라지다 áftereffect *n.* 후유증 preanesthétic *adj.* 전마취제 make sure 확실히 하다 redúce *v.* 줄이다 drówsy *adj.* 졸리는 náusea *n.* 메스꺼움, 멀미

1. Which is not a suggested statement about an ideal anesthetic?

① It should be pleasant to take.
② It should have the smallest possible effect on the heart and lungs.
③ It should put the patient to sleep rapidly.
④ It should wear off quickly, leaving no unpleasant aftereffects.
⑤ It should work smoothly and reduce anxiety.

풀이 ① 복용하기가 좋아야 한다. ② 심장과 폐에 가능한 최소한의 영향을 주어야 한다. ③ 환자를 신속하게 잠들게 해야 한다. ④ 불쾌한 후유증을 남기지 않고 신속히 사라져야 한다. ⑤ 부드럽게 작용하고 화를 삭여 주어야 한다. '이상적인 마취제'가 등장하는 곳을 찾는다. 셋째 단락이 'Ideally'라는 말로 시작한다. 한 문장씩 답지와 확인한다.

보너스 상식

하품(yawn)이란?

하품은 어쩌다 하게 되는 심호흡으로 졸리거나, 지겹거나, 다른 사람이 하품을 할 때 하게 된다. 근육의 긴장을 풀고 편안한 상태에서는 호흡이 얕아지게 된다. 얕은 호흡을 계속하게 되면, 체내로 들이마시는 산소량이 적어진다. 이 때, 하품이 발생한다. 입을 크게 벌려 많은 산소를 들이마셔서 부족한 산소를 보충하는 것이다.

1

The first successful blood transfusion was performed more than 500 years ago by the Incas of South America. When an Inca was injured and suffered a great blood loss, the victim was given blood from a healthy individual. Inca doctors used a hollow tube to link the injured person with the blood donor.

Doctors in other parts of the world also tried to perform transfusions, but the recipients often died when they did. Medical experts think the treatment worked for the Incas because it is likely that they all had the same blood type. Having the same blood type would mean that they could give and receive blood among themselves without the risk of a dangerous transfusion reaction.

transfúsion *n.* 수혈 ínjure *v.* 다치게 하다 suffer a great blood loss 피를 아주 많이 흘리는 고통을 겪다 hóllow tube 속 빈 튜브 dónor *n.* 기증자 recípient *n.* 수혈자 blood type 혈액형 reáction *n.* 반응

1. Which of the following does the passage mainly discuss?

① blood donor
② blood type
③ Inca doctors
④ recipients
⑤ transfusion

풀이 ① 혈액 기증자 ② 혈액형 ③ 잉카 의사들 ④ 수혈자 ⑤ 수혈
이 글에서 가장 자주 등장하는 단어가 핵심어이다. 첫 문장과 마지막 문장의 핵심어.

보너스 상식

골수이식

골수는 적혈구나 혈소판의 생산 등 혈액을 만드는 데 중요한 역할을 한다. 그러나 방사선에는 극히 약해 강한 방사선을 쪼이면 조혈 기능이 파괴되고 출혈 및 세균 감염으로 사망한다. 골수이식은 30여년 전 프랑스에서 강한 방사선을 쏘인 사람에게 시도한 것이 세계 최초이다. 제공자의 골수에서 세포를 채취하여 주사로 환자에게 주입한다. 방사선에 쪼인 피해자에 대한 치료법으로 시도되었지만, 백혈병이나 재생불능 빈혈 등 혈액병 치료에도 응용된다. 백혈병 등의 치료에는 환자에게 강한 방사선을 쬐어, 골수를 완전히 태워 버린 다음에 세포를 이식한다.

theme

07 Human Body 인체

1

The human body has more than a hundred different kinds of cells. Each has a special form that makes it fit with the special job it has to do. Cells of one kind are usually joined to make tissue. Blood cells are an exception. They are not joined. They travel alone through the blood vessels.

A tissue is a fabric of the same kind of cells. For example, muscles are tissue made up of muscle cells; nervous tissue is made up of nerve cells. There are four main kinds of tissue: Epithelial tissue, which covers the surface of the body; connective tissue, which helps support and join together parts of the body; muscle tissue, which makes body movement possible; and nervous tissue, which carries nerve signals throughout the body.

Different kinds of tissue are combined in the body's organs. An organ is a body part that does one or more special jobs for the rest of the body. The heart, lungs, stomach, brain, and skin are all organs.

A group of organs working together is called a system. For example, the heart, blood, and blood vessels make up the circulatory system. The nose, throat, windpipe, and lungs make the respiratory (breathing) system. The kidneys and bladder make up the urinary system. The systems of the body are like members of a team. Each one has a specific job, but together they make <u>it</u> possible for the body to work, play, grow, and carry out many other functions.

tíssue *n.* (신체의) 조직 excéption *n.* 예외 blood véssel 혈관 fábric *n.* 섬유질, 조직 make up of – ~을 구성하다 nérvous tíssue 신경 조직 epithélial *adj.* 상피의, 표피의 epithélial tíssue 상피 조직 connéctive tíssue 연결 조직 muscle tissue 근육 조직 nerve sígnal 신경 부호 órgan *n.* 기관 círculatory *adj.* 순환하는 círculatory system 순환계 throat *n.* 식도 wíndpipe *n.* 기도 réspiratory *adj.* 호흡의(= breathing) kídney *n.* 신장, 콩팥 bladder *n.* 방광 úrinary *adj.* 오줌의, 비뇨의 úrinary system 비뇨계 carry out 수행하다

1. The human body is made up of the following four main kinds of tissue **except**

① bone tissue.
② connective tissue.
③ epithelial tissue.
④ muscle tissue.
⑤ nervous tissue.

2. What kind of paragraphs are these?

① introductory paragraphs
② contradictory paragraphs
③ explanatory paragraphs
④ descriptive paragraphs
⑤ conclusive paragraphs

3. The underlined word it refers to

① a specific job.
② a team.
③ to work, play, grow and carry out many other functions.
④ the body.
⑤ each one.

풀이 1. ① 골 조직 ② 연결 조직 ③ 상피 조직 ④ 근육 조직 ⑤ 신경 조직
'tissue'에 대한 설명은 둘째 단락에 나와 있다. 4가지를 확인할 것.

2. ① 소개 ② 반박 ③ 설명 ④ 묘사 ⑤ 결론

3. ① 특정한 직업 ② 어느 팀 ③ 일하고, 놀고, 성장하고, 다른 많은 기능을 수행하는 것 ④ 신체 ⑤ 각개

보너스 상식

피부(skin)

피부는 인체에서 가장 큰 조직으로 성인의 신체인 경우, 전체 넓이가 2.04m²이고 무게가 3.6kg~4.5kg 정도 나간다.

theme 07 Human Body 인체

2 As you can see, the body is a complicated chemical machine. Simple chemicals are built into complicated macromolecules. Some macromolecules are woven into various structures that form the cell. Inside the cell hundreds of chemical reactions are going on and these reactions are catalyzed by other macromolecules, the enzymes. The chemical reactions provide the energy to make new cells and to carry out the functions of the body—moving muscles, thinking, and so on. Each cell is an independent unit, but it co-operates with other cells to make the body machine run smoothly and efficiently.

cómplicated *adj.* 복잡한 macromólecule *n.* 고분자, 거대분자 weave *v.* 엮다, 짜다(weave-wove-woven) reaction *n.* 반응 cátalyze *v.* 촉매작용 하다 énzyme *n.* 효소 carry out 수행하다 indepéndent unit 독자적인 단위 co-óperate *v.* 협력하다 effíciently *adv.* 효율적으로

1. What is the topic word of this passage?

① body　② cell
③ chemicals　④ machine
⑤ macromolecules

풀이 ① 신체 ② 세포 ③ 화학 물질 ④ 기계 ⑤ 고분자
이 글은 신체라는 화학 기계의 작용을 설명하고 있다. 첫 문장과 마지막 문장의 핵심어이다.

보너스 상식!

생체리듬(바이오리듬 biorhythm)

생물의 생체 활동이 주기적으로 변화하는 것으로 biological rhythm의 약칭이다. 인간을 포함한 모든 생물에게는 지구물리학적 주기(cycle)와 어느 정도 일치하는 여러 리듬이 있는데, 이를 '육체 시계' 또는 '생물 시계' 라고 한다. 그 중에서도 지구의 자전 주기와 거의 같은 '일주 리듬'(日周리듬 circadian rhythm : 교대 근무 노동자에게 나타나는 신체 증상)이 중요하다. 또 인간의 생체리듬은 출생일로부터 세상을 떠날 때까지 사인(sine)곡선을 그리는데, 신체리듬이 23일, 감성리듬이 28일, 지성리듬이 33일의 주기를 갖는다. 모든 리듬은 출생일과 꼭 일치한다. 총 생존 일수를 리듬 주기로 나누면 자신의 주기를 알 수 있다. 특별한 이유 없이 심신의 상태가 안 좋은 날이 그 주기이다.

1 How and where does the brain store the information that we call memory? That is an easy question to ask, but very difficult to answer. In the human brain, areas of the cortex appear to be involved. When these areas are excited by a weak electrical current, the person 'relives' past experiences. Apparently these electrical stimuli force the brain to reproduce experiences that are stored within it from the past. It is also known that injury to certain areas will result in loss of memory.

But this does not mean that these are the places in the brain where the information is stored. Nor does it tell us anything about the way information is stored. ______ scientists think that memory storage is chemical in nature. That is, they think that individual nerve cells have chemically coded information within them. ______ scientists believe that memory is a result of some permanent change in the structure of the nerve.

córtex *n.* 뇌의 피질 excíte *v.* 자극하다, 흥미를 주다 eléctrical cúrrent 전류 relíve *v.* 되살리다 appárently *adv.* 겉으로는 stímuli *n.* 자극 reprodúce *v.* 재생하다 ínjury *n.* 손상 result in ― ~의 결과를 낳다, 결국 ~이 되다 mémory stórage 기억 저장 in nature 사실은, 실제는

1. Which of the following is the best title for the passage?

① Brain and Memory ② Nerve Cells
③ The Loss of Memory ④ The Memory Procedure
⑤ The Structure of Brain

2. Which of the following is the suitable words for the blanks?

① One ― The other ② One ― The others
③ Some ― Other ④ Some ― Others
⑤ The One ― The Other

theme 08 Brain 두뇌

풀이 1. ① 두뇌와 기억 ② 신경 세포 ③ 기억상실 ④ 기억 과정 ⑤ 두뇌의 구조
이 글은 두뇌의 구조와 기억 과정을 설명하고 있다.
2. 괄호 뒤의 두 문장이 나란히 어떤 scientists를 설명하고 있다.

보너스 상식

뇌가 크면 더 똑똑할까?

반드시 그렇지는 않다. 인간은 동물들 가운데 가장 똑똑하다. 그러나 머리는 다른 동물들에 비해 작거나 가볍다. 인간의 뇌는 약 1.5kg 정도인데, 코끼리의 뇌는 인간의 뇌보다 3배는 된다. 지능의 단서는 뇌를 덮고 있는 표면인 대뇌 피질(cortex) 속에 있다. 지능은 대뇌 피질 속 '주름' 의 수량과 관련이 있는 것으로 알려져 있다.

2 Today scientists in many countries are studying the brains of people and other animals. In recent years electronic equipment has been developed that lets scientists observe the tiny electrical signals produced by nerve cells. These signals provide much important information about the operation of the brain. Other instruments permit experimenters to use tiny amounts of electricity to stimulate or prevent activity in certain parts of the brain. These methods have been used to trace pathways through the brain, to discover the connections between cells, and to see how signals are sent from one center to another. These experiments also tell us what functions are served by different areas of the brain.

Nevertheless, we have only begun to uncover the basic processes going on within the brain. As we learn more, many new questions arise. The brain is the most complicated of all organs. And it will be a challenge to scientists as long as people continue to wonder about the workings of the living body.

trace *v.* 추적하다 **páthway** *n.* 경로 **connéction** *n.* 연결 **uncóver** *v.* 찾아내다 **chállenge** *n.* 도전 **contínue to do** 계속해서 ~을 하다 **wonder about –** ~에 의문을 가지다

1. Which of the following is the best title for the passage?

① Brain of Animals ② Brain of People
③ Nerve Cells ④ Operation of Brain
⑤ Study on Brain

풀이 ① 동물의 뇌 ② 사람의 뇌 ③ 신경세포 ④ 뇌의 작용 ⑤ 뇌의 연구
첫 문장과 마지막 문장에서 핵심어를 유추할 수 있다.

보너스 상식!

뇌사(腦死)

뇌의 기능이 죽어 있으나 인공호흡 장치에 의해 심장이 뛰고 있는 상태를 가리킨다. 뇌사로 판정된 환사가 회생하는 일은 없다. 1974년 일본의 뇌파학회가 내놓은 뇌사 판정 기준은 ① 깊은 혼수상태로 강한 통증이나 자극에도 반응하지 않는 상태 ② 양쪽 눈의 동공이 열려 있어 빛에 대한 반응이 없는 상태 ③ 자발적인 호흡이 정지된 상태 ④ 혈압이 급격히 떨어져 저혈압인 상태 ⑤ 뇌파가 평탄한 상태 ⑥ 이상 5가지 조건을 갖춘 상태로 6시간 지속되는 경우이다. 일반적으로 심장과 호흡이 정지된 상태를 사망으로 보았으나, 뇌의 기능을 잃은 상태에서도 인공호흡 장치로 심장을 움직일 수 있게 되면서 뇌사 문제가 쟁점으로 떠올랐다.

theme **09** # Cancer 암

1 Nutritional disorders, hormonal imbalances, certain viral infections, and disorders of the immune system all have been identified as factors that can contribute to the development of cancer. For example, AIDS, caused by the human immuno-deficiency virus, leads to an increased risk of lymphoma and sarcoma. Genetic abnormalities also can cause cancer. If these abnormalities are inherited, an entire family may have a high risk of a particular kind of cancer.

Certain substances, called carcinogens, can transform a healthy cell into a cancerous one. They do this by interacting with genetic abnormalities in the cell. Examples of carcinogens are chemicals such as benzene, fibers such as asbestos, and radiation from a variety of sources, such as ultraviolet (UV) sunlight, X rays, and radioactive elements. Some substances, such as tobacco and tobacco smoke, contain many different carcinogens. Researchers have found that carcinogens can interact with each other to greatly increase the cancer risk. For example, the highest known risk of lung cancer is in a smoker who also works as a uranium miner.

nutrítional *adj.* 영양의 disórder *n.* 무질서 hormónal *adj.* 호르몬의 imbálance *n.* 불균형 viral *adj.* 바이러스의 inféction *n.* 감염 immúne system 면역 체계 idéntify *v.* 확인하다 fáctor *n.* 요소 contríbute *v.* 이바지하다 cáncer *n.* 암 human immuno-deficiency virus 인체 면역결핍 바이러스 lymphóma *n.* 림프종(腫) sarcóma *n.* 육종(肉腫) genétic *adj.* 유전적인 abnormálity *n.* 변이, 변종, 이상 inhérit *v.* 유전하다, 물려받다 carcínogen *n.* 발암물질 transfórm *v.* 변형시키다, 바꾸다 cáncerous *adj.* 암의, 암적인 interáct *v.* 상호작용 bénzene 벤젠 asbéstos *n.* 석면 radiation *n.* 복사, 방사 ultravíolet *n.* 자외선(UV) radioáctive *adj.* 방사능의, 방사성의 uránium miner 우라늄 광부

1. Which of the following is <u>not</u> included in the examples of carcinogens?

① alcohol ② asbestos
③ benzene ④ tobacco smoke
⑤ ultraviolet

풀이 ① 알코올 ② 석면 ③ 벤젠 ④ 담배 연기 ⑤ 자외선
'carcinogens'를 설명하는 둘째 단락에서 'Examples of carcinogens ...'이하를 찾아보면 그 종류가 열거되어 있다.

보너스 상식!

암의 일반적인 증세

1. 이따금 출혈이 있다.
2. 가슴이나 기타 부위에 덩어리나 굳은 부위가 만져진다.
3. 낫지 않는 어떤 통증이 있다.
4. 배변이나 배뇨에 이상이 있다.
5. 목이 쉬거나 기침이 계속된다.
6. 음식을 삼키기가 힘들거나 계속해서 소화가 잘 안 된다.

2 Special tests to detect some kinds of cancers can be performed even before any noticeable symptoms appear. Examples include a mammogram, which is an X ray that can detect breast tumors too small to be felt, and a laboratory test for blood in the stools, which may indicate colon cancer. When performed regularly, procedures such as these help with early diagnosis. They have reduced the incidences of certain cancers and increased the chances that people with cancer will be cured.

If a tumor is thought to be cancerous, a piece of tumor tissue is removed—in a procedure called a biopsy—and examined under a microscope. The appearance of the tumor cells reveals whether the tumor is benign or malignant and also helps in predicting the course of the disease.

An evaluation is used to determine the extent to which the cancer has spread. This information is necessary in order to plan an effective course of treatment.

detéct *v.* 찾아내다, 탐지하다 nóticeable *adj.* 눈에 띄는 symptom *n.* 증상 mámmogram *n.* 유방암 X선 사진 túmor *n.* 종양, 암 breast tumor 유방종양 láboratory test 실험실 검사 stool *n.* 대변 índicate *v.* 알려주다, 지적하다 colon cancer 대장암 procédure *n.* 절차, 과정 diagnósis *n.* 진단 early diagnosis 초기 진단 redúce *v.* 줄이다 íncidence *n.* 발생률 cáncerous *adj.* 암적인, 암의 tumor tissue 종양 조직 remóve *v.* 떼어내다 bíópsy *n.* 조직 검사 revéal *v.* 드러내다, 노출시키다 beníg‌n *adj.* [의학] (질병이) 양성인 malígnant *adj.* (질병이) 악성인, 적대적인 predíct *v.* 예측하다 evaluation *n.* 판정, 평가 detérmine *v.* 판단하다 extént *n.* 정도, 범위

1. Which of the following is the best title for the passage?

① Detection and Treatment of Cancers
② Diagnosis and Evaluation of Cancers
③ Early Diagnosis of Cancers
④ Incidences of Cancers
⑤ Kinds of Cancers

풀이 ① 암의 발견과 치료 ② 암의 진단과 평가 ③ 암의 초기 진단 ④ 암의 발생률 ⑤ 암의 종류
앞의 두 단락은 암의 진단(diagnosis)을, 마지막 단락은 평가(evaluation)를 설명하고 있다.

보너스 상식

암의 대표적인 치료법

① 수술 (surgery) ② 방사능 요법 (radiotherapy)
③ 화학요법 (chemotherapy) ④ 약물(drugs) 치료법

theme

10 Dentistry 치의학

1 In the old days, if you had had a toothache, your mother would have put a clove in your mouth and hoped that the hot spice would keep you from feeling pain. If the pain had continued, she would have taken you to the village blacksmith, the barber, or if you were lucky, to the physician.

There were no dentists in those days to repair a tooth and try to save it. The blacksmith or the barber would have taken a good, strong pair of pliers and given a mighty pull. The trouble with that kind of mouth care was that most people had few, if any, teeth left by the time they were middle-aged!

Today dentistry is an important part of modern health care. Dentists are the professionals whose primary job is to take care of the teeth and mouth. They are educated in the field of health care that involves the teeth, gums, cheeks, lips, tongue, and palate, as well as the occlusion, or 'bite.'

clove *n.* 정향(丁香), 향료로 쓰는 나무뿌리 hot spice 매운 맛 keep – from –ing 누가 ~하는 것을 막아주다, 방지하다 blácksmith *n.* 대장장이 bárber *n.* 이발사 physícian *n.* 의사 déntist *n.* 치과의사 déntistry *n.* 치의학 repair a tooth 치아를 치료하다 pliers *n.* 집게, 뺀찌 give a pull 잡아당기다 prímary job 주된 임무 gum *n.* 잇몸 tóngue *n.* 혀 pálate *n.* 입천장 occlúsion *n.* 아래 윗니의 맞물림 bite *n.* 묾

1. Which is <u>not</u> the part of human body which dentistry takes care of?

① gums ② palate
③ occlusion ④ throat
⑤ tongue

풀이 ① 잇몸 ② 입천장 ③ 아래 윗니의 맞물림 ④ 목구멍 ⑤ 혀
치의학이 담당하는 인체 부위는 마지막 단락에 열거되어 있다.

보너스 상식

치아를 가장 많이 뽑은 치과의사

기록상으로 세계에서 치아를 가장 많이 뽑은 치과의사는 'Giovanni Battista Orsenigo' 라는 사람으로 1868년부터 1903년까지 36년 동안 2,000,744개의 치아를 뽑았다고 한다.

2 Human beings grow two sets of teeth, a primary (first) set and a permanent (secondary) set. At birth no teeth are usually visible, but below the gums 20 primary teeth and 32 permanent teeth are beginning to form.

The primary teeth start to erupt, or grow out, between six months and a year after a baby is born. By the time children are 3 years old, they have a set of 20 teeth — 10 in the upper jaw and 10 in the lower jaw.

At about 6 years of age, permanent teeth begin to erupt in the back of the mouth behind the last primary teeth. At about the same age the primary teeth in the front of the mouth begin to loosen. Eventually all the primary teeth become loose and fall out. Every time a primary tooth is lost, it is replaced with a permanent tooth. By the time most children are 11 years old, all their primary teeth have been replaced with permanent teeth.

The last permanent tooth to erupt in the mouth is the <u>third molar</u>. Third molars are often called wisdom teeth, because they erupt in the mouth when a person is in his or her late teens or early 20' s—long after the primary teeth of childhood have been replaced.

prímary teeth 젖니 pérmanent teeth 영구치 gum *n.* 잇몸 erúpt *v.* 분출하다, 치아가 잇몸을 뚫고 나오다(= grow out) lóosen *v.* 느슨해지다, (치아가) 흔들거리다 (*opp.* tighten) fall out (치아가) 빠지다 repláce *v.* 교체하다 mólar *n.* 어금니 third molar 사랑니(= wisdom teeth)

1. The underlined expression <u>third molar</u> is closest in meaning to

① back teeth ② front teeth
③ permanent teeth ④ primary teeth
⑤ wisdom teeth

풀이 ① 뒷니 ② 앞니 ③ 영구치 ④ 젖니 ⑤ 사랑니
우선 글 가운데 'third molar'를 찾으면 마지막 단락에 있다. 그 의미(명칭)도 함께 나와 있다.

보너스 상식

치아 보호

1. 식사 후에는 반드시 양치질을 한다.
양치질은 치아에 붙은 음식물의 찌꺼기를 제거하고, 치아 표면의 박테리아를 제거한다.
2. 정기적인 치아 검진을 받아서 치아와 잇몸의 상태를 검사하고, 치석을 제거한다.

theme 11

Diseases 질병

1 An illness that comes suddenly, such as an attack of vomiting after eating spoiled food, is referred to as acute. In a chronic condition, on the other hand, symptoms either continue or return from time to time for a period of months or years. Some diseases can be chronic but then become acute. For example, diabetes is a chronic disease in which the body does not use and store sugars properly. By eating a special diet and taking certain drugs or injections of the hormone insulin, diabetics (people who have diabetes) can usually keep their symptoms under control and lead a relatively normal life. But a diabetic who takes in too much sugar or injects too much insulin may have a sudden acute attack that can result in unconsciousness.

attáck *n.* 공격 vómiting *n.* 구토 spoiled food 상한 음식 acúte *adj.* 예민한, 급성의(질병) acúte diséase 급성 질병 chrónic *adj.* 만성적인, 고질적인 chrónic cond tion 만성적인 상태 symptom *n.* 증상 take drugs 약을 복용하다 diabétes *n.* 당뇨병 injéct *v.* 주사하다 injéction *n.* 주사 diabétic *n.* 당뇨 환자 underócontrol 통제하여, 완화시켜서 uncónsciousness *n.* 무의식 result in unconsciousness 의식을 잃게 되다

1. Which of the following is the best title for the passage?

① Acute and Chronic Illness ② A Chronic Condition
③ An Illness That Comes Suddenly ④ Symptoms of Diabetes
⑤ Unconsciousness

풀이 ① 급성과 만성질환 ② 만성적인 상태 ③ 갑자기 찾아오는 질환 ④ 당뇨병의 증상 ⑤ 무의식
이 글은 급성(acute)질환과 만성(chronic)질환, 두 증상의 관계를 당뇨병(diabetes)을 통해 설명하고 있다.

보너스 상식!

세계에서 가장 치명적인 질병

1. Lassa fever(라사 열병) : 서아프리카의 바이러스에 의한 열병으로 사망률이 50%를 넘는 가장 치명적인 질병이다.
2. Marburg fever(마르부르크 열병) : 독일 원숭이 병이라고도 하며, 고열과 출혈을 동반한다.
3. Ebola fever(에볼라 열병) : 바이러스에 의해 전염되며, 고열과 내출혈을 일으키는 치명적인 병이다.
4. Cholera(콜레라) : 역시 치명적인 무서운 질병으로 치료를 하지 않으면 사망률이 50%나 된다.

2 Until the 1940's, infectious diseases were the major cause of death in many parts of the world. Bacteria and viruses are the main groups of microbes that can cause infectious diseases. Bacteria damage the body by producing poisons called toxins, and viruses may kill the cells they infect. Various parasites (tiny creatures that live off a host's body), including plantlike fungi, microscopic animal-like protozoa, and a number of worms, can also be pathogenic (disease-causing) for humans.

inféctious *adj.* 전염성의 (*cf.* infection *n.* 전염) mícrobe *n.* 세균, 미생물 dámage *v.* 손상시키다 póison *n.* 독 tóxin *n.* 독소 párasite *n.* 기생 생물 live off 기생하다, 기식하다 host *n.* 숙주 (*opp.* parasite 기생충) fúngus *n.* 버섯균 (*pl.* fungi) microscópic *adj.* 미세한 prótozoa *n.* 원생 생물 worm *n.* 벌레(지렁이, 구더기, 땅벌레, 거머리, 회충 등) pathogénic *adj.* 발병시키는, 병원성의(=disease-causing)

1. Which is <u>not</u> included in the microbes that can be disease-causing for humans?

① algae ② bacteria
③ fungi ④ protozoa
⑤ virus

풀이 ① 조류(말) ② 박테리아 ③ 버섯균 ④ 원생 생물 ⑤ 바이러스
이 글에는 발원성 미생물을 5가지 나열하고 있다. bacteria, virus, fungi, protozoa, worms 등이다.

보너스 상식

전염병의 전염 방법

1. Airborne transmission(공기에 의한 전염) : 공기 중에 있는 감염 물질이 호흡기나 상처 난 피부를 통해서 전염되는 경우
2. Contamination(오염에 의한 전염) : 오염된 물이나 음식을 먹고 전염되는 경우
3. Direct contact(직접 접촉) : 전염병 환자와 직접 접촉함으로써 전염되는 경우
4. Sexual transmission(성 관계에 의한 전염) : 직접 성교나 항문 성교, 구강 성교 등의 성 관계를 통해 전염되는 경우. 성 관계 시 콘돔을 사용하면 전염을 줄일 수 있다.
5. Blood-borne transmission(혈액에 의한 전염) : 혈액을 주사하거나, 정맥주사를 이용하는 약물 중독자 등에게 발병되기 쉽다. 문신과 침을 맞는 경우도 위험하다.
6. Animal borne transmission(동물에 의한 전염) : 모기(말라리아)나, 벼룩(역병) 등 해충에 물려서 전염되는 경우

theme 11

Diseases 질병

3 Hormones are chemical messengers produced in structures called endocrine glands. Hormones help control growth, reproduction, and many other important body functions. Endocrine disorders resulting in the production of too much or too little of a particular hormone can cause serious diseases. Disorders of the pituitary gland, for instance, can result in dwarfism (too little growth hormone) or giantism (too much growth hormone). Thyroid hormones help determine how fast the body's chemical reactions take place. With too little of these hormones, a person becomes sluggish and fat; too much makes a person 'hyper,' suffering from nervousness, weight loss, and sleeplessness.

The various endocrine hormones act on each other in many complicated ways. Normal sexual development, for example, is influenced not only by the sex hormones produced in the reproductive organs (ovaries in females and testes in males) but also by hormones that are released from the pituitary and adrenal glands.

méssenger *n.* 메신저, 전령 éndocrine *n.* 내분비선(= endocrine gland) reprodúction *n.* 생식 disórder *n.* 장애, 이상, 무질서 resúlt in – ~을 일으키다, 결국 ~이 되다 pitúitary *n.* 뇌하수체(= pituitary gland) dwárfism *n.* 왜소발육증 gíantism *n.* 거인증 thyroid *n.* 갑상선 slúggish *adj.* 둔한, 게으른 hyper *adj.* 매우 긴장한, 흥분 잘하는 nérvousness *n.* 신경과민 weight loss 체중 감소 act on each other 상호 작용하다 séxual devélopment 성 발육 reprodúctive órgan 생식기 óvary *n.* 난소 téstis *n.* 고환(*pl.* testes) reléase *v.* 방출하다 adrénal *n.* 콩팥, 부신(= adrenal gland)

1. 다음 중 이 글에 나오는 'thyroid hormones' 의 이상 증세로 <u>틀린</u> 것을 찾으시오.

① giantism ② nervousness
③ sleeplessness ④ sluggishness
⑤ weight loss

풀이 ① 거인증 ② 신경과민 ③ 불면증 ④ 둔함 ⑤ 체중 감소
글 중에서 'thyroid hormones'를 찾아 그 증세를 확인한다. 첫 단락에 있다.

보너스 상식

비전염 질병의 종류

① Allergies 알레르기 ② Arthritis 관절염
③ Cancer 암 ④ Genetic Diseases 유전병
⑤ Heart Diseases 심장병 ⑥ High blood pressure 고혈압
⑦ Environmental diseases 환경 질환 : 석면 중독, 납중독, 방사선 병 등

4 Alzheimer's disease is a form of dementia, a condition in which the mind becomes unable to function properly. The disease causes degeneration of the nerve cells in areas of the brain that are needed for processing information, acquiring new memories, and retrieving old memories. People with this disorder gradually lose the ability to remember and think clearly. As the disease progresses, people with Alzheimer's disease become unable to care for themselves. They may become confused and forget to eat, or they may wander away from home and get lost. The risk of developing Alzheimer's disease increases with age. About 20 percent of people over the age of 80 will develop the disorder.

Scientists are working to discover the cause and the treatment for the disease. Current research indicates that hereditary factors as well as environmental factors may play a role in its development.

deméntia *n.* 치매 degenerátion *n.* 변질, 쇠퇴 prócess informátion 정보를 처리하다 acquíre *v.* 습득하다 retríeve *v.* 상기하다, 되살리다 disórder *n.* 장애, 이상 progréss *v.* 진행하다 become unable to do ~할 수 없게 되다 confúse *v.* 혼동시키다 care for – ~을 돌보다 wander *v.* 방황하다 get lost 길을 잃다 cúrrent *adj.* 현재의 índicate *v.* 지적하다, 나타내다 heréditary factor 유전적 요인 environméntal factor 환경적 요인 play a role in – ~에 어떤 역할을 하다

1. According to the passage, which of the following is <u>not</u> stated about Alzheimer's disease?

① Environmental factors may play a role in its development.
② Hereditary factors cannot cause its development.
③ People with it become unable to care for themselves.
④ People with it gradually lose the ability to remember and think clearly.
⑤ The risk of developing the disease increases with age.

풀이 ① 환경적 요인이 발병에 어떤 역할을 할 수 있다. ② 유전적 요인이 병을 일으키지는 않는다. ③ 그 병의 환자들은 스스로를 돌볼 수 없게 된다. ④ 그 병의 환자들은 또렷하게 기억하고 생각하는 능력을 점차 잃게 된다. ⑤ 발병 위험도는 나이와 함께 증가한다.
마지막 문장에 환경 요인과 함께 유전 요인도 발병에 역할을 한다고 기술되어 있다.

보너스 상식!

식물인간

의식불명인 채 장기간 계속 누워 있는 상태에서 살아가는 환자를 말한다. 원인은 교통사고나 뇌졸중, 일산화탄소 중독 등이다. 인간에게는 운동, 감각, 정신작용 등의 '동물적 기능'과 음식물의 소화, 흡수, 호흡, 배설, 혈액순환 등의 '식물적 기능'이 있다. '식물인간'은 동물적 기능을 하지 못하고 식물적 기능만이 유지되는 경우이다. 그래서 인공 호흡기를 사용하지 않으면 살 수 없는 뇌사 상태의 환자와는 다르다.

theme **11** # Diseases 질병

5 Mumps is a viral disease that causes swelling of the salivary glands. These are the glands that make saliva, the moisture in the mouth. The glands are found under the tongue and jawbone and in front of the ear. The ones found in front of the ear are called the parotid glands. These are the ones that swell most often in mumps. When they become swollen, it hurts to chew and swallow. Headaches are another symptom of mumps.

Mumps may cause the swelling of other glands, such as the pancreas and testes, especially when adults get the disease.

But mumps is mainly a disease of children between 5 and 15 years of age. The virus is spread from one person to another through the air or through contaminated objects. It takes from 14 to 21 days for mumps to develop after a person has been exposed to the virus. Usually people have mumps only once. Most children are immunized against mumps when they are 15 months old.

mumps *n.* 볼거리 víral diséase 바이러스성 질병 swell *v.* 부어오르다(swell-swelled-swollen) salívary *adj.* 침의, 침샘의 salivary gland 침샘 sáliva *n.* 침 móisture *n.* 습기 jawbone *n.* 턱뼈 in front of — ~앞에 parótid *n.* 귀밑샘(= parotid gland) swállow *v.* 삼키다 symptom *n.* 증상 páncreas *n.* 췌장 téstis *n.* 고환 contáminate *v.* 오염시키다 be expósed to — ~에 노출되다 ímmunize *v.* 면역시키다, 면역 주사를 주다

1. When are the most children immunized against mumps?

① when they are 1 to 15 days old
② when they are 14 to 21 days old
③ when they are 5 to 15 days old
④ when they are 15 months old
⑤ when they are 5 to 15 years old

풀이 'mumps 면역'이란 말을 찾으면 해결된다. 글의 마지막 문장에 나와 있다.

보너스 상식

가장 오래 굶은 사람

사람은 아무 것도 먹지 않고 얼마나 버틸까? 음식물을 먹지 않고 가장 오래 견딘 사람은 오스트리아 Bregenz의 'Andreas Mihavecz' 라는 사람으로, 1979년 4월 1일에 경찰서 유치장에 갇혔는데, 경찰관이 그를 가둔 것을 까맣게 잊어 버린 것이다. 4월 18일, 18일만에 발견되었을 때는 거의 죽기 직전이었다고 한다.

Diagnosis and Treatment of Disease 질병의 진단과 치료

12 theme

1

In the past, lack of medical knowledge about disease often meant that a person' s chances of recovering from an illness were small. When a person became ill, doctors frequently were unable to identify the illness accurately or to determine its cause. Treatment often consisted mainly of sympathy, rest, and simple home remedies. As a result, the expected human life span was quite short.

This situation, which existed throughout most of human history, changed dramatically in the 20th century. An explosion of medical knowledge has enabled doctors to diagnose and treat many illnesses with great accuracy and success. In turn, improvements in diagnosis and treatment have helped people today live healthier and longer lives.

recóver *v.* 회복하다 idéntify *v.* 확인하다 áccurately *adv.* 정확하게 accúracy *n.* 정확성 sympathy *n.* 위로, 문병 rémedy *n.* 치료 expected human life span 인간의 기대 수명 explósion *n.* 폭발 diagnóse *v.* 진단하다 in turn 차례, 교대로 impróvement *n.* 향상

1. When was the medical knowledge exploded?

① in the 16th century ② in the 17th century
③ in the 18th century ④ in the 19th century
⑤ in the 20th century

풀이 둘째 단락에 '의학 지식의 폭발'이 설명되어 있다. 연대를 확인 할 것.

보너스 상식

질병의 종류

현재까지 인간에게 발생하는 것으로 알려진 각종 질환의 종류는 20,000가지가 넘는다고 한다.

Diagnosis and Treatment of Disease 질병의 진단과 치료

2 More often than not, your body will heal or 'treat' itself. Many of the signs and symptoms of disease actually give evidence of how your body fights a particular disease. Fever, even though it makes you uncomfortable, helps suppress or kill the germs that make you sick. The pus in an infected wound comes from your white blood cells, which ingest (take in) and kill the bacteria causing the sore. Your lymph glands enlarge while they manufacture antibodies, which fight infections. If you accidentally swallow a poisonous substance, you may react by vomiting and expelling the substance from your stomach. Or the substance may be expelled from the body by diarrhea.

One of the first rules in the treatment of disease should be to help the body's own defenses. For example, if you have a sore throat, you may be able to wash some of the infection away by gargling with a weak, hot salt water solution. When you suffer from diarrhea or vomiting, your body loses a large amount of water and salts, which need to be replaced by drinking liquids. And do not forget rest as a treatment. It helps your body use all of its energy to fight the illness.

more often than not 대개, 가끔 heal *v.* (병을) 고치다, 치료하다 uncómfortable *adj.* 불편한 suppréss *v.* 억제하다 germ *n.* 병원균, 세균, 미생물 pus *n.* 고름 infécted wound 감염된 상처 white blood cell 백혈구 세포 ingést *v.* 섭취하다 sore *n.* 종기, 상처, 통증 lymph *n.* 림프, 임파선(= lymph gland) enlárge *v.* 확대시키다 antibódy *n.* 항생제 swállow *v.* 삼키다 vómit *v.* 토하다 expél *v.* 쫓아내다, 배출시키다 diarrhéa *n.* 설사 defénse *n.* 방어 sore throat 후두염, 목이 아픔 gárgle *v.* 양치질하다 solútion *n.* 용액 líquid *n.* 액체, 물

1. All of the following are the evidences of how our body fights a disease **except**

① diarrhea. ② fever.
③ glands. ④ pus.
⑤ vomiting.

풀이 ① 설사 ② 발열 ③ 분비샘 ④ 고름 ⑤ 구토
첫 단락에서 찾는다. 열거된 증거들로는 fever, pus, enlarge of lymph glands, vomiting, diarrhea 등 다섯 가지이다.

보너스 상식

대체 의학(Complementary or alternative medicine)

1. Acupuncture(침술)
2. Aromatherapy(향기 요법)
3. Chiropractic(지압 요법)
4. Herbalism(본초(本草)요법)
5. Homeopathy(유사 요법) : 치료할 질병과 같은 증세를 일으키는 약을 극소량 쓰는 치료법
6. Iridology(홍채학) : 눈동자의 홍채를 검사하여 질병을 진단하는 의술
7. Osteopathy(정골(整骨) 요법) : 우리의 접골과 유사한 요법

Prevention of Diseases 질병의 예방

1

The body has many ways of defending against invading microbes. The skin that covers the body and the membranes that line the mouth, nose, and other openings act as barriers that keep most germs out. When microbes do manage to get into the bloodstream or body cells, several kinds of defenses go into operation. Cells damaged by the invading microbes send out chemical messengers. Some of the messengers cause blood vessels to leak, so that fluid accumulates in the tissues and causes swelling. Other chemical messengers may reach a special control center in the brain and produce a rise in the body temperature, known as fever.

White blood cells monitoring the tissues pick up the chemical 'Help!' signals and travel to the site of the infection. There they gobble up the microbes, literally eating and digesting them. Other types of white blood cells recognize 'foreign' particles such as disease microbes, distinguishing them from the body's own substances. Still other white cells produce antibodies, very specific defenses that attack particular kinds of germs.

Each of these defenses is important in preventing disease, but none of them are effective against every kind of illness.

invāde *v.* 침입하다 mícrobe *n.* 미생물, 세균 mémbrane *n.* 점막 line *v.* (안쪽을) 바르다, 입히다 bárrier *n.* 장벽 keep out 쫓아내다 germ *n.* 세균 manage to do 가까스로 ~하다 get into 들어오다 bloodstream *n.* 혈류 body cell 체세포 go into operation 작전에 들어가다 dámage *v.* 손상시키다 send out 파견하다, 내보내다 blood vessel 혈관 leak *v.* 누출하다 fluid *n.* 액체(혈액) accúmulate *v.* 축적하다 tíssue *n.* (세포)조직 swelling *n.* 부기 produce a rise in the body temperature 체온을 상승시키다 mónitor *v.* 감시하다 pick up 감지하다, 포착하다 góbble *v.* 먹어 치우다(- up) líterally *adv.* 말 그대로 digést *n.* 소화 white blood cell 백혈구 récognize *v.* 인식하다 párticle *n.* 분자, 요소 disease microbe 질병 미생물 distínguish *v.* 구별하다 antibódy *n.* 항생제 efféctive *adj.* 효과적인

1. According to the passage, white blood cells can

① defend against invading microbes ② gobble up the germs
③ monitor the tissues ④ produce antibodies
⑤ recognize foreign particles

풀이 ① 침입 세균 방어 ② 세균 먹어 치우기 ③ 조직 감시 ④ 항생제 생산 ⑤ 외부 요소들 인식
우선 'white blood cells'를 찾는다. 둘째 단락 전체가 그 기능을 설명하고 있다. 몇 가지 기능을 하나씩 확인한다.

보너스 상식!

체온의 한계

입안에 온도계를 넣어서 재는 체온은 보통이 37℃이며, 38℃ 이상이면 고열이라고 한다. 고 체온의 한계는 41℃이고, 저 체온의 한계는 29℃이다. 이 한계를 넘으면 죽음의 위험에 처한다.

theme 13

Prevention of Diseases 질병의 예방

2 It is important to do all that you can to protect your health. A healthy person is much better able to fight off disease germs than a person who is weak and run-down. A person who stays healthy while he or she is young also has a better chance of enjoying continuing good health in later years.

The best ways to protect your health are to have a balanced diet (including fish, meat, milk, green and yellow vegetables, and fruit), to enjoy some form of exercise every day, to sleep eight to ten hours every night, to keep your body clean, and to go to the doctor regularly.

In order to avoid disease, it is sensible to avoid going near people if you know they have illnesses that can be spread. If you get a cut or scrape, you can avoid diseases such as blood poisoning by cleaning the wound with soap and water and using local antiseptics to prevent infection.

If you do become ill, you can take steps to prevent your illness from becoming worse or being complicated by a more serious disease. The best way to do this is to follow your doctor's instructions for getting rest, eating properly, and taking medications.

fight off 이겨내다 disease germ 질병 세균 run-down 쇠약한 in later year 노년에 balanced diet 균형 있는 식사 éxercise *n.* 운동 spread *v.* 퍼지다, 전파시키다 get a cut 칼에 베이다 get a scrape 긁히다 blood poisoning 패혈증 antiséptic *n.* 소독제, 살균제, 방부제 local antiseptics 환부 소독제 take step 조치를 취하다 become worse 악화되다 be complicated by a more serious disease 더 심각한 질병에 합병되다 medication *n.* 약, 투약 take medication 약물치료를 받다

1. These are the best ways to protect our health **except**

① To enjoy some form of exercise every day.
② To go to the doctor regularly. ③ To have a balanced diet.
④ To keep your body clean. ⑤ To sleep six to eight hours every night.

풀이 ① 매일 어떤 형태의 운동을 한다. ② 정기적으로 의사의 검진을 받는다. ③ 균형 있는 식사를 한다. ④ 신체를 청결히 유지한다. ⑤ 매일 밤에 6~8시간의 수면을 취한다.
'건강을 보호하는 최선의 방법'이 둘째 단락에 다섯 가지 나와 있다. 한 가지씩 확인할 것.

보너스 상식!

정신-신체적 치료법

① 요가 (Yoga) ② 태극권 (Tai chi) ③ 무용 요법 (Dance therapy)
④ 감각 요법 (Sense therapy) : 빛깔 요법, 음악 요법, 미술 요법
⑤ 명상 (Meditation) ⑥ 최면 요법 (Hypnotherapy)

1 Medical ethics are the rules that tell doctors how to behave when caring for patients. For example, doctors must honor patients' privacy. Any information a patient tells the doctor or any diagnostic findings cannot be told to anyone without the patient's permission.

Since modern medical technology may prolong a very sick person's life, doctors today sometimes face serious problems with medical ethics. When a patient permanently loses consciousness, for example, or has no hope of recovery, the doctor and the patient's family must decide when to treat the illness, how long to treat it, and when to stop treatment. These are very difficult decisions to make. Some people believe that stopping treatment is a form of euthanasia, or mercy-killing. The ethics of such actions are an issue of intense debate and disagreement. Doctors must weigh these issues and at the same time respect their patients' rights and wishes.

éthics *n.* 윤리 care for 보살피다 pátient *n.* 환자 hónor *v.* 존중하다 diagnostic findings 진단 결과 permíssion *n.* 동의, 허가 prolóng *v.* 늘이다, 연장하다 face *v.* 부딪치다 cónsciousness *n.* 의식 recóvery *n.* 회복 make a decision 결정을 내리다 euthanásia *n.* 안락사(= mercy-killing) inténse *adj.* 격렬한 disagréement *n.* 의견 불일치, 불화 weigh *v.* 숙고하다

1. 이 글의 둘째 단락에 나오는 'euthanasia'란 단어의 뜻을 다음에서 찾으시오.

① 과실치사 ② 뇌사
③ 법의학 ④ 안락사
⑤ 의료 사고

풀이 우선 둘째 단락에서 'euthanasia'를 찾으면 그 뒤에 바로 다른 쉬운 말로 부연되어 있다. 'mercy-killing'이란 안락사이다.

보너스 상식!

가장 오랜 수술 시간

세계에서 가장 오래 진행된 수술은 1951년 2월 4일에서 8일까지 계속된 난소 제거 수술이었다. 96시간 동안 진행되었다. 환자는 미국 시카고의 'Gertrude Levandowski' 라는 사람으로, 수술 전 280kg이던 몸무게가 수술 후에 140kg으로 절반이나 줄었다고 한다.

theme 14

Doctors 의사

2 When the doctor and patient meet, a number of things usually happen. First, the doctor talks with the patient and asks many questions about the patient's problem or concern. These questions include information about the patient's health history (such as broken bones or severe illness), family, habits (such as smoking), and daily routines (such as diet and number of hours of sleep). All of this is called the patient's medical history.

Next the doctor performs a physical exam. This is a careful examination of the body that gives the doctor additional information about the patient's physical health. Sometimes the doctor uses special lights or instruments for looking at and listening to the workings of the body.

After the medical history and physical exam, the doctor may need even more information. This is obtained from laboratory tests of body fluids (such as blood or urine), X rays, or other special procedures. With all this information, the doctor comes to a conclusion, or diagnosis, about the patient. Then the patient receives treatment or recommendations from the doctor. These might include taking medicines, having an operation, or starting a special diet or an exercise program.

concérn *n.* 관심 health history 건강 기록, 병력 dáily routínes 일상 addítional *adj.* 부가적인, 추가적인 médical hístory 의료 기록 obtáin *v.* 얻다 láboratory test 실험실 검사 body flúids 체액 úrine *n.* 오줌 come to a conclúsion 결론에 도달하다 recommendátion *n.* 권고 take médicines 약을 먹다 have a operation 수술을 받다

1. Which of the following is <u>not</u> stated in the passage as the patient' s medical history?

① daily routines ② family
③ habit ④ health history
⑤ friends

풀이 ① 일상 ② 가족 ③ 습관 ④ 건강 기록 ⑤ 친구
의사가 질문하는 '환자에 관한 정보'는 첫 단락에 열거되어 있다.

보너스 상식 **세계 첫 심장 이식자**

세계에서 처음으로 심장을 이식한 것은 1967년 12월 3일, 남아프리카의 Cape Town에 있는 Grote Schuur 병원에서 시술되었다. 의사는 'Christiaan Neethling Barnard'라는 교수였고, 환자는 55세의 'Louis Washkansky'라는 사람으로, 수술 후 18일 동안 살았다고 한다.

3 Because modern medical care and the issues facing doctors are continually changing, medical schools must adapt their content and style according to the times. In today's schools, students study medical subjects ranging from anatomy, biochemistry, and physiology to pediatrics, surgery, and psychiatry. Their learning takes place in the classroom as well as the hospital and clinic. They also discuss problems in medical ethics. Equally important, they learn how to relate to their patients in an understanding and helpful way.

After four years of college and four years of medical school, the student receives a medical degree. He or she then enters a residency training program in a hospital to become a specialist in a chosen area. This is called graduate medical education and can last from two years to more than ten years. It gives the new doctor additional experience in patient care.

During medical school or residency, the student completes a special examination. This exam plus the M.D. degree and the residency training allow the doctor to obtain a license to care for patients in his or her state. No doctor in the United States can practice without a license. Look for it on the wall of your doctor's office.

face *v.* 당면하다 adápt *v.* 적응하다 cóntent *n.* 내용 according to – ~에 따라 ranging from – to – (범위가) ~에서 ~에 이르는 anátomy *n.* 해부학 biochémistry *n.* 생화학 physiólogy *n.* 생리학 pediátrics *n.* 소아과학 súrgery *n.* 외과학 psychiátry *n.* 정신의학 take place 일어나다 medical ethics 의료 윤리 médical degrée 의사 학위 résidency *n.* 수련의 교육과정(= residency training program) graduate medical education 의학대학원 교육 compléte *v.* 마치다 M.D. 의학박사(Medical Doctor) práctice *v.* 진료하다

1. For how many years do American students study at the medical school?

① 2years ② 3years
③ 4years ④ 6years
⑤ from 2 to 10 years

풀이 미국에서는 대학(학부) 과정에 의과대학이 없다. 의과대학은 4년제 대학원이다.
참고로, 법과대학도 학부가 아니고 3년제 대학원 과정이다.

보너스 상식

공중보건의 제도

의사가 병역의무 대신 3년간 무의촌(無醫村)에 가서 활동하게 한 제도이다. 의료 인력이 대도시에 편중되어 있는 현상을 시정하려고 1979년부터 시행되었다. 그러나, 공중보건의들이 의과대학을 졸업한 후 임상수련 경험이 부족하다는 자질의 문제, 공중보건의들의 근무 의욕이 낮아 지역 주민과 유대 관계가 적다는 점, 의료 장비와 시설의 부족 등 문제점도 많이 남아 있다.

theme

15 First Aid 응급 처치

1 Exposure to heat, certain chemicals, electricity, or radiation can cause a type of skin injury known as a burn. Burns are classified by degree. First-degree burns are red and painful and involve only the topmost layer of skin. Second-degree burns are marked by redness, swelling, and blisters. They extend into the second layer of skin. Third-degree burns can be black or brown, sometimes with white patches. They extend to the tissue beneath the skin and are life-threatening.

How a burn is treated depends on its cause. Heat burns and sunburns should be immersed in cool water or covered with a damp cloth. Once the burned area is cool, it can be loosely covered with sterile bandages. Chemical burns should be flushed with cool running water. First aid for electrical burns should be given only if the scene is safe and the electricity that caused the burns is disconnected. If CPR is not necessary, the burns should be covered with a dry, sterile bandage.

expósure *n.* 노출 chémicals *n.* 화학 물질 radiátion *n.* 방사능 burn *n.* 화상 clássify *v.* 분류하다 topmost layer of skin 피부의 가장 바깥 층 swelling *n.* 부기 blíster *n.* 물집 exténd to – ~까지 확장하다 patch *n.* 반점 life-threatening 생명이 위험한 immérse *v.* 담그다 damp *adj.* 축축한, 젖은 stérile *adj.* 살균한 bándage *n.* 밴드 flush *v.* 담그다 running water 흐르는 물 first aid 응급 처치 scene *n.* (사고)현장 disconnéct *v.* 단절시키다 CPR(cardiopulmonary resuscitation) 심폐기능소생술 : 심장마비나 전기 충격, 기타 원인으로 환자의 심장 박동이 멈췄을 때, 가슴을 압박하여 혈액이 신체로 공급되는 것을 도와준다. 인공호흡도 효과가 있다.

1. Which of the following is not stated in the passage as the causes of burns?

① chemicals ② electricity
③ heat ④ light
⑤ radiation

풀이 ① 화학 물질 ② 전기 ③ 열 ④ 빛 ⑤ 방사능
첫 문장에 화상의 요인들이 열거되어 있다.

보너스 상식

응급 처치(First Aid)

원래는 소방 업무만을 하던 '119 소방대'가 이제는 긴급한 사고나 재난에서 인명을 구조하는 일까지 업무를 넓혔다. 119 구급차에는 반드시 간호사 1명이 동승하여 병원으로 이송하는 도중에 필요한 응급 처치를 한다. 미국에서는 긴급구조 신고 번호가 911이다.

2 Volunteers who know first aid are the first link in the chain of people who help during medical emergencies. Backing them up are the medical professionals who save thousands of lives every year. Police, fire fighters, paramedics, and emergency medical technicians arrive at the scene of an accident and take over the treatment started by first aid volunteers. Doctors and nurses in hospital emergency rooms continue this care. Dispatchers who operate the telephones of a community's emergency medical services and poison control center coordinate emergency care. Without the help of all these people, including volunteers trained in first aid by the American Red Cross, everyone would be in much greater danger during any type of medical emergency.

link *n.* 연결, 단계 médical emérgency 의료 긴급사태 back up 지지하다, 후원하다 fire fighter 소방관 paramédic *n.* 의료 보조원 emérgency médical technícian 긴급 의료 기술진 scene *n.* (사고)현장 take over 넘겨받다, 인수하다 hóspital emérgency room 병원 응급실 dispátcher *n.* 배송반원, 전화 교환원 poison control center 독극물 관리 센터 coórdinate *v.* 조정하다 be in danger 위험에 처하다

1. According to the passage, who is <u>not</u> included in the chain of people who help medical emergencies?

① fire fighters ② paramedics
③ police ④ soldiers
⑤ volunteers

풀이 ① 소방관 ② 의료 보조원 ③ 경찰 ④ 군인 ⑤ 자원 봉사자
이 글에 등장하는 직업 명칭들을 모두 찾아 확인하는 것도 하나의 방법이다.

보너스 상식!
'착한 사마리아인'(a good Samaritan)이란?

성경에 나오는 비유담으로, 한 낯선 사람이 강도를 당해 다쳐서 쓰러져 있었는데, 지나가는 사람들 누구도 도와주질 않았다고 한다. 이때 한 사마리아 시민이 길을 멈춰 도와주었다고 한다. 오늘날도 위급한 상황에 처한 사람을 돕는 사람들을 '착한 사마리아인'(Good Samaritans)이라고 한다.

theme 16 Hospitals 병원

Hospitals 병원

1 There are many different kinds of hospitals. Some hospitals only treat patients suffering from mental illness, or chronic diseases, or cancer. Other hospitals specialize in treating patients of a certain age group, such as children or senior citizens. However, the largest number of hospitals in the United States are short-term, general hospitals. These hospitals treat patients with all kinds of illnesses or injuries that do not require hospitalization of longer than 30 days.

There are approximately 6,800 hospitals in the United States. These hospitals range in size from small rural facilities with beds to accommodate fewer than 25 patients to large urban hospitals with more than 3,000 beds.

méntal íllness 정신 질환 **chrónic diséase** 만성 질병 **sénior cítizens** 노인들, 어른들 **short-term, general hospital** 단기 치료 종합병원 **hospitalization** *n.* 입원 **rúral facílity** 시골 의료시설 **accómmodate** *v.* 수용하다 **úrban hospital** 도시 병원

1. According to the passage, the kinds of hospitals can be classified by the following conditions **except**

① its size ② kinds of disease
③ patient's age group ④ province
⑤ term of treatment

풀이 ① 규모 ② 질병의 종류 ③ 환자의 연령 집단 ④ 지역 ⑤ 치료 기간
이 글에는 병원의 종류를 분류하는 조건을 네 가지 설명하고 있다. 순서대로, 질병의 종류, 특정 연령 집단, 진료 기간, 병원의 크기 등이다.

보너스 상식

오픈 병원(Open Hospitals)

외부의 의사에게 시설의 이용을 개방하는 병원. 개업 의사가 특정 병원과 계약하고 입원 치료가 필요한 환자나 값비싼 의료 장비를 필요로 하는 치료는 그 병원의 시설을 이용하게 된다. 미국의 개업의는 보통 오픈 병원을 이용하여 자신이 입원시킨 환자의 주치의가 되며, 병원측의 의사와 협력해서 치료에 임하기 때문에 보다 적절한 의료를 기대할 수 있다.

2 Most hospitals work very hard to be a visible and important part of a community. Many employ public relations specialists whose job is to keep the public aware of all the services the hospital has to offer.

Most hospitals offer many patient education programs for free or at a small cost. These programs include classes for expectant parents, weight-control and stop-smoking clinics, and group meetings for members of the community suffering from certain diseases. Many hospitals also teach cardiopulmonary resuscitation (CPR). They may also offer free blood-pressure testing and operate programs to treat alcohol and drug abuse.

vísible *adj.* 눈에 띄는 public relation PR홍보 spécialist *n.* 전문가 for free 무료로, 공짜로 expéctant *adj.* 기대되는, 예상되는, 잠재의 weight-control 체중 관리 cardiopulmonary resuscitation 심폐기능소생술(CPR) blood-pressure 혈압 drug abuse 약물 남용

1. According to the passage, all of the following are the services which hospitals usually offer to a community **except**

① Establishing medical school
② Stop-smoking clinic
③ Teaching CPR
④ Treating programs for alcohol and drug abuse
⑤ Weight-control clinic

풀이 ① 의과대학 설립 ② 금연 클리닉 ③ 심폐기능 소생술 강좌 ④ 알코올과 약물 남용 치료 과정 ⑤ 체중 조절 클리닉
둘째 단락에 병원이 주민들에게 하는 여러 가지 교육이 설명되어 있다.

보너스 상식

보건소

우리 나라에는 각 지방의 기초 단체마다 보건소가 있다. 지역 주민에게 보건에 관한 각종 교육을 실시하고, 각종 전염병을 예방하며, 모자 보건에 관한 교육과 필요한 진료 등을 제공하여 주민의 보건을 관리하고 있다. 지역 주민이면 누구나 무료로 이용할 수 있다.

theme 17 Kidney 신장(콩팥)

1 Some people are born with only one kidney. Others can lose a kidney because of a disease. And even though the fragile kidneys are protected by thick layers of fat, they can be injured by a hard blow to the body. That is why kidney punches are illegal in boxing. But whichever way a kidney is damaged, it is possible to live a normal, healthy life with only one kidney.

Both kidneys do exactly the same jobs of removing waste and toxins from the body, regulating the balance of body fluids, and maintaining the proper range of blood pressure. In a lifetime, these remarkable organs clean more than 1 million gallons of liquid—enough to fill a small lake! But one kidney can handle this gigantic task. In fact, if one kidney is removed, the remaining kidney can increase in size by 50 percent within two months to take over the whole job.

kídney *n.* 신장(콩팥) frágile *adj.* 연약한, 다치기 쉬운 protéct *v.* 보호하다 layer *n.* 층 hard blow 강한 타격 kidney punch 신장을 가격하는 것 illégal *adj.* 규정에 어긋나는, 불법의 remóve *v.* 제거하다 tóxin *n.* 독소 régulate *v.* 조절하다 body fluid 체액 maintáin *v.* 유지하다 proper range of blood pressure 적당한 혈압 범위 remárkable *adj.* 놀라운 gigántic *adj.* 거대한, 엄청난 take over 넘겨받다, 인수하다

1. What is the conclusion of the passage?

① Both kidneys do exactly the same jobs.
② In a lifetime, kidneys clean more than 1 million gallons of liquid.
③ It is possible to live a normal, healthy life with only kidney.
④ Some people can lose a kidney because of a disease.
⑤ Some people are born with only one kidney.

풀이 ① 두 개의 신장이 똑 같은 일을 정확하게 수행한다. ② 일생 동안, 신장은 1백만 갤런이 넘는 액체를 정화한다. ③ 신장을 하나만 가지고 정상적이고 건강한 삶을 사는 것이 가능하다. ④ 어떤 사람들은 어떤 질병 때문에 신장을 하나 잃기도 한다. ⑤ 어떤 사람들은 신장을 하나만 가지고 태어난다.
첫 단락의 마지막 문장에 이 글의 결론이 압축되어 있다. 둘째 단락은 그것을 보충 설명하고 있다.

보너스 상식

신장(콩팥 kidney)

신장은 두 개로 되어 있는데, 진한 갈색의 콩 모양의 기관으로 길이가 약 10센티 된다. 1분에 1리터의 혈액이 신장을 통해 걸러져 정화되고 재생된다. 하루에 약 1,609리터의 혈액이 재생되는 셈이다.

Mental Health 정신 건강

1 Mentally healthy people are glad to be alive and glad to be themselves. This does not mean that they are always completely happy and confident. They have successes and failures, ups and downs. But they are generally hopeful about the future. And they are reasonably successful in meeting the everyday problems of life.

Having good mental health does not mean being just like everyone else. You may be a quiet person who enjoys spending a lot of time alone, or you may be very sociable and outgoing. You may have different feelings, ideas, and interests from other people.

The important thing is that you are able to live in reality. You can meet the challenges of life in such a way that you use your talents and strengths and enjoy your relationship with other people.

Mentally healthy people have an understanding of themselves. They recognize their limitations, but they like themselves and have a sense of their own worth. They accept the fact that they are human and not perfect. Still, they try to grow and change. They understand that it is normal to have many kinds of feelings — including anger, fear, frustration, and jealousy. But they also learn to control what they do about these feelings.

méntally *adv.* 정신적으로 cónfident *adj.* 만족스러운 ups and downs (인생의) 오르막과 내리막 réasonably *adv.* 합리적으로 being just like – ~와 똑 같아짐 quiet person 조용한 사람 sóciable *adj.* 사교적인 outgóing *adj.* 개방적인 in reálity 현실적으로, 실제에 chállenge *n.* 도전 relátionship *n.* 관계 limitátion *n.* 한계 frustrátion *n.* 좌절 jéalousy *n.* 질투

1. Which of the following is <u>not</u> stated in the passage about the mentally healthy people?

① They accept the fact that they are human and not perfect.
② They are generally hopeful about the future.
③ They are glad to be alive and glad to be themselves.
④ They recognize their limitations, and they don't understand their own worth.

풀이 ① 인간이며 완전하지 않다는 사실을 받아들인다. ② 미래에 대해서 일반적으로 희망적이다. ③ 살아 있는 것이 즐겁고 자신들에 대해서도 만족스럽다. ④ 자신의 한계를 인식하고 있으며, 자신의 가치를 알지 못한다.
정신적으로 건강한 사람들의 특징은 모두 긍정적인 서술일 것이라는 점을 유추하여 답지를 읽어보는 것도 의 한 방법이다.

theme 18

Mental Health 정신 건강

보너스 상식!

1. 정신 건강에 필요한 마음가짐

1. 화내고, 미워하고, 난폭한 감정은 누구에게나 있다. 이런 감정이 든다고 부끄러워 할 필요는 없다. 다른 사람에게 해를 끼치지 않기 때문이다. 다만 행동으로 옮기면 문제가 된다.
2. 자신의 감정을 받아들이고 문제에 직접 부딪치는 것이 자신의 인생을 통제하고 스스로가 주인이 되는 첫걸음이다.
3. 어떤 문제에 부딪쳐서 다른 사람에게 도움을 구하는 것은 나약한 모습이 아니라 성숙하고 강한 모습이다.
4. 몸과 마음은 하나이다. 신체적으로 영향을 미치는 것은 정신적으로도 영향을 미치고, 정신적으로 영향을 미치는 것은 신체적으로도 영향을 미친다.
5. 자기 자신을 찾는 것은 정신 건강의 열쇠이다. 자신이 잘 할 수 있는 것 — 관심이 있는 것과 특별한 재능이 무엇인지 — 을 발견하는 것은 자신의 정체성을 찾는 것이다. 사람은 평생 이것을 목표로 산다.
6. 희망을 가지고 미래를 바라보는 것이 정신 건강에 필요하다.

2. 정신 질환의 종류

1. Character disorder(성격장애) : 정서적으로 미숙한 상태이거나, 불안정한 상태.
2. Neurosis(신경증) : 흔히 노이로제라고 하는 것으로 많은 사람들에게 있을 수 있는 약한 정도의 질환이다.
3. Psychosis(정신이상) : 가장 심각한 정신 질환으로 정신분열증(Schizophrenia)과 조울증(Manic-depressive psychosis)이 있다.

Mental Illness 정신 질환

19 theme

1

Most mental illnesses, unlike many physical diseases, have no single known cause. Many different things can cause a person to become mentally disturbed. But some types of mental illness have a clearly understood physical cause. Persons who have a high fever caused by an infection can become so confused that they do not know who or where they are. This condition is called delirium. It will disappear when the infection goes away. Other persons may become mentally ill when they have not had proper food for a long time. They will recover when their diet is corrected. An elderly person may lose the ability to think clearly. This can be caused by hardening of the arteries of the brain, a disease of old age that harms the brain cells that control behavior.

There is no simple answer to why some other people become mentally ill. Many of them have lived under unhappy conditions, where they could not build up feelings of self-confidence. Some of them may have been kept by themselves, away from the company of others. They may have been made to feel unwanted or unloved. They may not have received approval from their families for their accomplishments. They may have been laughed at for something in their appearance or manner over which they had no control. Any of these persons would be more likely to develop mental illness than those brought up in a home where they were loved and appreciated.

distúrb *v.* 혼란하게 하다 confúse *v.* 혼동시키다 delírium *n.* 정신착란 go away 사라지다(= disappear) proper food 적절한 식사 corréct *v.* 수정하다, 바로잡다 élderly person 노인 hárden *v.* 굳게 하다 ártery *n.* 동맥 hardening of the arteries 동맥경화 harm *v.* 해를 입히다 build up 쌓다 feelings of self-confidence 자신감 by themselves 홀로 cómpany *n.* 일행 unwánted *adj.* 쓸모 없는, 필요 없는 appéarance *n.* 외모 bring up 성장하다 be appréciated 인정을 받다

1. Which of the following is the main idea for the passage?

① Many different things can cause a person to become mentally disturbed.
② Many physical diseases have no single known cause.
③ People with mental illnesses have lived under unhappy conditions
④ Some types of mental illness have a clearly understood physical cause.
⑤ There is certain simple answer to why some people become mentally ill.

풀이 ① 많은 다른 것들이 어떤 사람을 정신적으로 혼란하게 한다. ② 많은 신체적 질병은 알 수 있는 한 가지 원인을 가지고 있다. ③ 정신 질환을 가진 사람들은 불행한 조건에서 살아왔다. ④ 어떤 정신 질환은 신체적 원인을 분명하게 알 수 있었다. ⑤ 어떤 사람들이 정신 질환을 일으키는 이유에는 어떤 한 가지 해답이 있다.
각 단락의 첫 문장이 글의 주제문이다. 답지에는 첫 단락의 둘째 문장이 같은 뜻을 나타내고 있다.

theme 20 Muscular System 근육계

1 Every moment of your life, even when you are asleep, some of the muscles of your body are working. As you read this article, tiny muscles move your eyeballs back and forth and help to give you a clear view of the words. Muscles in your arm and hand work when you turn a page. Even if you try to sit very still, muscles in your back are working to keep you from slumping over. At the same time, other kinds of muscles in your inner organs are helping you to breathe and to digest your most recent meal.

More than 650 muscles make up the muscular system of the human body. These tough, elastic tissues, which account for nearly half the weight of the whole adult body, are responsible for all body movements. Movements such as walking, running, or jumping are easily observed. However, muscles are also responsible for other movements such as those that open and close the pupil of the eye, force food through the intestines, and keep blood flowing through the body.

mόment *n.* 순간 múscle *n.* 근육 árticle *n.* 글 back and forth 앞뒤로 turn a page 책장을 넘기다 sit still 가만히 앉아있다 slump over 구부러지다 ínner órgans (신체의) 내부 장기 digést *v.* 소화하다 make up 구성하다 muscúlar system 근육계 elástic *adj.* 탄력 있는 accóunt for – ~에 해당하다, 설명하다 be respónsible for – ~을 책임지는 púpil *n.* 동공, 학생 intéstine *n.* (대, 소)장

1. Which of the following is the key word for the passage?

① body ② life
③ movements ④ muscle
⑤ tissues

풀이 ① 신체 ② 삶 ③ 운동 ④ 근육 ⑤ 조직
핵심어는 글에서 가장 많이 등장하는 단어이고, 각 단락의 첫 문장과 마지막 문장에서도 알 수 있다.

보너스 상식

근육(Muscles)

사람의 근육은 인체의 30%를 차지한다. 각각 임의로 작용하는 근육이 600개나 있는데, 이들이 한꺼번에 함께 작용하여 힘을 쓰면 무게 25톤의 물건을 들어올릴 수 있다고 한다.

Narcotics 진통제

1

All narcotics are alike in their effects on the body. They act on nearly all the body systems, but their strongest and most noticeable effects are on the nervous system. Narcotics reduce the activity of the central nervous system, which is made up of the brain and spinal cord. The result is that all behavior is reduced, irritability and anxiety are lessened, and drowsiness and sleep take place. Even low doses of narcotics may cause a person to slip in and out of awareness.

For a person who is sick or in severe pain, the effects that narcotics produce can provide much needed relief. In fact, the ability of narcotics to relieve pain is their most important medical application.

Other effects of narcotics include shrinking in size of the pupils of the eyes, dizziness, nausea, vomiting, itching, and lowering of blood pressure. The precise effects on a particular individual depend on the type of narcotic, how much is taken, the way it is taken, and how often it is taken.

narcótics *n.* 진통제 efféct *n.* 효과 nóticeable *adj.* 두드러진 redúce *v.* 완화시키다, 줄이다 be made up of – ~로 구성되다 spínal *adj.* 척추의 spinal cord 척수 behávior *n.* 행동 irritabílity *n.* 과민성 anxíety *n.* 노여움 léssen *v.* 줄이다 drówsiness *n.* 졸음 take place 생기다, 일어나다 dose *n.* (약의) 한번 복용 량, 한 첩 slip *v.* 미끄러지다 awáreness *n.* 의식 slip in and out of awareness 의식을 들게도 하고 나가게도 하다 sevére pain 심한 통증 relíef *n.* 위안, 구원 relíeve *v.* 구원하다 application *n.* 적용 shrink in size of pupils of the eyes 눈동자 동공의 축소 dízziness *n.* 현기증 náusea *n.* 메스꺼움 ítching *n.* 가려움 precíse *adj.* 정확한

1. Which of the following is the most important medical application of narcotics?

① dizziness
② drowsiness
③ lessening of irritability
④ lowering of blood pressure
⑤ relief of pain

풀이 ① 현기증 ② 졸음 ③ 과민성의 약화 ④ 혈압 저하 ⑤ 통증 제거
'narcotics'의 '가장 중요한 의학적 효과'는 둘째 단락에 적고 있다.

보너스 상식

생활 속의 집중

1. 스스로 집중할 수 있는 자신만의 때, 장소, 자세를 정해 둔다.
2. 1층보다는 2층, 천장이 높은 곳보다는 낮은 곳이 집중이 더 잘된다.
3. 공부나 일에 대한 목표를 의식하게 해주는 것을 항상 옆에 둔다.
4. 복장 등 주변의 상황을 바꾸어 본다.
5. 몸을 의식적으로 격렬하게 움직임으로써 '권태'를 해소한다.

theme

22 Florence Nightingale (1820~1910) 나이팅게일

1 In 1854 the Crimean War broke out. News soon reached London of the terrible state of the hospitals in the Russian Crimea. Florence Nightingale had made such a success of her hospital that Sidney Herbert, secretary at war in the British Government, asked her to conduct a party of nurses to the war area. She agreed to do so, and on October 21, 1854, she sailed for the Crimea with 38 nurses. There she found more than 5,000 wounded and sick men in so-called hospitals. These were bare buildings lacking facilities not only for medical care but even for ordinary cleanliness.

Working night and day, often for 20 hours at a time, Florence Nightingale personally inspected every ward each day. Although she was hampered by the jealousy of officials and medical staff alike, she triumphed. She equipped the hospitals and made them sanitary. Because the army worshiped her, she was able to bring about a revolution in the treatment of soldiers.

Crimea *n.* 크림, 오늘날 우크라이나 지방 break out 발발하다 reach – of – ~을 ~에 전해주다 térrible *adj.* 끔찍한 sécretary *n.* 장관, 비서 condúct *v.* 지휘하다 a party of nurse 간호 부대 so-called 소위 bare building 벌거벗은 건물 facílity *n.* 시설 cléanliness *n.* 청결 at a time 한번에 inspéct *v.* 검열하다 ward *n.* 병동 hámper *v.* 방해하다, 곤란하게 하다 jéalousy *n.* 질시 offícial *n.* 장교 medical staff 의료진, 군의관 tríumph *v.* 승리하다, 이기다 equíp *v.* 장비를 갖추다 sánitary *adj.* 위생적인 wórship *v.* 숭배하다, 존경하다 bring about 일으키다 revolution *n.* 혁명

1. With how many nurses did Nightingale sail for Crimea in 1854?

① 12 ② 24
③ 38 ④ 40
⑤ 5,000

풀이 간호사의 수를 찾으면 된다. 첫 단락에 '38 nurses'가 있다.

보너스 상식

야전 병원

야전 병원은 전쟁 부상자들을 수용하여 치료할 목적으로 전장의 가까운 후방에 설치하는 병원이다. 제네바 협정으로 야전 병원은 적십자 마크를 표시하며, 적군 병원이든 아군 병원이든, 소속 의료진과 함께 보호된다.

Nurses and Nursing 간호사와 간호 23 theme

1

Helping people is the business of nursing. Because nurses deal with life-and-death situations, they must be accurate and alert and have good judgement. They must really care about, and want to help, people. They need to be physically and mentally healthy themselves.

In return, nursing offers a satisfying career in health care to people with a wide range of abilities—from the abilities needed by nursing aides to those needed by nurse scientists. A person should consider his or her academic abilities and career goals before choosing a training program. The career possibilities are many and different. That is why careful early planning may save both time and money in meeting the desired goal.

Throughout the world there is a great need for nurses. But in some countries the need is desperate. Where there is a great shortage of nurses, aided and other auxiliary personnel may actually do much of the nursing of patients, under the supervision of professional nurses. Professional nurses are needed to teach, to supervise, and to do the most highly skilled nursing.

nursing *n.* 간호 nurse *n.* 간호사 deal with ~ ~을 다루다 situation *n.* 상황 áccurate *adj.* 정확한 alért *adj.* 방심 않는, 정신 바짝 차린 júdgement *n.* 판단 care about 돌보다 sátisfying caréer 만족스러운 직업 health care 건강 관리 nursing aide 간호 보조사 nurse scientist 간호학자 académic abílity 학구적인 능력 caréer goal 직업 목표 caréer possibílity 직업 선택권 desíred *adj.* 바라는 (*cf.* desírable *adj.* 바람직한) désperate *adj.* 필사적인, 절대절명의 shórtage *n.* 부족 personnél *n.* 요원 aided personnel 간호 보조 요원 auxíliary *adj.* 보조의 supervísion *n.* 감독 súpervise *v.* 감독하다 proféssional nurse 전문 간호사

1. Which of the following is <u>not</u> stated in the passage as the qualities which nurses need?

① accuracy ② alertness
③ good judgement ④ physical and mental health
⑤ a sense of balance

풀이 ① 정확성 ② 경계심 ③ 훌륭한 판단력 ④ 신체적 정신적 건강 ⑤ 균형 감각
간호사에게 필요한 자질들은 첫 단락에 열거되어 있다.

보너스 상식

남자 간호사

외국 병원에서나 볼 수 있었던 남자 간호사가 요즈음에는 우리 나라에도 가끔 눈에 띈다. 남자 간호사들이 점점 늘어나는 이유는 첫째, 간호 분야에서 남성들도 동등한 기회를 가지게 되었고, 둘째, 간호사의 보수가 다른 직업의 보수와 비교할 때 경쟁력을 가지게 된 것이다.

theme 23 Nurses and Nursing 간호사와 간호

2 Many sick people need nurses to help them get well. In hospitals there are nurses to care for patients and to give them treatments and medicines. But sometimes a sick person is cared for at home. Then a home nurse is needed.

The people who are in charge of running the household usually perform the duties of home nurse. Under the doctor's supervision, they provide the normal nursing care. When people are extremely ill and must have highly skilled nursing care, the services of a professional nurse may be necessary.

The first duty of the person who is acting as home nurse is to consult the family doctor and describe the signs of illness. The doctor will then examine the patient and leave complete instructions about nursing care and treatment. The doctor might also prescribe medicines and a special diet.

get well 병이 낫다 care for – ~을 돌보다 médicine *n.* 약 home nurse 가정 간호사 be in charge of – ~을 책임지다 hóusehold *n.* 가족, 가정 run the household 가정을 운영하다 supervísion *n.* 감독 consúlt *v.* 자문하다 family doctor 가정의, 주치의 descríbe *v.* 설명하다 exámine *v.* 진찰하다 leave a instruction 지시를 내리다 prescríbe *v.* 처방하다

1. According to the passage, which of the following is the first duty of nurses?

① To consult the family doctor
② To examine the patient
③ To leave instructions about treatment
④ To prescribe medicines
⑤ To prescribe a special diet

풀이 ① 주치의에게 자문을 해줌 ② 환자를 진찰함 ③ 치료에 대한 지시를 내림 ④ 약품 처방 ⑤ 특별한 식단 처방
'가정 간호사의 첫째 임무'는 마지막 단락의 첫 문장에 나와 있다.

보너스 상식

구급상자(First Aid Kit)의 내용물

장갑 (gloves) 가위 (scissors) 반창고 (adhesive tape) 솜 (cotton balls) 붕대 (gauze) 핀셋 (tweezers) 안전핀 (safety pins) 면봉 (cotton swabs) 소독 천 (antiseptic wipes) 일회용 밴드 (adhesive bandage)

Occupational Health and Safety 직업적인 건강과 안전

24 *theme*

1

People have always had to obtain food, make clothing and shelters to protect themselves from the climate, and produce other things to make their lives more comfortable. In short, people must work to live. And in working, people are exposed to many dangers that threaten life and health.

The field of occupational health and safety is concerned with lessening these dangers. The people who work in this field include doctors, nurses, and other health-care professionals, as well as chemists and safety engineers. They try to find ways to reduce or eliminate accidents and diseases that are common to certain kinds of work.

obtáin *v.* 구하다, 얻다 shélter *n.* 은신처, 피난처 cómfortable *adj.* 편안한 be expósed to ─ ~에 노출되다 thréaten *v.* 위협하다 occupátional *adj.* 직업적인 be concérned with ─ ~와 관계되다, 관련되다 léssen *v.* 줄이다 chémist *n.* 화학자 safety engineer 안전 기술자 redúce *v.* 줄이다(= lessen) elíminate *v.* 제거하다 be common to ─ ~에 흔한

1. Who is <u>not</u> the person who works in the field of occupational health and safety?

① chemists ② doctors
③ lawyers ④ nurses
⑤ safety engineers

풀이 ① 화학자 ② 의사 ③ 변호사 ④ 간호사 ⑤ 안전 기술자
둘째 단락에 그 분야와 종사자들이 설명되어 있다. 직업 명칭을 하나씩 확인 할 것.

보너스 상식

산업재해보상법

현대인은 모두 각자 종사하는 직업과 관련한 질병 곧, '직업병' 을 얻거나 사고를 당할 위험에 노출되어 있다. 거의 모든 산업 국가들이 각 사업장에서 작업과 관련하여 일어날 수 있는 모든 사고와 질병으로부터 노동자를 보호하고 있다. 각국에서 시행하고 있는 '산업재해보상법' 이 그것이다.

theme 24 Occupational Health and Safety 직업적인 건강과 안전

2 There are many people who have disabilities, or handicaps, that make it difficult for them to perform even the easiest tasks. Some disabilities, often those that are present at birth, are permanent. Disabilities that are a result of an accident or an illness may be temporary. Disabled people may be paralyzed (unable to move parts of the body), crippled, blind, or deaf. They may have lost an arm or a leg, or the ability to control certain muscles.

These physical problems often lead to emotional ones. Frequently, disabled people become depressed because they cannot do what they once did, or what their friends and members of their family can do. Sometimes the emotional problems are as difficult to cure as the physical ones.

Occupational therapy is a form of treatment that helps the handicapped lead happier lives. Through a carefully planned program, occupational therapists teach the disabled to perform the activities that are part of self-care, school, work, and leisure.

disabílity *n.* 장애(= handicap) task *n.* 일 présent *adj.* 나타나는, 존재하는 pérmanent *adj.* 영구적인 témporary *adj.* 일시적인 disabled people 장애자들(= the disabled, the handicapped) páralyze *v.* 마비시키다 crípple *v.* 불구로 만들다 blind *adj.* 시각장애의 deaf *adj.* 청각장애의 occupátional thérapy 작업요법(재활요법). 치료하면서 가벼운 작업을 시켜 직업보도를 겸한다. occupátional thérapist 작업 치료사(재활 치료사) self-care 스스로 돌보기

1. Occupational therapists teach the handicapped all of the following **except** which of the following?

① business ② leisure
③ school ④ self-care
⑤ work

풀이 ① 사업 ② 레저 ③ 학습 ④ 스스로 하기 ⑤ 작업
마지막 단락에 작업 요법에서 하는 활동들이 열거되어 있다.

보너스 상식! 재활 치료사

재활 치료사가 되려는 사람은 무엇보다 다른 사람을 도우려는 마음이 깊어야 한다. 교사처럼, 재활 치료사는 참을성이 있어야 하고, 친근하고, 마음을 열고 다른 사람과 쉽게 친할 수 있어야 한다. 대학에도 재활 의학과가 있어서 해부학(anatomy), 생물학(biology), 심리학(psychology) 등을 중심으로 필요한 공부를 한다.

Physical Fitness 신체 건강

1

For a long time, most people did not realize how important physical fitness was. Today, however, we know that staying in good physical condition not only makes life more enjoyable but also quite possibly helps us live longer. That is why millions of people today participate in some sort of strenuous exercise several times each week.

There are four foundations to physical fitness. First, you must eat in an intelligent way, based on principles of good nutrition. Second, you must get plenty of rest and sleep. This is vital when you are growing, and it is important at all times of your life. Third, you must practice good hygiene and health habits, and you should avoid dangerous substances such as tobacco and narcotics. Fourth, you must get plenty of exercise. Exercise keeps your muscles, heart, and lungs in good working order. There are many different exercises, but just three basic kinds are necessary for physical fitness. They are aerobic exercises, stretches, and strengtheners.

physical fítness 신체 건강 staying in good physical condition 양호한 신체 조건 유지하기 partícipate *v.* 참가하다
strénuous *adj.* 노력하는, 분투하는 éxercise *n.* 운동 foundation *n.* 기초, 기본 intélligent *adj.* 똑똑한, 지적인, 현명한
based on – ～에 기반을 둔 prínciple *n.* 원칙 nutrítion *n.* 영양 hygiene *n.* 위생, 건강 narcótic *n.* 진통제, 마취제
aeróbic exercise 유산소 운동 strétche *n.* 탄력 운동 stréngthener *n.* 근육 강화 운동

1. Which of the following is <u>not</u> mentioned as the four foundations to physical fitness?

① You must eat in an intelligent way, based on principles of good nutrition.
② You must follow your doctor's instructions.
③ You must get plenty of rest and sleep.
④ You must get plenty of exercise.
⑤ You must practice good hygiene and health habits.

풀이 ① 좋은 영양 원칙에 기반을 둔 현명한 방식으로 식사를 한다. ② 의사의 지시를 따른다. ③ 휴식과 수면을 많이 취한다. ④ 운동을 많이 해야 한다. ⑤ 좋은 위생과 건강 습관을 실천한다.
둘째 단락에서 First부터 Fourth까지 하나씩 확인한다.

보너스 상식

체력 단련의 종류

① Aerobic exercises(유산소 운동) : running, jogging, bicycling, swimming, rope skipping(줄넘기), skiing, cross-country, basketball, soccer 등 대부분의 스포츠
② Stretching exercises(탄력 운동) : bend and sway(몸통 굽히기와 흔들기), wing flaps(양팔 흔들기) 등 대부분의 체조
③ Strengthening exercises(근육 강화 운동) : push-ups(팔굽혀펴기), sit-ups(윗몸 일으키기), pull-ups (턱걸이) 등

theme

26 Public Health 공중 보건

1 Public health is the measurement, improvement, and maintenance of a community's health by people who use specialized scientific methods, skills, and beliefs to control and prevent disease. Public health programs are usually funded and administered by government agencies. These agencies develop special programs for people at high risk for disease, such as the elderly, persons with chronic disease, disability, or addiction, and those living in poverty.

In a manner similar to how a medical doctor diagnoses and treats a patient, a public health agency also diagnoses and treats a community. First, an agency performs an assessment by asking careful questions of and about those people possibly affected by a particular disease. After deciding which people or groups may be at risk, the agency makes estimates of how much actual risk of disease or disability there is. The agency uses this information to design and implement preventive solutions tailored to each unique community. For example, during an infectious disease outbreak, a public health agency responds by investigating its cause and the likelihood of further spread of disease. It then develops and coordinates a program to treat all infected people as well as protect those not infected. After the emergency is over, the agency formulates a plan to prevent future outbreaks.

públic health 공중 보건 méasurement *n.* 측정 impróvement *n.* 개선, 향상 máintenance *n.* 유지 spécialized *adj.* 전문화된 fund *v.* 자금을 대다 admínister *v.* 행정을 관리하다 ágency *n.* 기관 the élderly 노인들 chrónic diséase 만성 질병 disabílity *n.* 장애 addíction *n.* 중독 povérty *n.* 가난 díagnose *v.* 진단하다 perfórm an asséssment 진단을 내린다 make an éstimate 판단하다 desígn *v.* 계획하다 ímplement *v.* 이행하다 prevéntive solútion 예방책 táilored to ~에 맞추어진 uníque *adj.* 독특한 inféctious diséase 전염병 óutbreak *n.* 발병 respónd *v.* 대응하다 invéstigate *v.* 조사하다 líkelihood *n.* 가능성 coórdinate *v.* 조정하다 be over 끝나다 fórmulate *v.* 공식화하다, 처방하다

1. According to the passage, who takes charge of public health?

① Communities ② Each individuals
③ Government agencies ④ Health-care professionals
⑤ Large businesses

풀이 ① 지역사회 ② 각 개인 ③ 정부 기관 ④ 보건 전문가들 ⑤ 대기업
첫 단락에 'funded and administered by government agencies'가 있다.

보너스 상식!

공중위생법

숙박업법, 공중목욕탕법, 이 · 미용사법, 유기장업법 등으로 구분되어 있던 우리 나라 위생관계 법령을 통합한 것이다. 이 법은 퇴폐 행위를 한 업소를 처벌할 수 있도록 벌칙을 강화하였고, 무허가 업소나 영업 정지 등 행정처분을 받고도 계속 영업을 한 업소에 대한 벌칙도 엄격히 하였다. 또, 이 · 미용업을 신고제에서 허가제로 바꾸고 세탁업과 위생관리 용역업을 자유 업종에서 신고 업종으로 바꾸었다.

2 Many people do not realize the importance and scope of public health services because the outcomes are often hidden. Public health services prevent major disasters: epidemics, polluted waters, unsafe food, and so on. Ignoring the importance of good health is costly. The AIDS epidemic emerged as a major public health threat to all people in the 1980's, as did the re-emergence of syphilis and tuberculosis.

Good health is not just the responsibility of the public health system, a network of hardworking and dedicated professionals including physicians, dentists, nurses, and public health workers. Good health is the responsibility of all individuals. By keeping public health recommendations in mind, now more than ever, people can protect their health and the health of others in their community.

scope *n.* 범위, 영역 óutcome *n.* 결과물, 성과 hide *v.* 숨기다, 숨다 (hide-hid-hidden) prevént *v.* 예방하다 disáster *n.* 재난 epidémic *n.* 유행병, 전염병 pollúte *v.* 오염시키다 and so on 등등 ignóre *v.* 무시하다 costly *adv.* 대가를 치르는, 비싼 emérge *v.* 부상하다, 떠오르다 threat *n.* 위협 reemérgence *n.* 재등장 syphilis *n.* 매독 tubérculosis *n.* 결핵 nétwork *n.* 네트워크, 수평조직 dédicate *v.* 헌신하다 physícian *n.* 의사 déntist *n.* 치과의사 public health worker 공중보건 종사자 keep – in mind ~을 명심하다 now more than ever 이제 전보다 더

1. According to the passage, why people do <u>not</u> realize the importance and scope of public health services?

① Because good health is not the responsibility of the public health system.
② Because good health is the responsibility of all individuals.
③ Because the outcomes are often hidden.
④ Because people can protect their health for themselves.
⑤ Because public health services prevent major disasters.

풀이 ① 건강이 공중 보건 체제의 책임이 아니기 때문에 ② 건강이 모든 개인의 책임이기 때문에 ③ 성과가 흔히 드러나지 않기 때문에 ④ 사람들이 스스로 자신의 건강을 보호할 수 있기 때문에 ⑤ 공중 보건 서비스가 주요 재난을 예방하기 때문에
바로 첫 단락의 첫 문장에 나타나 있다.

보너스 상식!

공중보건의 용어

① Biostatistics 생물통계학	② Environmental Health 환경 보건
③ Epidemiology 유행병학	④ Maternal and Child Health 모자 보건
⑤ Nutrition 영양학	⑥ Population and International Health 인구와 국제 보건

theme

27 Red Cross 적십자

1 Over the last 100 years the Red Cross has changed from an organization with a program of wartime services alone to one that serves at all times. In some European countries the Red Cross owns and operates hospitals and clinics that serve as nurse-training centers. It also helps to train community public-health workers. Part of the daily work of Red Cross societies in the new African and Asian nations is to educate people to good habits of health and hygiene. In Canada, the Red Cross Society has programs for children and adults that include water safety, first aid, and general health care.

A large number of society have, or take part in, blood service programs. Blood is collected from volunteers, processed, and distributed to civilian and military hospitals and doctors. Most Red Cross societies have Junior Red Cross branches and disaster-relief programs. The disaster-relief program is a broad one, covering community preparedness, emergency relief activities, and finally the care of the disaster victims until they are able to care for themselves. Several countries have trained Red Cross ambulance corps.

All Red Cross societies take part in an international search in order to bring together members of families who have become separated or have been lost to one another through wars or other disasters.

wártime sérvice 전시(戰時) 봉사 public-health worker 공중 보건 종사자 hygiene *n.* 위생 water safety 수질 안전 blood service program 헌혈 프로그램 colléct *v.* 수집하다 prócess *v.* 보존 처리하다 distríbute *v.* 나누어주다, 유통시키다 disáster-relíef prógram 재난 구조 프로그램 cóver *v.* 범위가 미치다 prepáredness *n.* 준비 태세 emérgency relíef actívity 긴급구조 활동 Red Cross ambulance corps 적십자 구급단 séparate *v.* 헤어지다 be lost 길을 잃다 one another 서로

1. Which is not stated in the passage as the activities of the red cross?

① Blood service programs ② Disaster-relief programs
③ Education for health care ④ Search for lost family members
⑤ Public health service

풀이 ① 헌혈 프로그램 ② 재난 구조 프로그램 ③ 건강 교육 ④ 이산가족 찾기 ⑤ 공중 보건 서비스
첫 단락은 의료 교육, 둘째 단락은 헌혈과 재난 구조 프로그램, 마지막 단락은 이산가족 찾기 등의 역할이 서술되어 있다.

Red Cross 적십자

27 theme

보너스 상식!

적십자의 창설

1859년, 스위스인 앙리 뒤낭(Henry Dunant, 1828~1910)이 이탈리아를 여행하던 중, 오스트리아 군과 나폴레옹 3세의 군대가 전투를 하고 지나간 곳을 보았다. 수천 명의 사망자와 부상자들이 돌보는 사람도 없이 쓰러져 있었다. 뒤낭과 자원자들이 서둘러 응급 병원을 설치하고 양쪽 군대의 부상병들을 치료해 주었다. 귀국한 뒤, 뒤낭은 전시에 부상자들을 도울 자원자들의 중립적인 기구를 각국에 설립하자는 제안을 하게 되고, 많은 사람들이 공감하여 마침내 1863년에 적십자(Red Cross)가 창설된다.

적십자 협약인 제네바 협정은 도움이 필요한 사람의 생명과 존엄성이 인종, 국적, 정치 동맹이나 신분에 관계 없이 존중되어야 한다는 것이었다. 협정은 또 전쟁 부상자, 전쟁 포로, 피점령국의 민간인, 군대 병원과 그 의료진이나 장비들을 보호하고 있다.

theme **28** # Vaccination and Immunization 백신과 면역

1 Vaccinations work because they stimulate the body to build defenses against infection. These defenses are part of the body's immune system. The immune system's job is to protect the body from infections and illnesses.

When disease-causing organisms (germs), such as bacteria and viruses, enter the body, certain cells in the immune system begin to make antibodies. Antibodies are chemical substances that can stop disease organisms from causing a massive infection. The immune-system cells make a special antibody for each type of disease organism. Other cells directly attack the organisms and work to remove them from the body.

After a person recovers from an infectious disease, some of the antibodies and defensive cells for that particular disease remain in the body. If the same disease organisms enter the body again, the defenses are ready to help prevent the illness. This is why we rarely experience two episodes of certain infectious diseases, such as measles or rubella. When the body's defenses prevent an infection of a disease, a person is said to have an immunity to that disease.

vaccinátion *n.* 백신 stímulate *v.* 자극하다 defénse *n.* 방어 immúne system 면역 체계 inféction *n.* 감염, 전염 germ *n.* 세균, 병원균 ántibody *n.* 항생제 diséaser óganism 질병 조직체 attáck *v.* 공격하다 remóve *v.* 제거하다, 떼어내다 recóver *v.* 회복하다 inféctious diséase 전염성 질병 épisode *n.* 에피소드, (재발성 질병의) 발현, 재발 méasles *n.* 홍역 rubélla *n.* 풍진(= German measles)

1. Which of the following is the best title for the passage?

① Antibodies and Defensive Cells ② Body's Immune System
③ Disease-causing Organisms ④ Infections and Illnesses
⑤ Vaccinations

풀이 ① 항생제와 방어 세포 ② 신체의 면역 체계 ③ 질병을 일으키는 조직체 ④ 감염과 질환 ⑤ 백신
첫 단락에 핵심어로 나와 있으며, 글 전체에 가장 자주 등장한다. 결론인 마지막 문장에도 immunity가 핵심어이다.

보너스 상식
어린이 면역권장계획(Recommended Schedule for Immunization of Children)

① 생후 2개월 : DTP(Diphtheria 디프테리아, Tetanus 파상풍, Pertussis 백일해), Polio(소아마비)
Hib(Haemophilus Influenzae type b : b형 혈우병 인플루엔자)
② 생후 4개월 : DTP, Polio, Hib
③ 생후 6개월 : DTP, Hib
④ 생후 15-18개월 : MMR(Measles 홍역, Mumps 볼거리, Rubella 풍진, Hib, DTP, Polio
⑤ 생후 4-6년 : DTP, Polio, MMR
⑥ 생후 14-16년 : Tb(Tetanus 파상풍, diphtheria 디프테리아)

Vaccination and Immunization 백신과 면역

2 Immunization helps the body to defend itself against invading disease germs. When the body is attacked by disease germs, it makes substances called antibodies. The antibodies fight the germs and the poisons, or toxins, that the germs produce.

Some diseases can be prevented by purposely putting the disease germs or their toxins into the body. This is called a vaccination, or inoculation, and the material is called a vaccine. In some types of vaccine the germs or toxins have been weakened to make them harmless. In other vaccines, the germs are dead. But even the weak or dead germs or toxins cause the body to make antibodies. Later on, if the body is invaded by the germs causing these diseases, it is protected by the antibodies needed to fight that disease.

Most vaccines are given by injection. Immunization procedures can provide protection against a wide variety of diseases, including polio, diphtheria, tetanus, measles, mumps, whooping cough, and one kind of pneumonia.

During the first year of life, a baby is usually given vaccines against a number of diseases. The older child is given booster shots. The boosters strengthen the immunity produced by the original vaccination.

immunizátion *n.* 면역 inváding diséase germ 침입 병원균 púrposely ad*v.* 일부러, 고의적으로 inoculátion *n.* 예방 접종, 백신(= vaccination) weaken *v.* 약화시키다 hármless *adj.* 무해한 later on 나중에 injéction *n.* 주사 immunizátion procédure 면역 절차 a wide varíety of – 다양한 pólio *n.* 소아마비 diphthéria *n.* 디프테리아 tétanus *n.* 파상풍 méasles *n.* 홍역 mumps *n.* 볼거리 whooping cough 백일해 pneumónia *n.* 폐렴 booster shot(injection) (첫 번째 백신의 약효 지속을 위한) 두 번째 예방주사 stréngthen *v.* 강화하다 (*opp.* weaken 약화시키다)

1. Which of the following is the main role of the booster shots?

① They cause the body to make antibodies.
② They can provide protection against a wide variety of diseases.
③ They help the body to defend itself against invading disease germs.
④ They put the disease germs or their toxins into the body.
⑤ They strengthen the immunity produced by the original vaccination.

풀이 ① 신체가 항생제를 만들게 해준다. ② 다양한 질병에 대항하여 보호를 해준다. ③ 신체가 침입 병원균으로부터 스스로 방어하도록 도와준다. ④ 병원균이나 그 독소를 신체 속에 넣어 준다. ⑤ 처음의 백신에 의해 생산된 면역을 강화해 준다.
마지막 문장에 그 역할이 나와 있다.

보너스 상식

WHO(**세계보건기구** World Health Organization)

1948년 창설된 국제연합(UN)의 세계보건기구이다. 전세계에서 발생되는 각종 질병을 감시하여 그 대책을 발표하며, 각종 대규모의 보건 캠페인을 수립하여 전세계에 홍보하여 지구촌의 보건을 위해 노력한다.

theme 28 Vaccination and Immunization 백신과 면역

3 Sometimes illness or an accident damages body tissue so much that it is no longer able to function normally. Then an operation, called a tissue graft, or transplant, may be performed to replace the damaged part. Healthy tissue, such as skin, may be taken from one part of the body and grafted to another part of the body. The body accepts the transplanted tissue because it has the same self label. Problems arise when the tissue or organs are taken from one person and transplanted to another. Then the immune system recognizes the transplant as foreign and launches an attack against it. When this happens, special drugs are used to lessen the immune system attack.

Although the body attacks cells that have a different self label, some self labels are chemically more similar than others and cause less of an immune response. The self labels are coded by genes inherited from each parent, so brothers and sisters are more likely to have similar, but not the same, self labels. The only people who would have the very same self labels would be identical twins, because they share the same genes.

nórmally *adv.* 정상적으로 **operátion** *n.* 수술 **graft** *v.* 접합하다, 접붙이다 **tissue graft** 조직 접합 **tránsplant** *n.* 이식, 옮겨심기(= graft) **transplánt** *v.* 이식하다 **repláce** *v.* 대체하다, 교체하다 **self label** 유전 지표 **launch** *v.* 착수하다, 시작하다 **léssen** *v.* 줄이다, 완화하다 **immúne respónse** 면역 반응 **gene** *n.* 유전인자 **inhérit** *v.* 물려받다, 유전하다 **idéntical** *adj.* 똑같은 **identical twins** 일란성 쌍둥이

1. 이 글에서 말하는 다른 사람의 장기를 이식하였을 때 면역 반응이 일어나는 것은 무엇 때문인지 다음에서 고르시오.

① Different self labels　② Identical twins
③ Illness or an accident　④ Same gene
⑤ Special drugs

풀이 ① 다른 유전 지표 ② 일란성 쌍둥이 ③ 질환이나 사고 ④ 같은 유전자 ⑤ 특별한 약
이 글에서 가장 자주 등장하는 핵심어는 'self label'이다. 이것이 같은 경우에는 면역 반응이 일어나지 않고, 다른 경우에 면역 반응이 일어난다.

보너스 상식!
면역 체계의 이상 현상

① Allergy(알레르기) : 면역 체계의 과민 반응
② Autoimmune Disease(자기 면역 이상 질환) : 자신과 다른 침입 항체를 구분하지 못하는 증세
③ AIDS(후천성면역 결핍증) : 면역 체계가 파괴된 증세

Viruses 바이러스

1

Each virus needs a certain type of cell in which to multiply: Plant viruses multiply only in plant cells; animal viruses multiply only in animal cells. Some viruses are even more particular, such as the animal viruses that only infect certain types of cells in animals.

After infecting a host cell, a single virus can produce hundreds or even thousands of similar viruses. The virus carries the essential information for its life cycle in its genes, while the host cell supplies the energy, machinery, building blocks, and production enzymes necessary for the virus to live and multiply. The new viruses are made in an orderly, step-by-step process. The steps used by all viruses are 1) attachment, 2) entry, 3) synthesis of virus parts, 4) assembly, and 5) release.

múltiply *v.* 증식하다 host cell 숙주 세포 carry *v.* 가지고 다니다, 보유하고 있다 life cycle 생의 주기 machínery *n.* 조직, 기계 building block 서식 공간 énzyme *n.* 효소 órderly *adj.* 질서 있는 attáchment *n.* 접착, 흡착 synthesis *n.* 합성 assémbly *n.* 조립, 조합 reléase *n.* 방출, 방면

1. All of the following are the things which the host cell supplies **except**

① building blocks ② energy
③ machinery ④ plant cells
⑤ production enzymes

풀이 ① 서식 공간 ② 에너지 ③ 조직 ④ 식물 세포 ⑤ 생산 효소
'host cells'는 둘째 단락에 있다. 제공하는(supplies) 것을 찾아 하나씩 확인할 것.

보너스 상식

바이러스의 발견

러시아 식물학자 '드미트리 이바노프스키'(Dmitri Ivanovski)가 박테리아보다 더 작은 물질이 질병을 일으키는 것을 발견한다. 이것이 식물성 바이러스의 첫 발견이다. 이후 네덜란드 식물학자 '마르티누스 베이체링크'(Martinus Beijerinck)는 '이바노비치'가 발견한 이 물질이 박테리아와는 다른 활동을 하는 것을 발견하고, '바이러스'(Virus)라고 이름 붙였다.

theme 29 Viruses 바이러스

2 It will be remembered as one of the biggest killers of all time. Since 1157 B.C., when Pharaoh Ramses V became its first known victim, smallpox has swept through the countries of the world, killing, blinding, and disfiguring millions of people.

The first step toward wiping out the deadly virus was made in 1796 when Edward Jenner, an English doctor, developed a smallpox vaccine. Although the vaccine prevented smallpox, there was no treatment for those who contracted the disease. Over time it became clear that a global vaccination program was needed in order to fight smallpox.

In 1967, the World Health Organization (WHO) began an intensive vaccination program. Hundreds of health personnel went through infected countries, isolating those who had smallpox and vaccinating those who did not. The campaign was successful,. In 1980, WHO declared the world free of smallpox—the first disease conquered by human beings.

smállpox *n.* 천연두 víctim *n.* 희생자 sweep *v.* 휩쓸다(sweep-swept-swept) blind *v.* 눈멀게 하다 disfígure *v.* 얼굴을 추하게 만들다, 일그러뜨리다 wipe out 일소하다, 박멸하다 deadly *adj.* 치명적인 contráct *v.* 병에 걸리다 glóbal *adj.* 지구의, 세계적인 inténsive *adj.* 강력한 health personnél 보건 요원 go through — ~를 가다, 경험하다 ísolate *v.* 격리시키다 decláre *v.* 선언하다 free of — ~가 없어진, ~에서 자유로운 cónquer *v.* 정복하다

1. When was the world freed of smallpox?

① 1157 B.C. ② A.D. 1796
③ A.D. 1967 ④ A.D. 1980
⑤ A.D. 1990

풀이 '지구상에서 없어진' 해를 찾는다. 마지막 문장에 WHO의 공식 선언이 기술되어 있다.

보너스 상식

바이러스 하나가 사람에게 질병을 일으킬 수 있을까?

사람, 곤충, 물, 음식 등은 바이러스를 가지고 있어서 다른 것에 옮길 수도 있다. 그러나 감염되기 위해서는 노출될 뿐 아니라 충분한 양의 바이러스를 섭취해야 한다. 많은 양으로 감염시키는 바이러스가 있고, 적은 양으로도 감염시키는 바이러스가 있다. 하지만 바이러스 분자 하나가 질병을 일으키는 일은 거의 없다.

제 4 장

환경문제 Environmental Problems

theme 01 Acid Rain 산성비

1 When fossil fuels—oil, coal, and gas—are burned, in industrial plants or automobile engines, for example, sulfur oxides and nitrogen oxides are released into the air. One industrial smokestack without pollution controls may produce as much as 500 tons of sulfur oxides each day.

Nitrogen oxides and carbon particles produced by motor vehicles are so plentiful in some large cities that the air is colored by them. Nitrogen oxides also enter the air from the breakdown of agricultural fertilizers. Other acid-forming chemicals also occur but in smaller amounts. Hydrochloric acid often comes directly from smokestacks. Carbon monoxide and carbon dioxide are produced by motor vehicles.

fóssil fúels 화석 연료 **indústrial plant** 산업 공장 **súlfur óxide** 아황산가스 **nítrogen óxide** 산화질소 **reléase** *v.* 배출하다, 방출하다 **smókestack** *n.* 굴뚝 **mótor véhicle** 자동차 **bréakdown** *n.* 분해 **fértilizer** *n.* 비료, 거름 **ácid-fórming** *adj.* 산성의, 산성을 함유하는 **hydrochloric acid** 염산 **cárbon monóxide** 일산화탄소 **cárbon dióxide** 이산화탄소

1. Which of the following is <u>not</u> stated in the passage as the matters of pollution?

① carbon monoxide ② carbon dioxide
③ hydrogen dioxide ④ nitrogen oxide
⑤ sulfur oxide

풀이 ① 일산화탄소 ② 이산화탄소 ③ 과산화수소 ④ 산화질소 ⑤ 아황산가스
이 글에 열거된 오염 물질 5가지를 하나씩 확인하면 명칭이 틀린 것이 있을 것이다.

보너스 상식!
대기오염의 주범

산성비의 원인이 되는 가장 큰 주범은 자동차에서 내뿜는 배기가스와 공장에서 배출되는 매연과 유독가스이다. 대기오염을 줄이기 위해 개인이 가장 하기 쉬운 방법은 걷기와 자전거 타기, 대중 교통을 이용하는 일이고, 국가적으로는 모든 산업체에 정화 시설을 강화하고 철저히 감독하는 일일 것이다.

Acid Rain 산성비

2 Millions of tons of acids fall in rain on the United States and Canada each year. The concentration of these acids are too weak to cause burns, but they do produce other less severe effects.

When acid rain falls on metal objects, the objects can begin to change in undesirable ways. Shiny objects become dull and, if the process continues for many years, the metal objects can corrode and lose strength or crumble. Acid rain also affects the surfaces of stone statues and stone or brick buildings.

The way in which acid rain reacts with aluminum causes another serious problem. Aluminum is normally present in soil. If acid rain causes soil acidification, the aluminum in the soil may dissolve in water and be absorbed by plants, where it can damage root cells. Animal cells are also very sensitive to aluminum.

Human beings may also be at risk from the effects of acid rain. In moist air, high levels of pollutants from acidic aerosols have been found to affect lung function in experimental studies. People who suffer from asthma, emphysema, and chronic bronchitis are more sensitive to acid environments. Additional studies are necessary to determine whether people are affected at current levels of aerosol acidity.

concentrátion *n.* 농도 burn *n.* 화상 ácid rain 산성비 undesírable *adj.* 바람직하지 않은 dull *adj.* 둔한, 희미한 corróde *v.* 부식하다 crumble *v.* 부서지다 stone státue 석상(石像) brick building 벽돌 건축물 reáct *v.* 작용하다, 반응하다 be présent in – ~에 있는, 존재하는 soil acidificátion 토양 산성화 dissólve *v.* 용해되다, 녹다 sénsitive *adj.* 민감한 be at risk 위험에 처한 moist air 습한 공기 pollútant *n.* 오염 물질 acídic áerosol 산성 에어로졸 suffer from – ~로 고생하다 ásthma *n.* 천식 emphyséma *n.* 기종(氣腫), 폐기종 chrónic *adj.* 만성적인 brónchitis *n.* 기관지염 áerosol acídity 에어로졸 산성도

1. Which of the following is <u>not</u> the object which acid rains affect?

① metals ② people ③ plants
④ oil ⑤ stones

풀이 ① 금속 ② 사람들 ③ 식물 ④ 석유 ⑤ 석재
둘째 단락부터 산성비의 영향을 받는 것을 한두 가지씩 설명하고 있다.

보너스 상식!

가장 심한 삼림의 피해

유럽에서 산성비에 의한 삼림 피해가 가장 큰 사례는 영국으로, 전체 삼림의 67%가 산성비로 인해 피해를 입었다고 한다. 우리 나라도 근처 산에 가면 산성비에 병든 삼림을 쉽게 볼 수 있다.

theme 02 Atmosphere 대기

1 Many scientists think that small changes in its composition will cause the atmosphere at the Earth's surface to become warmer. They are alarmed because the amounts of gases such as carbon dioxide, methane, and nitrous oxide in our atmosphere are increasing. These gases tend to trap the radiation that reaches the Earth from the sun. Because the amount of radiation we receive tends to be constant, if less radiation escapes from our atmosphere, the atmosphere could become warmer.

The problem is complex because many factors need to be considered. For example, if the surface atmosphere of the Earth warms, more water may evaporate from the Earth's surface. This would affect the formation of clouds and the amounts and patterns of wind and rainfall. Both of these changes could affect temperatures around the world but precisely how and whether or not the effects would be long-lasting is not fully understood.

Records going back many years show a temperature increase, but the increase has been interrupted by periods of cooling. So far, the evidence does not clearly show whether or not 'global warming' is occurring. However, the possible effects of global warming, should it occur, would be so serious that research is continuing on a global scale.

compositíon *n.* 성분 alárm *v.* 놀라게 하다, 경계시키다 méthane 메탄가스 nítrous óxide 이산화질소 trap *v.* 가두다, 붙잡다 cónstant *adj.* 끊임없는, 불변의, 항구적인 escápe *v.* 탈출하다, 빠져나가다 factor *n.* 요인, 요소 eváporate *v.* 증발하다 precísely *adv.* 정확하게 interrúpt *v.* 방해하다 so far 지금까지 évidence *n.* 증거 global warming 지구 온난화 global scale 세계적 규모

1. Which of the following is the topic word for the passage?

① Atmosphere ② Earth's surface
③ Global warming ④ Global scale
⑤ Temperatures

풀이 ① 대기 ② 지표면 ③ 지구 온난화 ④ 세계적 규모 ⑤ 기온
이 글의 핵심어는 주제문인 첫 문장에 포함되어 있지만, 마지막 단락에 용어로 등장하고 있다.

보너스 상식

오존 감소(Ozone Depletion)

지구 대기의 성층권에 있는 오존층은 태양으로부터 오는 해로운 자외선(ultraviolet radiation)을 차단해 주는 방패 역할을 한다. 1970년대 중반 남극대륙 상공에서 오존 감소의 징후가 처음 포착되었다. 남극기지 상공의 전체 오존의 양은 1970년대 중반에서 1980년대 중반 사이에 3분의 1이나 줄었다. 위성에서 보내 오는 관측 자료는 전 대륙 상공에서 오존이 감소하고 있음을 보여준다. 1990년대 초 남극 상공의 오존은 1970년대 중반 처음 포착되었을 때의 절반이 되었다. 인류가 지구의 환경문제를 심각하게 걱정해야 한다.

Conservation 환경 보호

03 *theme*

1

Clean water is essential to life, but we often use lakes and rivers—and especially the oceans—as sewers and dumping places for wastes, some of them poisonous. Most bodies of water can dilute and recycle some wastes. But many have been overloaded, or polluted. Sewage treatment plants have helped, as have measures taken by industries to clean up their wastes. Accidental pollution from oil spills at sea is an increasing problem. Informed and concerned citizens must take the lead in seeing that the waters of the world are protected by laws and that the laws are obeyed.

There are many simple things that individuals can do to conserve water. We can turn off the tap while brushing our teeth. We can water lawns and gardens in the evening, when less moisture will evaporate. And we can fix leaky faucets. Large quantities of water could be saved each year in these ways.

séwer *n.* 하수구 dúmping place 투기 장소 póisonous *adj.* 유독한 dilúte *v.* 희석시키다, 묽게 하다 recycle *v.* 재생하다 waste *n.* 폐기물 óverload *v.* 과적 하다 séwage tréatment plant 오물 처리 공장 méasures *(pl.)* 조치, 처치 áccidental *adj.* 우연한 oil spills at sea 바다에 유출된 기름 infórmed and concérned cítizen 배워서 관심 있는 시민 take the lead 앞장서다 seeing that – ~한 이상, 이니까 protéct *v.* 보호하다 obéy *v.* 준수하다 consérve *v.* 보존하다, 보호하다 turn off – ~을 끄다, 잠그다 tap *n.* 꼭지 lawn *n.* 잔디 móisture *n.* 습기 fix *v.* 고치다 leaky *adj.* 물이 새는, 흐르는 fáucet *n.* 수도꼭지

1. Which of the following is the best title for the passage?

① Clean Water ② Sewage Treatment
③ Waste Recycling ④ Water Conservation
⑤ Water Pollution

풀이 ① 깨끗한 물 ② 오물 처리 ③ 폐기물 재생 ④ 수자원 보호 ⑤ 수질오염
이 글의 첫 단락은 물의 오염 보호, 둘째 단락은 물의 절약을 설명하고 있다.

보너스 상식

수자원 보호

우리 나라는 부족한 수자원 공급을 위해 국토 곳곳에 거대한 새로운 댐을 건설하는 계획을 세운다. 댐은 생태계의 가장 큰 파괴자이다. 부족한 물을 댐을 만들어 증산하자는 발상보다는 산림을 보존하고, 물을 쓰는 방식을 계도하는 것도 적극 검토해 보아야 한다. 우리 나라 사람들의 1인당 물 소비량이 세계에서 가장 많다고 한다.

theme 03 Conservation 환경 보호

2 One of our most important resources is soil. Topsoil, the uppermost layer of fertile soil, is the only type of soil that will produce high yields of food crops. As many as 100 years of careful management are needed to make 1 inch of good topsoil. Yet it can be lost quickly—eroded by wind, rain, or flood. During the 1930's, overgrazing, poor farming practices, and years of drought stripped the grass from vast areas of the Great Plains in the United States. With no grass to hold it in place, precious topsoil was blown away. The area was known as the Dust Bowl until grass and trees were planted and reservoirs were built to hold water for irrigating the land.

Contour plowing—plowing horizontally across slopes—helps prevent erosion by water. Planting trees or bushes between fields prevents erosion by wind. Crop rotation slows the loss of nutrients from soil.

tópsoil *n.* 표토(表土), 상층토 yield *n.* 수확량 eróde *v.* 침식하다 (*cf.* erosion *n.* 침식) flood *n.* 범람, 홍수 overgrázing 지나친 방목 drought *n.* 가뭄 strip *v.* 헐벗기다, 황폐화시키다 précious *adj.* 귀중한 blow away 날아가다 Dust Bowl 흙모래 폭풍이 심한 건조 지대로, 미국 중서부의 황진(黃塵) 지대를 말한다 réservoir *n.* 저수지 írrigate *v.* 관개하다, 물을 대다 cóntour plówing 등고선 경작 horizóntally *adv.* 수평으로 bush *v.* 관목 crop rotátion 윤작(輪作) slow *v.* 늦추다

1. Which is <u>not</u> mentioned in the passage as the ways of presentation of soil preservation?

① Contour plowing ② Crop rotation
③ Overgrazing ④ Reservoir building
⑤ Tree planting

풀이 ① 등고선 경작 ② 윤작 ③ 지나친 방목 ④ 저수지 건설 ⑤ 나무심기
첫 단락 후반부와 둘째 단락 등 후반에 토양의 보존 방법들이 나온다.

보너스 상식!

땅을 오염시키는 주범

땅에는 많은 화학 분자가 있고, 여러 가지 박테리아 또한 서식하므로 어떤 물질이 유입되더라도 그것을 소화하여 자연의 균형 속에 녹여 넣는다. 그러나 인간이 저지르는 환경오염이 땅의 이런 자정 능력을 극도로 저하시켰다. 땅의 자정 능력을 저하시키는 주 오염원들은 다음과 같다. 산성비, 비료, 산업 폐유, 가정 쓰레기 및 산업 폐기물 등으로 수질오염 및 대기오염과 서로 연관되어 있다.

3 There are many careers in conservation in addition to the traditional ones of forest, park, and wildlife management. There is a great need for specialists in the conservation of all forms of energy. Engineers can develop new methods of recycling manufactured goods and using wastes. Soil conservationists study how soils can be made more productive. Lawyers help with the growing number of conservation regulations. Urban planners and landscape architects also contribute to conservation efforts.

For a career in conservation, courses in basic sciences, mathematics, and ecology are especially useful. A broad education is necessary because many conservation problems are very complex and do not fall under a single field of study.

caréer *n.* 직업 in addítion to – ~외에도 spécialist *n.* 전문가 manufáctured goods 제조품 soil conservátionist 토양 보호론자 regulátion *n.* 규정 úrban plánner 도시 계획자 lándscape árchitect 조경사 ecólogy *n.* 생태학

1. Which is <u>not</u> stated in the passage as the careers in environmental conservation?

① educators ② engineers
③ landscape architects ④ lawyers
⑤ urban planners

풀이 ① 교육자 ② 엔지니어 ③ 조경사 ④ 법률가 ⑤ 도시 계획자
첫 단락에 등장하는 직업 명칭들을 모두 찾아 확인한다.

보너스 상식

환경공학

최근에는 우리 나라에도 각 대학에 환경공학과가 생겼다. 그 동안 우리의 건설 산업 분야에서는 오로지 토목과 건축만이 통했으나, 이제 건설에서 환경을 빼놓을 수 없는 시대적인 요구를 받아들인 것이다. 환경에 대한 관심과 관리가 비교적 앞선 유럽에서도 환경공학은 독일이 가장 앞섰다고 한다. 그래서 유럽 전체의 환경에 대한 문제 제기와 관리에서 독일이 가장 적극적이다. 상대적으로 우수한 자국의 환경공학을 상품화하겠다는 의도 또한 포함되어 있다.

theme 04 # Detergents and Soap 세제와 비누

1 Although soap is a good cleaning agent, it tends to leave deposits—such as a ring in the bathtub—when used in water with a lot of mineral salts. Therefore, after World War II many people began to use detergents instead of soap. Unfortunately, the increased use of large quantities of detergents created several environmental problems that neither the manufacturers nor the public had expected.

One problem involved the surfactants. Certain bacteria feed on the natural waste materials in sewage and break them down into harmless substances. Soap molecules are rapidly broken down by these bacteria. But the bacteria could not break down the molecules of the surfactants that were first used in detergents. Keeping all their original foaming ability, surfactants caused the masses of foam in sewage plants and in rivers and lakes. To help solve the foaming problem, detergent manufacturers developed new types of surfactants whose molecules would break down quickly after use. By 1965 the changeover to the new surfactants was complete.

depósit *n.* 퇴적물 báthtub *n.* 욕조 detérgent *n.* 합성 세제 invólve *v.* 수반하다, 포함하다 surfáctant *n.* 표면 활성제 (surface-active agent) feed on – ~을 먹고살다 séwage *n.* 하수, 오수 break down 분해하다 soap molecules 비누 분자 foam *n.* 거품 chángeover (to) 대체 compléte *v.* 완성하다

1. Which of the following most likely follows this passage?

① Another problem from using detergents
② Another type of surfactants
③ The nature of new detergent
④ The condition of new sewage plants
⑤ The problem of new surfactants

풀이 ① 합성 세제 사용의 또 다른 문제 ② 또 다른 표면 활성제 ③ 새로운 합성 세제의 본질 ④ 새로운 하수처리장의 상태 ⑤ 새로운 표면 활성제의 문제
첫 단락의 마지막 문장에 'several environmental problems'가 있고, 이어지는 둘째 단락이 'One problem ...'으로 시작하고 있으므로, 다음 단락은 'Another problem ...'으로 시작할 것임을 유추할 수 있다.

보너스 상식!

비누와 환경

머리를 감을 때, 샴푸보다는 비누로 감는 것이 수질오염을 줄이는 방법이다. 비누 거품이 빨리 분해되기 때문이다. 환경을 생각하는 많은 사람들이 빨래 비누로 머리를 감는다. 빨래 비누가 가장 환경 친화적이기 때문이라고 한다. 최근에는 동네에서 폐 식용유를 모아 빨래 비누를 만들어 나누어 가지는 것을 볼 수 있다. 좋은 일이다. 기업들도 세탁용 세제 역시 분해가 잘되는 제품을 앞다투어 내놓고 있다.

1 People can do things that make drought worse. In the Sahel region of Africa, people cut down many trees. Trees absorb some of the sun's heat. Without the trees, some scientists think, temperatures were hotter in north central Africa than they were when the forests were still there. So, human actions—in this case, the cutting of trees—probably worsened the effects of drought.

Some scientists also believe that the residents of New York City made their drought worse by using much more water than residents of other cities normally use. The city's reservoirs were drained very quickly. Finally, city authorities had to order people to stop watering lawns, washing cars, and otherwise using water unnecessarily. These steps were taken so that the half-filled reservoirs would have enough water to last through the summer.

Careful conservation of the water supply is perhaps the best way that people can prepare for the possibility of drought. However, during periods of good rainfall, people tend to forget that drought can occur quickly and can quite rapidly reduce the water supply.

make drought worse 가뭄을 악화시키다 résident *n.* 주민 réservoir *n.* 급수 탱크, 저수지 drain *v.* 물을 빼다, 배수하다 authórity *n.* 당국(자) take steps 조치를 취하다 prepáre for – ~을 준비하다 redúce *v.* 줄이다

1. Which of the following is the best way that we can prepare for the possibility of drought?

① Careful conservation of the water supply
② Cutting down the trees
③ Filling reservoirs for the water supply
④ Stop watering lawns and washing cars
⑤ Using much more water

풀이 ① 물 수급의 주의 깊은 보호 ② 나무 베기 ③ 물 수급용 급수 탱크들을 채우기 ④ 잔디에 물 주기나 세차를 중단하기 ⑤ 훨씬 많은 물을 사용하기
문제의 '가뭄의 가능성에 대비하는 최선의 방법'(... the best way that people can prepare for the possibility of drought.)을 글 가운데서 찾으면 바로 답을 알 수 있다. 마지막 단락에 나와 있다.

보너스 상식!

산림과 가뭄 예방

풍부한 산림은 비가 올 때 많은 양의 수분을 흡수하여 홍수를 예방할 뿐 아니라, 가뭄에도 물의 공급에 큰 도움을 준다. 예로부터 치산치수(治山治水)라고 하여, 산에 나무를 많이 심어 산을 먼저 다스리고, 다음에 저수지를 건설하여 물을 공급하거나, 하천의 제방을 건설하여 물길을 다스리는 것이 국사 중에 으뜸이었다.

theme 06

Endangered Species 멸종 위기의 생물들

1 At one time, living things were primarily endangered by natural events such as the cold climate of the Ice Age or the geological changes caused by an earthquake or volcano. Now the greatest problems facing plants and animals—and people, too—are the human activities that harm the environment on which plants, humans, and other animals depend. Although many different human activities can threaten or endanger a species, the greatest problems occur because of habitat destruction. Illegal hunting and trading and introduction of new species can also cause serious problems.

prímarily ad*v.* 우선, 먼저 endánger *v.* 위험에 빠뜨리다 nátural evént 자연의 격변 face *v.* 부닥치다 thréaten *v.* 위협하다 spécies *n.* 생물의 종(種) habítat *n.* 서식지, 주거지

1. Living things are primarily endangered by all of the following **except**

① Climatic changes. ② Geological changes.
③ Human activities. ④ Habitat destruction.
⑤ Trade barriers.

풀이 ① 기후 변화 ② 지질 변화 ③ 인간 활동 ④ 서식지 파괴 ⑤ 무역 장벽
이 글은 생물 멸종 위기의 원인들을 열거하고 있다. 하나씩 대조하거나, 먼저 답으로 나온 5가지를 읽어보면 찾을 수도 있다.

보너스 상식

황소개구리(bullfrogs)의 한국 유입

70년대에 우리 나라에 들어온 미국산 황소개구리가 토착 생태계를 파괴하였다. 미국에서는 뒷다리를 요리해서 먹는 식용개구리이지만, 우리 나라에 들어와서는 거대한 체구에 맞게 대단한 식성과 번식력으로 한국의 토착 생태계를 파괴한 것이다. 농촌에서는 벌써 생태계 파괴의 피해를 입고 있다. 정부와 관련 단체들이 나서서 직접 황소개구리 소탕 작전을 벌이는가 하면, 식용 캠페인도 벌였다. 30여년 전, 환경에 무지한 관리들이 무심코 들여온 외국 개구리 몇 마리가 이제 나라 전체의 골칫거리가 되었다.

2 Saving habitat is the cornerstone of protecting species. However, even if their habitat is saved, some species have too few members in the wild to repopulate. Many of these have been taken to zoos or parks and bred there. Within these captive-breeding programs, species are bred with the hope that offspring can be raised and then returned to the wild. Programs such as this, combined with laws, awareness, and commitment, will help maintain the delicate balance of nature that is necessary for the survival of all living things.

córnerstone *n.* 초석 repópulate *v.* 다시 서식하다 breed *v.* 양육하다 captive-breeding program 사육 프로그램 óffspring *n.* 새끼 awáreness *n.* 의식, 자각, 경계 commítment *n.* 실행, 책임 délicate *adj.* 미묘한 balance of nature 자연의 균형 survíval *n.* 생존

1. Which of the following is the best title for the passage?

① The Captive-breeding Programs
② The Delicate Balance of Nature
③ Protecting Endangered Species
④ Saving Habitat for Species
⑤ The Survival of Living Things

풀이 ① 사육 프로그램 ② 미묘한 자연의 균형 ③ 멸종 위기의 생물 보호 ④ 종의 서식지 구하기 ⑤ 생명체의 생존
제목은 주제문에 등장하는 핵심어들로 유추할 수 있다. 첫 문장이 주제문이다.

보너스 상식!

세계 지정 보호동물

① 중국 Giant Panda(팬더곰)
② 인도네시아 Sumatran Orangutan(오랑우탄)
③ 뉴질랜드 Tuatara(도마뱀)
④ 아프리카 Black Rhinoceros(코뿔소)
⑤ 미국 Florida Panther(표범)
⑥ 태평양 Humpback Whale(고래)
⑦ 중남미 Galapagos Hawk(매)

Environment 환경

1 Human beings have made many changes in the environment. They have cut down forests and planted crops in their place. They have hunted some animals and learned to raise others. Human inventions have put smoke and dangerous chemicals into the air, have polluted lakes and streams, and have worn out or damaged parts of the earth. These human-caused environmental problems have endangered not only humans, but also most other living creatures.

Environmentalists are people who have become concerned about <u>such problems</u>. They are looking for ways in which humans can live and prosper without harming the environment for future generations.

raise *v.* 기르다 invéntion *n.* 발명 stream *n.* 시냇물 wear out 소모하다, 소진시키다 human-caused 인간이 일으킨 concérn about ─ ~을 염려하다 prósper *v.* 번영하다

1. According to the passage, which is <u>not</u> included in the underlined expression <u>such problems</u>.?

① Cutting down forests
② Damaging parts of the earth
③ Polluting lakes and streams
④ Putting smoke and chemicals into the air
⑤ Saving habitat for animals

풀이 ① 삼림 베기 ② 지구의 여러 지역 훼손 ③ 호수와 시냇물 오염 ④ 연기와 화학 물질을 공기 중에 보내기 ⑤ 동물의 서식지 보호
문제의 'such problems'는 인간이 만든 환경오염으로 부정적인 내용들이다. 답 가운데 긍정적인 것이 있으면 그것이 정답이다.

보너스 상식

그린피스(Greenpeace)

환경문제에 관심을 가지고 1971년에 창설된 국제적인 환경 보호 단체. 핵폐기물이나 유독 산업폐기물의 무단 유기, 해양 동물의 상업적인 남획 등을 막는 일을 한다. 이들은 오염 화학 물질을 방류하는 파이프를 손수 틀어막는 등 직접적인 방법을 써서 환경문제를 공론화하기도 한다. 또, 환경을 보호하는 국제적인 협약을 장려한다.

2 In every environment, the substances that make up all living things are used and re-used continually. For example, plants use carbon dioxide and water in the presence of sunlight to make their own food. During this process, plants release oxygen, the gas that animals must have for breathing. Animals exhale carbon dioxide, which is then available to be used by plants.

As plants grow, they take minerals from the soil. Some plants are eaten by animals. When the animals die, their bodies decay and minerals are returned to the soil where they can be absorbed again by other plants.

These substances—carbon dioxide, water, oxygen, and minerals—are examples of both resources and wastes in the environment. Although considered wastes by one organism, some substances are important resources to another. Because of this, there is a natural balance between resources and wastes. Each is important in the continuous cycle of life on earth.

Human beings also use resources in their environment and create waste. Unfortunately, as we have attempted to provide for our growing population, we have upset the balance of resources and wastes. Wastes are now being produced faster than they can be re-used. These wastes are no longer resources. Instead, they are considered pollutants because they are damaging to the environment. And the faster our population grows, the more pollutants are produced.

make up 구성하다 contínually *adv.* 계속해서 in the présence of – ~가 있을 때 bréathing 호흡 exhále *v.* 숨을 내쉬다 míneral *n.* 무기물 decáy *v.* 썩다 resóurce *n.* 자원 órganism *n.* 생명체, 기관, 유기체 contínuous *adj.* 계속되는 upsét *v.* 뒤엎다 pollútant *n.* 오염 물질

1. Which of the following is the best title for the passage?

① The Balance of Resources and Wastes
② The Cycle of Life on Earth
③ The Difference between Wastes and Pollutants
④ The Growing Human Population

풀이 ① 자원과 폐기물의 균형 ② 지상의 생명의 순환 ③ 폐기물과 오염 물질의 차이 ④ 증가하는 인구
이 글의 핵심어는 resources와 wastes이고, 이 두 가지의 관계를 설명하는 글이다.

보너스 상식

주요 환경 오염원

① 수질 오염 (비료, 세제, 하수, 기름)
② 대기 오염 (자동차 배기가스, 가정과 공장의 연소가스)
③ 토양 오염 (산성비)
④ 열대 우림의 파괴 (남벌)
⑤ 열 오염 (공장의 더운 폐수)
⑥ 고체 폐기물 (가정 및 산업 폐기물)

3 A significant amount of air pollution is caused by the fuels burned in power plants. But another type of pollution, called thermal (heat) pollution, is also caused by power plants. Both fuel-burning and nuclear power plants use huge amount of cold water to cool the steam coming from the turbines. As a result the water is warmed. When this warm water is returned to rivers or ocean harbors, it may stimulate the growth of weeds. It may also kill fish and their eggs, or interfere with their growth.

Physicists are studying new ways of generating electricity that may be less damaging to the environment. In the meantime, many power plants are being modernized to give off less polluting material. Also, engineers try to design and locate new power plants to do minimum damage to the environment.

signíficant *adj.* 상당한, 중요한 power plant 발전소 thérmal *adj.* 열의 as a result 그 결과 ócean hárbor 항구 stímulate *v.* 자극하다 weed *n.* 잡초, 해초 interfére with ~ ~을 방해하다 génerate electrícity 전기를 발생시키다, 발전하다 in the meantime 한편 give off 방사하다, 내다(= emít) locáte *v.* 짓다, 설립하다

1. What is the key word of the passage?

① Air pollution ② New power plants
③ New ways of generating electricity ④ Less polluting material
⑤ Thermal pollution

풀이 ① 공기 오염 ② 새로운 발전소 ③ 새로운 발전 방식 ④ 오염이 덜한 물질 ⑤ 열 오염
주제문인 둘째 문장에 나와 있다.

보너스 상식

환경보호 수칙

① 전기를 절약한다 : 필요 없는 전등을 끄고, 에어컨 사용을 자제한다.
② 난방을 줄인다 : 실내 온도를 낮춰 생활하고, 대신 옷을 따뜻하게 입는다.
③ 대중 교통 이용 : 이동할 때, 가능하면 걷거나, 자전거, 카풀, 대중 교통을 이용한다.
④ 포장을 줄인다 : 물건을 살 때, 최소 포장으로 구입한다. 비닐, 플라스틱, 스티로폼 등 썩지 않는 포장 물품은 피한다. 식품 구입 때는 더욱 해당된다.
⑤ 쓰레기 분리 수거 : 쓰레기를 재활용품, 음식물, 썩는 것, 썩지 않는 것 등으로 분리하여 수거한다.

1 Fire is an essential part of our lives. Although it has many beneficial uses, it can be dangerous if it is uncontrolled or allowed to contribute to environmental problems.

During combustion, the chemical reaction that takes place produces water vapor and carbon dioxide. Water vapor is harmless to the environment. But too much carbon dioxide, which traps radiation and heat close to the Earth's surface, may contribute to the greenhouse effect, a gradual warming of the Earth's surface and atmosphere.

Fires also can release pollutants into the atmosphere. The burning of fuels in industrial processes produces large amounts of gases such as sulfur dioxide and nitrogen oxides. When these combine with moisture in the atmosphere, they produce acid rain, which can damage vegetation and aquatic life and erode the stone on buildings and monuments.

Air pollution is a matter of worldwide concern. People must devise better and more efficient ways to produce energy without burning fuels and ways to trap the pollutants from fires instead of releasing them into the atmosphere. When fire is used carefully, its benefits outweigh its dangers.

esséntial *adj.* 필수적인 benefícial *adj.* 유익한 combústion *n.* 연소 chemical reaction 화학작용 close to ─ ~에 가까이 gréenhouse efféct 온실효과 súlfur dióxide 아황산가스 nitrógen óxide 산화질소 vegetátion *n.* 식물 aquátic life 수상생물 mónument *n.* 비석, 기념비 worldwide *adj.* 세계적인 concérn *n.* 관심사 devíse *v.* 고안하다 trap *v.* 붙잡아두다 instead of ─ ~대신에 bénefit *n.* 혜택 outwéigh *v.* ~보다 무겁다, 가치가 있다

1. Which of the following is the best title for the passage?

① Air Pollution by Fire
② The Burning of fuels
③ Fire and the Environment
④ The Pollutants from Fires
⑤ The Uses of Fire

풀이 ① 불에 의한 공기 오염 ② 연료 연소 ③ 불과 환경 ④ 불에서 나오는 오염 물질 ⑤ 불의 이용
이 글의 핵심어는 fire이고, 주제문인 첫 단락에서 알 수 있듯이, 그것이 환경에 미치는 영향을 설명하고 있다.

보너스 상식

세계 최초의 성냥(match)

세계 최초의 성냥은 577년에 중국에서 발명되었다. 당시 적군에게 포위되어 외부로부터의 물자 공급이 끊어진 어느 궁궐에서 불씨를 책임지고 있던 궁녀가 발명하였다. 불씨가 있던 자리에서 불씨를 얻기 위해 작은 부싯깃을 사용하면서 성냥을 만들었던 것이다. 오늘날과 같은 성냥은 영국의 화학자 John Walker가 1826년에 발명하였는데, 새로운 폭약을 개발하면서 나무막대기로 화학 물질을 섞던 중에 아이디어를 냈다고 한다.

theme 09 Forests and Forestry 산림과 산림조성

1 Reforestation and the fight against fires, insects, and diseases are important parts of forest management. Another is forest improvement. Many forests, especially in the eastern United States, need selective cutting. If diseased and cooked trees and trees of undesirable species are removed, the remaining trees grow more quickly. Where good trees grow close together, some are cut to increase the total annual growth of the remaining trees. In some places the land is cleared of trees and brush, and new forests are started with healthy, properly spaced seedlings. Forestry research is developing new tree strains that grow faster, taller, and straighter and are more resistant to disease.

reforestátion 산림 재조성 **fórest mánagement** 산림 관리 **imprόvement** *n.* 향상 **seléctive cutting** 선별적 벌목 **cooked tree** 벌레 먹은 나무 **undesírable spécies** 바람직하지 않은 수종(樹種) **remóve** *v.* 제거하다 **be cleared of –** ~을 제거하다 **prόperly spaced séedling** 간격을 잘 맞춘 묘목 **strain** *n.* 혈통, 수종(樹種)

1. Which of the following is the key word for the passage?

① Forest improvement
② Forest management
③ Forestry research
④ Reforestation
⑤ Selective cutting

풀이 ① 산림 개선 ② 산림 관리 ③ 산림 연구 ④ 산림 재조성 ⑤ 선별적인 벌목
주제문이 있는 첫 두 문장을 통해서 알 수 있다.

보너스 상식

산림의 남벌률(Rates of Deforestation)

현재 인류는 나무를 10그루 벌채할 때, 겨우 1그루를 심는다고 한다. 이 비율로 가면 2035년에는 지구상에 남아 있는 모든 열대 우림이 완전히 파괴된다고 한다.

2 Diseases, insects, and fires take an annual toll of trees almost equal to the volume cut by people. Diseases do more damage than fires and insects combined.

There are about 100,000 forest fires in the United States every year. Most of them are caused by people. Quick detection by observers in fire towers and by aircraft patrols makes it possible to control the size of most fires.

Heavy insect infestations can be fought by spraying chemicals from aircraft or from the ground. But these chemicals kill harmless insects too, and they may kill birds and fish. Foresters are seeking better methods of insect control.

Some diseases are fought by using chemicals; some by removing diseased trees; others by removing plants that transmit the disease. But present methods make only a small reduction in disease damage.

take a toll of – ~으로 희생자를 내다 ánnual *adj.* 연간 do dámage 피해를 입히다 detéction *n.* 탐지, 추적 obsérver *n.* 감시원, 관찰자 fire tower 산불 감시탑 áircraft patróls 항공기 순찰대 infestátion *n.* (질병이나 해충의) 습격, 감염 fórester *n.* 산림학자 ínsect contról 해충 방제 transmít *v.* 옮기다, 전염시키다 make a redúction 줄이다

1. Which is not stated in the passage as the things that do damage to forests?

① chemicals ② cutting
③ diseases ④ fires
⑤ insects

풀이 ① 화학약품 ② 벌목 ③ 질병 ④ 산불 ⑤ 해충
이 글의 주제어인 '산림의 적(敵)'은 첫 문장에 모두 다 열거되어 있다.

보너스 상식

세계 열대 우림의 연간 파괴율(1981~1990)

① Jamaica 7.2 %
② Haiti 4.8 %
③ Bangladesh 3.9 %
④ Pakistan 3.5 %
⑤ Philippines 3.3 %
⑥ Thailand 3.3 %
⑦ Costa Rica 3.0 %
⑧ Diminican Republic 2.75 %
⑨ Paraguay 2.75 %
⑩ El Slavador 2.25 %

3 Air pollution problems are made worse by the destruction of tropical rain forests. Each year many thousands of acres of rain forest are cleared for farming, animal grazing, lumbering, and building.

The great number of plants in a rain forest absorbs enormous amounts of carbon dioxide gas. As rain forest trees are cut and can no longer absorb this gas, carbon dioxide in the atmosphere increases and helps create what is called the greenhouse effect.

The greenhouse effect occurs when carbon dioxide traps certain kinds of radiation and heat close to the earth's surface. This results in increases in worldwide temperatures, changed weather patterns, increases in sea level, and other serious modifications of the world environment.

Rain forests must be saved if the greenhouse effect is to be reversed. To accomplish this, some conservation organizations are buying and preserving large areas of rain forest. In some countries rain forests are promoted as tourist attractions. In some cases this has proven to generate more needed income than farming or lumbering while at the same time preserving an essential natural resource.

trópical rain fórests 열대 우림 ánimal grázing 목축 lúmbering *n.* 목재, 제재(= timbering) result in ― ~의 결과를 낳다 wéather páttern 기상 패턴 sea lével 해수면 modificátion *n.* 변화, 수정 revérse *v.* 되돌리다, 뒤집다 promóte *v.* 증진시키다, 장려하다 tourist attráction 관광지, 관광객 유치 prove to do ~을 나타내다, 증명하다 génerate *v.* 산출하다, 발생하다

1. According to the passage, which is the most important function of the tropical rain forests?

① They absorb enormous amounts of carbon dioxide gas.
② They help create what is called the greenhouse effect.
③ They are promoted as tourist attractions.
④ They generate more income than farming or lumbering.
⑤ They result in serious modifications of the world environment

풀이 ① 엄청난 양의 이산화탄소를 흡수한다. ② 온실효과를 창출하는 데 도움이 된다. ③ 관광지로 장려된다. ④ 농사나 목재보다 더 많은 수입을 낳는다. ⑤ 심각한 세계의 환경 변화를 낳는다.
식물의 가장 큰 역할은 이산화탄소를 흡수하고 산소를 내뿜는 것이다.

보너스 상식!

열대 우림(tropical rain forests)

지구의 허파라고 할 수 있는 열대 우림은 한때 지구 육지 표면의 20%를 차지하였으나, 오늘날에는 12%로 줄었다. 또, 열대 우림에는 약 2백여만 종의 식물과 동물이 서식하는 것으로 추정되나, 산림이 남벌되면서 멸종으로 치닫고 있다.

4 Some forests actually need fire. In many forests, especially in the western United States where there is little moisture, dead branches, twigs, needles, and leaves quickly become dry and brittle. When a fire starts, perhaps due to lightning or human carelessness, a dry forest can immediately become engulfed in flames.

To decrease the risk of raging fires, Forest Service rangers actually start fires, called prescribed fires, that they can carefully control. In this way, they can burn away the dry bush that would cause an unplanned fire to spread and burn out of control. After a forest has been treated with a prescribed, or controlled, fire, it is possible that when an unplanned fire does occur, it will not have enough 'fuel' to get hot enough to burn most of the larger trees.

branch *n.* 나뭇가지 twig *n.* 잔가지 needle *n.* 솔잎, 침엽수의 잎 brittle *adj.* 파삭파삭한, 부서지기 쉬운 cárelessness *n.* 부주의 immédiately *adv.* 즉시, 순식간에 engúlf *v.* 휘말아들이다, 휩싸다 flame *n.* 화염, 불꽃 decréase *v.* 줄이다 raging *adj.* 맹렬한, 분노하는 Forest Service rangers (미국) 산림 순찰 prescríbed fires 예방 산불, 산불의 확산을 막기 위해 미리 내는 산불 unplanned fire 뜻하지 않은 화재

1. Which of the following is the best topic for the passage?

① A dry forest ② Forest Service rangers
③ Prescribed fires ④ The risk of raging fires
⑤ Unplanned fires

풀이 ① 건조한 산림 ② 산림 순찰대 ③ 예방 산불 ④ 맹렬한 산불의 위험 ⑤ 뜻하지 않은 산불
첫 단락의 첫 문장에 개념이 나왔고, 둘째 단락의 첫 문장에 그 용어가 나와 있다.

보너스 상식

레인저(rangers)란?

미국 국유림을 경비하는 순찰 대원을 'Forest Rangers'라고 한다. 군대에서는 밀림이나 특수 지역의 전투나 게릴라전 등 특수 훈련을 받은 특별 공격 대원, 즉 유격 대원을 'rangers'라고 한다.

theme

10 Lead 납

1 It is now known that lead compounds are toxic to humans and other living things. In many homes built before 1980, the paint used on walls, ceilings, and trim is likely to contain lead. If children eat pieces of this paint or inhale lead-contaminated dust from peeling or cracking paint, they risk developing lead poisoning. Adults as well as children can also be exposed to lead in drinking water, soil, some types of ceramic dishes and cookware, and some canned foods. People who work in industries that use lead or that refine lead ores should also be concerned. In addition, the waste disposal from these plants can damage the environment.

The symptoms of lead poisoning include headaches, loss of appetite, stomachaches, and short-term loss of memory. Even if there are no physical symptoms, lead poisoning can interfere with the development of a child's brain. For that reason, children from ages 1 to 6 should have their blood tested for lead every year.

In response to these health hazards, the law now requires that paints produced for use in homes contain no lead, and most gasoline used today is unleaded. Also, there is a greater awareness of the risk of exposure to lead in homes and in the workplace. Older homes, apartments, and offices are often tested to determine the amount of lead in existing paint on walls, in drinking water, and in the plumbing, particularly the pipes used to carry drinking water. In industrial plants, waste disposal is monitored more closely.

lead cómpound 납 복합물 tóxic *adj.* 유독한, 독성의 ceiling *n.* 천장 trim *n.* 장식, 흔히 나무로 된 내부 장식 부분 inhále *v.* 흡입하다, 숨을 들이마시다 contáminate *v.* 오염시키다 peeling or cracking paint 벗겨지고 갈라지는 페인트 be expósed to – ~에 노출되다 cóokware 그릇 canned food 통조림 refíne *v.* 제련하다 lead óre 납 광석 concérn *v.* 염려하다 waste dispósal 폐기물 symptom *n.* 증후군 loss of áppetite 식욕 상실 stómachache *n.* 복통 loss of mémory 기억 상실 interfére with – ~을 저해하다 in respónse to – ~에 대비하여 health házard 건강상의 위험 unléaded *adj.* 무연의, 납이 없는 awáreness *n.* 자각, 인식 plumbing 배관 closely *adj.* 자세히, 철저하게

1. Which of the following is the best topic for the passage?

① Health hazards ② Lead compounds ③ Lead hazards
④ Uses of lead ⑤ Waste disposal

풀이 ① 건강상의 위험 ② 납 복합물 ③ 납의 위험성 ④ 납의 용도 ⑤ 폐기물
각 단락의 첫 문장과 마지막 문장을 읽으면 핵심어를 유추할 수 있다.

Lead 납

10 theme

보너스 상식

연필의 속 심, lead는 무엇인가?

우리가 흔히 연필의 '심'을 영어로 'lead'라 하는데, 이 lead는 납(lead)이 아니다. 탄소의 부드러운 형태인 '흑연'이다. 그런데 '연필'을 왜 'lead pencil'이라고 했을까? 그것은 옛날에 납(lead)이 연필로 쓰였기 때문이다. 부드러운 납을 종이에 문지르면 회색의 선이 그려진다. 흑연이 발견되기 전에 납이 필기 도구의 하나로 쓰였다.

theme 11 The U.S. National Park System 미국의 국립공원 제도

1

The National Park System is a collection of the most beautiful, as well as the most historic, places in the country. They have been set aside to be enjoyed but also to be protected for many generations to come. There are more than 365 units of the National Park System that are visited every year by approximately 280 million visitors from all over the world. The system contains more than 80 million acres of land. This is slightly less than 4 percent of the total land area of the United States. This remarkable collection of natural places, monuments, historic sites, and other areas is one of America's finest accomplishments.

Establishing and protecting the national parks depends upon vision, care, and hard work. The U.S. National Park System is viewed with pride by Americans and with admiration by people of other countries. In fact, more than 100 other countries have used the United States' park system as a model for establishing their own collections of natural and historic places.

colléction *n.* 집합, 수집 set aside 따로 마련하다 slightly *adv.* 약간 remárkable *adj.* 놀라운 mónument *n.* 기념관, 기념비, 비석 históric site 사적지 accómplishment *n.* 업적 estáblish *v.* 설립하다 admirátion *n.* 경탄

1. According to the passage, how much land area does the U.S. National Park System have?

① 4 million acres
② 80 million acres
③ 100 million acres
④ 280 million acres
⑤ 365 million acres

풀이 ① 4백만 에이커 ② 8천만 에이커 ③ 1억 에이커 ④ 2억8천만 에이커 ⑤ 3억6천5백만 에이커
이 글에 서술된 숫자 가운데 면적을 가리키는 말을 찾으면 쉽게 확인할 수 있다.

보너스 상식

미국에서 가장 큰 국립공원은?

알래스카 남동부에 있는 Wrangell-St. Elias National Park and Preserve로 8백30만 에이커가 넘는다. Yellowstone National Park보다 4배나 된다. St. Elias 산은 미국에서 가장 큰 Mckinley 산 다음으로 높은 산이다. 그리고 북미에서 가장 큰 빙산도 있다.

1 Although there is no way to escape noise pollution completely, experts agree that noise control is possible. Today the responsibility for establishing and carrying out most environmental noise regulations is left to local governments. These regulations range from planning city housing and transportation systems with sound control in mind to banning the playing of radios in buses.

Industry contributes to noise-induced hearing impairment. When noise interferes with speech or masks warning signals, it also increases the chances for on-the-job accidents. Wearing ear-protection devices and adding mufflers to power tools can save workers' hearing and increase safety.

Through research, new products to help control noise have been developed, such as electronic anti-noise devices and building materials that isolate and absorb sound. But new technology is not enough. Government support is needed to enact and enforce noise-control measures. Together, technology and effective regulation can lead to a quieter, safer workplace and community.

noise poll tion 소음 공해 expért *n.* 전문가 noise contról 소음 통제 carry out 실행하다 noise regulátion 소음 규정 transportátion *n.* 교통 noise-induced 소음이 유발한 noise-induced hearing impairment 소음성 청각장애 impáirment *n.* 장애, 상실 mask *v.* 차단하다 warning sígnal 경고 신호음 on-the-job áccident 업무상의 사고 ear-protéction devíce 청각 보호 장치 múffler *n.* 소음기, 머플러 power tools 동력 장치 anti-noise devíce 반소음 장치 ísolate *v.* 분리하다, 고립시키다 enáct *v.* 실행하다 enfórce *v.* 집행하다 méasures *(pl.)* 조치 noise-control méasures 소음 규제 조치

1. Which of the following is the best topic for the passage?

① Anti-noise devices
② Hearing impairment
③ Noise control
④ Noise pollution
⑤ Noise regulations

풀이 ① 반소음 장치 ② 청각 장애 ③ 소음 통제 ④ 소음 공해 ⑤ 소음 규정
주제문인 첫 단락의 첫 문장에 핵심어가 제시되어 있다.

보너스 상식

소음 정도

매일 5시간 이상을 85 decibels 이상의 고음에 노출되거나, 100 decibels 이상의 고음에 자주 노출되는 사람은 청력을 잃을 수도 있다고 한다. 각 소음의 정도는 다음과 같다. 교통 소음은 80 decibels, 사람의 고함소리는 85 decibels, 잔디 깎기, 전기드릴, 스테레오 등 기계 소음은 110 decibels 등이다.

theme **13**

Ocean Pollution 해양 오염

1

At present, our oceans remain in relatively good condition. We cannot permit the resources of the sea to be over-exploited or polluted. As a result, many countries such as the United States have the laws that control the use of the seas and restrict the destruction of marine resources through overharvesting and pollution.

Technological advances have also enabled us to prevent many harmful effects of pollution. Toxic wastes can be burned aboard incineration ships at sea to avoid the dangers of burying these chemicals on land. New knowledge and special equipment have helped to contain most oil and chemical spills on the ocean and have reduced the damage they usually inflict on coastlines.

Limiting the amount of seafood harvested from the oceans has allowed fish and valuable invertebrates to reproduce and therefore restore their depleted populations.

These preventive measures and others will continue to help us improve the condition of our oceans. They will also protect the ocean's bountiful resources for generations to come.

rélatively *adv.* 비교적 permít *v.* 허용하다 óver-explóit *v.* 남획하다, 지나치게 이용하다 restríct *v.* 제한하다 destrúction *n.* 파괴 maríne resóurce 해양 자원 overhárvesting *n.* 남획 enable – to do ~가 ~을 할 수 있게 하다 prevént *v.* 못하게 하다, 막다 tóxic waste 유독성 폐기물 aboard (배나 비행기를) 타고서, 위에서 incineration *n.* 소각 incinerátion ship 소각선 avóid *v.* 피하다 contáin *v.* 억제하다 spill *n.* 유출 inflíct *v.* (주로 피해를) 가하다, 입히다 cóastline *n.* 해안 límit *v.* 제한하다 hárvest *v.* 수확하다 invértebrate *n.* 무척추동물 (*cf.* vertebrate 척추동물) reprodúce *v.* 번식하다, 재생하다 restóre *v.* 회복하다 depléte *v.* 고갈시키다 prevéntive *adj.* 예방의 méasures *(pl.)* 조치 bóuntiful *adj.* 풍부한 generation to come 다음 세대

1. Which is <u>not</u> stated in the passage as the measures that protect the ocean's resources?

① fishery ② knowledge
③ laws ④ special equipment
⑤ technology

풀이 ① 수산업 ② 지식 ③ 법규 ④ 특수 장비 ⑤ 기술
첫 단락에는 법률(laws)조처, 둘째 단락에는 기술(technology) 발달, 새로운 지식(knowledge)과 특수 장비(special equipment), 셋째 단락에는 어획고의 제한(limiting)의 순서로 서술되어 있다.

Ocean Pollution 해양 오염

13 theme

보너스 상식

바다의 이용

1. 수산업의 터전 : 어로와 양식의 터
2. 에너지원 : 석유와 천연가스가 매장되어 있고, 바닷물로 발전을 할 수도 있다.
3. 광물의 보고 : 염소, 나트륨, 황산염, 칼륨, 마그네슘, 칼슘 외에 철, 망간, 코발트 등 광물의 보고이다.
4. 선박의 운송로와 통신케이블 설치 장소 제공
5. 각종 레저의 장소

theme 14 Petroleum and Pollution 석유와 오염

1 During recent decades, environmental rules and practices have helped prevent pollution in two ways: by controlling how oil is produced, refined, transported, and stored; and by controlling the quality of the refined product that is burned as a fuel.

Environmental rules also dictate how to prevent pollution from an oil well after it is no longer producing and how far apart oil wells should be. Oil refineries once produced great amounts of air and water pollution. However, now they must obey many regulations that prevent or greatly reduce the output of pollutants during the refining process. For example, before water used in refining can be returned to waterways, it must be purified and cooled. Serious environmental problems can result if oil is spilled into the sea by oil tankers.

Oil spills can injure or kill fish, marine animals, and aquatic birds. They can also foul beaches and damage microscopic organisms living in tidal basins. Oil spills can affect not only the environment, but also industries, such as fishing and tourism, that depend on the sea.

Because burning petroleum products can also cause pollution, the quality of fuels is also controlled. For example, environmental rules require gasoline to evaporate more slowly in the summer to prevent smog and other forms of air pollution. Other petroleum products must also meet stricter environmental standards. Many rules, for example, limit the amount of sulfur that petroleum products can contain.

décade *n.* 십 년 práctice *n.* 조례, 판례, 실습 refíne *v.* 정제하다, 제련하다 transpórt *v.* 이송하다 store *v.* 저장하다 dictáte *v.* 지시하다, 다스리다 oil well 유정(油井) oil refínery 정유공장 redúce *v.* 줄이다 óutput *n.* 산출, 배출 púrify *v.* 정화하다 spill *v.* 유출하다 aquátic birds 수상 조류 foul *v.* 오염시키다 microscópic órganism 미세한 생물 tídal básin 해양 분지 tóurism *n.* 관광 petróleum product 석유 제품 eváporate *v.* 기화하다, 증발하다 strict *adj.* 엄격한 súlfur *n.* 황산

1. Which of the following is the best title for the passage?

① Damages by Oil Spills ② Environmental Rules
③ Environmental Standards ④ Petroleum and Pollution
⑤ Petroleum Products

풀이 ① 석유 유출의 피해 ② 환경 법규 ③ 환경 기준 ④ 석유와 오염 ⑤ 석유 제품
주제 단락인 첫 단락에서 핵심어를 유추하면 제목을 알 수 있다.

Petroleum and Pollution 석유와 오염

14 theme

보너스 상식

석유의 환경오염

석유는 환경오염의 가장 큰 주범이다. 오늘날 모든 기계문명을 움직이는 동력의 연료가 바로 석유이다. 대기오염의 주범인 탄산가스는 바로 석유의 연소에서 나온 것이다. 과학자들이 태양열 주택이나 전기 자동차 같은 무공해 에너지 개발에 몰두하는 것도 석유의 환경오염 때문이다.

theme 15 Population 인구

1 The rapid population growth now taking place is sometimes called a population explosion. Many persons fear that population will grow faster than the resources—such as food, fuel, and housing—needed to support all the people. If this should happen, the first result would be lower standards of living. Then, as living standards fell below what was needed to keep the poorest people alive, the death rate would rise. If living standards were reduced to a point where dangerous diseases could not be controlled, death rates would rise among the wealthy as well as the poor.

Concern with overpopulation is not new. Almost two centuries ago, the English economist Thomas R. Malthus (1766~1834) argued that the growth of human population eventually takes away any gains made in living standards. He wrote at the beginning of the industrial age. He did not foresee the increase in material wealth that industry has produced or the safe, reliable ways to control fertility that have been developed.

rápid *adj.* 빠른, 신속한 take place 일어나다, 발생하다 populátion explósion 인구 폭발 suppórt *v.* 부양하다 standard of living 생활 수준 death rate 사망률 the wealthy 부자들 the poor 가난한 사람들 concérn *n.* 염려, 관심 árgue *v.* 주장하다 evéntually *adv.* 결국 take away 앗아가다 gain *n.* 소득 foresée *v.* 내다보다, 예견하다 matérial wealth 물질적인 부(富) relíable *adj.* 믿을 만한 fertílity *n.* 출산력, 다산성

1. Which of the following is the best topic of the passage?

① Concern about overpopulation ② Death rate
③ Material wealth ④ Population growth
⑤ Standards of Living

풀이 ① 인구 과잉의 염려 ② 사망률 ③ 물질적인 부(富) ④ 인구 증가 ⑤ 생활 수준
두 단락의 첫 문장들을 보면 바로 알 수 있다.

보너스 상식

영아사망률 (1년 미만의 신생아 100명 중 사망아 수) — 1996

고비율 국가
① Afghanistan 아프가니스탄 20.5 % ② Sierra Leone 시에라 레온20.0 %
③ Gambia 갬비아 19.3% ④ Malawi 말라위 16.5 %
⑤ Kampuchea 캄푸치아 16.0 % ⑥ Guinea 기니아 15.5 %
⑦ Yemen 예멘 15.4 %

저비율 국가
① Finland 핀란드 0.6 % ② Japan 일본0.6 %
③ Sweden 스웨덴 0.7 % ④ Iceland 아이슬란드 0.7 %
⑤ Switzerland 스위스 0.8 % ⑥ Norway 노르웨이 0.8 %
⑦ Denmark 덴마크0.8 %

2 Is there truth in Malthus' view of the world as a place of limited resources? This remains an important question. If Malthus was right, then the growth of human population must stop sometime. The only questions are how and when. Will population growth be stopped by low birth rates or by a return to the high death rates of the pre-industrial past? Will this happen soon or not for several decades?

Answers to such questions can be given only for specific countries. In several countries of Western Europe, the population has already stopped growing, because of balanced birth and death rates. But these countries do not have all the resources they need. They must import metallic minerals, fuels, and food from other regions of the world. In fact, very few countries have the right combinations of resources to support their present populations—to say nothing of populations two or three times larger. In less developed regions of the world the situation is even more ominous.

view of the world 세계관 pre-industrial 산업화 이전 metállic mínerals 금속 광물 combinátion *n.* 결합, 조합 to say nothing of – ~은 말할 나위도 없이, 제쳐놓고 óminous *adj.* 험악한, 불길한

1. According to the passage, why has the population stopped growing in several countries of Western Europe?

① By the balanced birth and death rates
② By enough food to support populations
③ By importing all the resources
④ By the low birth rates
⑤ By the high death rates

풀이 ① 출생률과 사망률의 균형을 이루어 ② 인구를 부양할 충분한 식량이 있어서 ③ 모든 자원을 수입하여서 ④ 낮은 출생률로 ⑤ 높은 사망률로
둘째 단락의 둘째 문장에 문제와 답이 있다. '서유럽의 몇 나라'(several countries of Western Europe)에 대한 서술을 찾으면 된다.

보너스 상식!

세계 10대 인구 대국 (1996)

① 중국 1,140,000,000명	② 인도 844,000,000명
③ 미국 250,000,000명	④ 인도네시아 180,500,000명
⑤ 브라질 150,500,000명	⑥ 러시아 148,000,000명
⑦ 일본 123,500,000명	⑧ 방글라데시 115,600,000명
⑨ 파키스탄 112,500,000명	⑩ 나이지리아 108,500,000명

theme 16 Rain, Snow, and Hail 비, 눈, 우박

1 Rain is measured with a rain gauge, which is often simply a hollow tube with a vertical measuring scale on its side. The size of the tube and the length of the vertical scale may vary, allowing the measurement of widely differing amounts of rain. Many rain gauges have a partial cover to help lessen the amount of evaporation that may occur between the time of rainfall and the time of measurement.

Snow can be measured by using a ruler and sticking it through the snow until it touches the ground. However, since wind causes snow to drift to varying depths, it is often difficult to get an accurate measure with this method. Several measurements often must be taken within an area, and the numbers are then averaged.

The liquid equivalent of snow can be determined by filling a rain gauge with snow. When the column of snow in the gauge melts, the amount of water can then be measured. The ratio of snow to liquid varies depending on the consistency of the snow. Typically, 10 inches (25.4 centimeters) of snow will equal about 1 inch (2.54 centimeters) of water. However, with a dry, powdery snow, it takes about 12 inches (30 centimeters) of snow to equal 1 inch of water. The wetter the snow, the lower the snow-to-liquid ratio.

méasure *v.* 측정하다 rain gauge 우량계 hóllow *adj.* 속이 빈 vértical *adj.* 수직의 vertical scale 수직계수 vary *v.* 변하다, 달라지다 léssen *v.* 줄이다 evaporátion *n.* 증발 stick *v.* 찌르다 drift *v.* 날려보내다 get a measure 재다, 측정하다 méthod *n.* 방법 áverage *v.* 평균을 내다 equívalent *n.* 등가물 detérmine *v.* 판단하다 cólumn *n.* 기둥 rátio *n.* 비율 depending on ~ ~에 따라 consístency *n.* 밀도, 농도 typically *adv.* 전형적으로 pówdery *adj.* (물기가 없이) 가루 같은 wet *adj.* 젖은, 물기가 많은 snow-to-liquid ratio 눈-액체 비율

1. Which of the following is the best title for the passage?

① The Consistency of Snow
② The Liquid Equivalent of Snow
③ Measuring Rain and Snow
④ Rain Gauge and Ruler
⑤ Snow-to-liquid Ratio

풀이 ① 눈의 밀도 ② 눈의 액체 등가물 ③ 비와 눈의 측정 ④ 우량계와 자 ⑤ 눈-액체 비율
각 단락의 첫 문장을 읽고 '공통된 핵심어' 들로 제목을 만들 수 있다.

보너스 상식! **세계에서 가장 큰 우박 덩어리**(hailstones)

기록상으로는 1970년 9월, 미국 캔자스주 Coffeyville에 떨어진 것으로 지름이 5 ½ 인치로 측정되었다.

1 The most practical approach to water shortages is to conserve water. This means using—and wasting—less. Factories can reuse the water they use for cooling. Older cities, such as New York and Chicago, can save great amounts of water simply by repairing leaking water mains. And people can use less water in their homes.

Farmers can switch to irrigation methods that use less water, and they can line watercarrying channels with plastic or concrete so that water will not seep away into the ground. In areas that often suffer from water shortages, people can grow crops that require little water. Where the water is brackish, special crops can be grown. These include certain kinds of tobacco, oats, and wheat that will tolerate brackish water.

Some people think that the best way to reduce waste is to raise the price of water. In most places, water is now very cheap, and not many people feel the need to conserve. Perhaps if people paid more for water, they would be more careful about how they used it.

A great deal of water leaves lakes and reservoirs through evaporation. No easy way to stop this loss has been found. Some solutions that have been tried include storing water in underground reservoirs, adding chemicals to form a film on top of the water to prevent evaporation, and building reservoirs that are sheltered from the sun and the wind.

appróach *n.* 접근 shórtage *n.* 부족 repáir *v.* 수리하다 leak *v.* (물이) 새다 main *n.* 배관 water mains 배수관, 급수관 switch *v.* 바꾸다, 교체하다 irrigátion méthod 관개 방법 wátercarrying channels 급수 통로 seep away 새어나가다 suffer from — ~으로 고생하다 brákish *adj.* 염분이 있는 oat *n.* 귀리 tólerate *v.* 견디다 réservoir *n.* 저수지 solútion *n.* 해결책, 해답 form a film 피막을 형성하다 be sheltered from — ~을 피하는, ~로부터 안전한

1. What is the main subject for the passage?

① Building reservoirs ② Irrigation methods
③ The price of water ④ Water conservation
⑤ Water shortage

풀이 ① 저수지 건설 ② 관개 방법 ③ 물 값 ④ 물의 보존 ⑤ 물 부족
주제어나 핵심어 등은 주로 주제문인 첫 문장에 제시된다.

보너스 상식

가정에서의 물 절약

1. 물이 새는 수도꼭지를 바꾼다. 2. 샤워 꼭지를 개폐용으로 바꾼다. 3. 변기의 물통에 벽돌을 넣는다.
4. 이를 닦을 때처럼 아주 잠시 동안이라도 물을 사용하지 않을 때는 수도꼭지를 잠근다.
5. 설거지를 할 때, 물을 틀어 놓고 씻는 것보다는 싱크대 안에 물을 담아서 씻는다.

theme

17 Water 물

2 Water may look clean, but many materials can get into it and make it unsafe. Then the water is called polluted. Dangerous substances can pollute any water source—streams, lakes, oceans, and even the water that comes into homes. In our world today, thousands of hazardous substances end up in our water. These substances are hazardous to the health of the aquatic life that inhabit the water, to wild creatures that live near the water, and to people who drink the water and eat the contaminated fish. Almost all pollution is caused by people.

When the population of the world was small, the streams and rivers could handle the trash and sewage that people dumped into them. Nature's purification system helped to make the water clean again. Water from the oceans, lakes, and rivers—and even from the land—rose as water vapor, leaving any impurities behind. The water then fell again as clean rain or snow. This cycle still works, but now the impurities left behind are far more numerous and dangerous. Long ago most of the pollutants were biodegradable. That is, bacteria in the water and soil could break the waste down into less harmful substances. Today many of our pollutants are nonbiodegradable. These pollutants are chemicals that cannot be digested by bacteria, broken down by sunlight, or made simpler by any material process. For example, plastics will remain unchanged for hundreds of years. Nature has no way of disposing of them.

end up in – 결국 ~에 들어가다 aquátic life 수상생물 inhábit *v.* 서식하다 contáminate *v.* 더럽히다, 오염시키다 trash *n.* 쓰레기 séwage *n.* 오물, 오폐수 dump *v.* 던져버리다 nature's purification system 자연의 정화체계 impúrity *n.* 불순물 númerous *adj.* 수많은 biodegrádable *adj.* 미생물에 분해되는 (*opp.* nonbiodegradable 미생물에 분해될 수 없는) break down 분해하다 pollútant *n.* 오염물질 dispóse *v.* 처리하다

1. Which of the following is the best title for the passage?

① Impurities ② The Population of the World
③ Nature's Purification System ④ Water Pollution
⑤ Water Vapor

풀이 ① 불순물 ② 세계의 인구 ③ 자연의 정화 체계 ④ 수질오염 ⑤ 수증기
주제문인 첫 문장에 기술된 핵심어로 유추가 가능하다

대표적인 수질 오염원

① 화학 제품이나 금속 제품 등의 산업폐기물 (Industrial Chemicals and Metals)
② 공장에서 강이나 호수로 나오는 뜨거운 물 (Hot Water)
③ 산성비 (Acid Rain)
④ 강이나 바다에 유출되는 기름 (Oil Spills)
⑤ 각종 농약 (Agricultural Chemicals)
⑥ 가정이나 식당, 모든 건물에서 나오는 생활 오수 (Sewage)
⑥ 방사능 물질 (Radioactivity)

theme **18**

Wetlands 습지

1

Because wetlands can hold water, they help control flooding caused by rain and melted snow. They store and gradually release the large amounts of water that otherwise would cause damage or flow quickly to the ocean carrying away nutrient-rich soil.

The dense vegetation in wetlands traps soil and nutrients, such as those in run-off from farmland and sewage. In many places, people use wetlands as natural sewage plants. As sewage flows through the wetlands, plants remove phosphates and other pollutants.

For a long time, people thought of wetlands as mosquito-infested wastelands that were obstacles to land development. They drained or filled wetlands, turning them into land for houses, farms, and factories. Shore vegetation was destroyed as channels for shipping were made by dredging the waterways. People used wetlands as garbage dumps, emptying sewage and other waste into them. Additional wetlands were lost as water was diverted for human use, dams were constructed, and the courses of rivers were changed. Experts estimate that over time, approximately 50 percent of the world's wetlands have been lost.

In recent years, the destruction of wetlands has slowed as people have become aware of the importance of wetlands. Not only are their products, such as fish and crops, recognized as valuable, but so are their invisible services, such as water purification and flood control.

wétland *n.* 습지 flooding 범람 reléase *v.* 방류하다 carry away 실어 가다 nutrient-rich soil 자양분이 풍부한 흙 dénse *adj.* 울창한, 조밀한 végetation *n.* 식물 trap *v.* 품다, 가두다 run-off 유실물, 흘러가는 것 natural sewage plant 자연의 오폐수 공장 phósphate *n.* 인산염 mosquíto-infésted 모기가 득실대는 wásteland *n.* 황무지 óbstacle *n.* 장해물 drain *v.* 물을 빼다 shore végetation 물가 식물 chánnels for shípping 선박의 통로 drédge *v.* 준설하다 wáterway 수로 gárbage dumps 쓰레기 투기장 émpty – into – ~을 ~에 버리다 divért *v.* 전환하다 éstimate *v.* 진단하다, 평가하다 over time 시간이 지나면서 váluable *adj.* 귀중한 invísible service 눈에 보이지 않는 서비스 purificátion *n.* 정화 flood control 범람 억제

1. Which of the following is the best title for the passage?

① The Conservation of Wetlands ② The Destruction of Wetlands
③ The Importance of Wetlands ④ The Invisible Services of Wetlands
⑤ The Vegetation in Wetlands

풀이 ① 습지의 보존 ② 습지의 파괴 ③ 습지의 중요성 ④ 습지의 눈에 보이지 않는 서비스 ⑤ 습지 식물
마지막 단락이 이 글의 주제와 결론을 모두 함축하여 포함하고 있다.

보너스 상식

습지(wetlands)의 종류

① swamps : 숲이 우거진 소택(沼澤) 지대 ② bogs : 이끼를 포함한 물풀들이 자라는 늪지대
③ marshes : 초지 늪, 습지대

정답과 번역

Living and Health Care

제 1 장

1 ① 2 (1) ⑤ (2) ② 3 (1) ⑤ (2) ③ 4 1. ④ 2. ③ 5 1. ⑤ 2. (1) ④ (2) ④ (3) ① 6 ② 7 1. ① 2. ⑤ 8 ① 9 ④ 10 ③ 11 ⑤ 12 ⑤ 13 ⑤ 14 1. ④ 2. (1) ② (2) ⑤ (3) ⑤ 15 ③ 16 ④ 17 ⑤ 18 ① 19 ① 20 1. ① 2. ④ 21 ③ 22 ① 23 ④ 24 ⑤ 25 ④ 26 ④ 27 ④

1. 많은 사람들에게 야영은 천막 속에서 자는 것을 의미한다. 어떤 사람들은 자기 집 뒤뜰에다 천막을 치고서 밤을 보내기도 한다. 그러나 대체로 야영은 자동차에 천막과 식량, 소지품들을 꾸려서 바라던 야영지로 떠나는 것을 의미한다. 천막 야영자들은 주립 공원, 지방 공원, 국립 공원 또는 사설 캠프장에 천막을 칠 수 있다.

다른 사람들은 레저용 자동차를 이용해 야영을 하기도 한다. 레저용 자동차들은 작은 트레일러에서부터 커다란 이동 주택에 이르기까지 크기가 다양하다. 이 자동차들은 야영자들에게 주거 막사를 제공하고, 싱크대, 냉장고, 화장실 같은 현대적인 편의 시설들을 싣고 다닌다.

2. 화장의 스타일은 끊임없이 변하고 있다. 남자들이 흔히 여자들보다 향수와 파우더, 오일을 더 많이 사용했다. 18세기에는 여성들이 뺨을 너무 빛나게 화장을 해서 영국 의회가 화장에 관한 법을 제정하였다. 그 법은 남편을 유혹하기 위해 화장을 사용하는 것을 금지하였다. 빅토리아 시대에는 모든 화장을 불쾌하게 여겼다.

오늘날 화장은 머리에서 발끝까지 모든 연령의 사람들에 의해 사용된다. 화장에는 3가지가 있다. 한 가지는 립스틱, 눈 화장, 매니큐어 에나멜같이 보여주는 것이다. 다른 하나는 핸드 로션, 향수, 이발(미용), 땀 냄새 억제제 같이 바르고 덮는 것이다. 세 번째 종류의 화장은 가꾸기 과정에서 사용한 다음 닦아내거나 씻어내고 벗겨낸다. 예로는 면도 크림, 샴푸, 양치질 약, 목욕 용품 등이 있다. 비누는 흔히 화장품으로 여기지 않는다.

3. 악몽은 거의 모든 사람이 경험한다. 악몽은 아주 실재 같아 보이는 장시간의 무서운 꿈이다. 예를 들어, 괴물이나 야생 동물, 무서운 사람들, 위험으로부터 도망쳐 달리거나, 벼랑이나 나무에서 떨어지는 꿈을 꾸기도 한다. 때때로 정상적이고 일상적인 물체들이 그런 꿈의 무서운 부분이 되기도 한다.

악몽은 흔히 밤잠을 자면서 후반 몇 시간 동안에 생긴다. 악몽은 사람이 스트레스를 받을 때 일반적으로 더 자주 꾸고, 전쟁 같은 잊지 못할 사건 중에도 꾸게 된다. 악몽은 어린 시절에 더 흔하다. 최소한 어린이들의 절반은 악몽을 경험한다.

4. (1) 최초의 의복은 아마도 추위로부터 사람을 보호하기 위해 만들어졌을 것이다. 그러나 남자나 여자나 다같이 곧 의복이 실용적이기보다는 그 이상이기를 원했다. 그들은 의복이 예쁘기를 원했다. 사회가 점점 더 발전할수록, 더 많은 관심이 의상의 방식에 쏠렸다. 이집트인들이 거대한 피라미드를 건설할 때까지는, 옷차림이 오늘날처럼 중요하였다.

최근까지도 예쁜 옷은 손으로 만들어진다. 그 옷들은 일반적으로 정교하고 늘 비싸다. 패션은 왕족들과 부자들, 유명 인사들을 위한 것이었다. 이제 대량생산은 거의 모든 사람들에 유용한 멋진 의복들을 만들어 냈다. 현대 패션 산업은 디자인 실에서 쇼 윈도우까지 세계에서 가장 활발하고, 가장 상상력이 풍부하고, 가장 매력적인 활동이다.

(2) 좋은 패션의 한 가지 기본 요소는 잘 입는 것이다. 가장 멋진 의상도 자세가 좋지 못한 사람에게는 좋아 보이지 않는다. 또 다른 중요한 요소는 개성이다. 잘 입은 사람의 옷은 그 사람의 인격을 반영한다. 멋진 패션이 되기 위해서는 어떤 모양, 직물, 색상이 가장 돋보이는지, 무엇이 어울릴지를 아는 것이 필수적이다. 예를 들어, 키가 작은 사람들은 흔히 커 보이게 하는 옷을 고르는 반면, 키가 큰 사람들은 자신들의 키에서 주의를 돌리려고 한다.

5. (1) 불붙는 것보다 더 무서운 것은 거의 없다. 그러나 겁에 질린 상태에서의 반응은 죽거나 평생 남게 될 상처를 남기기도 한다. 사람이 불이 붙었을 때, 일반적인 반응은 달리는 것이다. 그러나 이것은 화재를 더 악화시킬 뿐이다. 기억해 두어야 할 것이 3가지 있다. 멈추고, 눕고, 구른다. 옷에 불이 붙었다면, 즉시 동작을 멈추고 땅바닥에 누워서 화염이 꺼질 때까지 계속해서 구른다. 코와 입을 손으로 막는다. 어떻게 해야 하는지를 알고 있는 구경꾼이 있으면, 구르는 것을 도와주고, 화재가 진화될 때까지 코트나 담요로 불이 붙은 사람을 덮어 준다. 화염은 연기가 나는 의복 밑에서 날 수도 있기 때문에 멈추기 전에 화재를 완전히 진화시킨다. 다치게 되면, 즉시 긴급 구조를 요청한다.

(2) 요리를 하는 동안 음식을 잘 지켜 보든가, 요리사에게 경보를 해주거나 자동적으로 오븐이나 전기 프라이팬 등을 꺼 주는 타이머를 사용하면 요리 화재는 피할 수 있다. 커다란 덮개와 적당한 소화기를 스토브 근처에 두면, 그 사용법을 아는 사람이 유성(油性) 화재를 진압하는 데 사용할 수 있다. 스토브의 배기 팬에 기름이나 때가 많으면 제거해 준다. 또, 늘어진 옷은 조리대 근처에서 입어서는 안 되며, 커튼이나 행주 등은 불꽃이나 전기 버너 가까이 두어서는 안 된다. 야외용 그릴은 실내에서나 차고에서 사용해서는 안 된다.

6. 제물 낚시 릴은 아래쪽에 달리는 것도 있지만, 대부분 미끼 낚시 릴처럼 낚싯대 끝에 달린다. 낚싯대 손잡이 밑에 방아쇠라고 하는 작은 돌출부가 있다. 방아쇠 위에다 검지손가락을 얹고, 릴의 뒷부분에 있는 낚싯줄을 푸는 버튼 위에 엄지손가락을 대고, 손잡이를 움켜쥔다. 미끼 낚시에서처럼 낚싯대와 릴은 편안한 각도인 45 ° 정도 되게 한다.

던지는 동작은 미끼 낚시와 제물 낚시의 던지기와 비슷하다. 차이는 낚싯줄을 다루는 방법에 있다. 제물 낚시에서는 낚싯줄을 엄지손가락에 있는 줄 푸는 버튼을 눌러서 풀어 준다. 멈추려면 엄지손가락을 들어올려 버튼을 놓는다.

7. (1) 깨끗한 모발은 감촉이 좋고, 보기도 좋고, 냄새도 좋다. 머릿기름과 섞인 땀은 머릿결을 미끈하고 실오리처럼 말리게 한다. 모발을 신선하고 윤기 있게 유지하기 위해서는 자주 감아 주어야 한다. 부드러운 샴푸를 사용하면, 매일 감아도 머릿결을 손상하지 않는다. 비눗물을 잘 헹구는 것을 명심해야 한다. 모발에 남아 있는 샴푸는 머릿결을 건조시킬 수 있다.

스포츠에서 활동하는 사람이라면 모자를 쓰고 모발을 보호한다. 실외 스포츠는 대체로 모발을 건조시키는 경향이 있다. 수영을 한 뒤에는 반드시 모발을 철저히 헹군다. 태양, 바람, 염소, 소금물 등도 모발을 건조시킬 수 있다.

항상 모발을 부드럽게 다루고, 젖은 경우는 특히 그래야 한다. 그때가 가장 부서지기 쉬울 때이다. 성긴 빗으로 엉킴을 풀어 준다. 젖은 모발을 빗지 마라. 빗이나 솔은 모발만큼이나 깨끗해야 한다는 것을 명심한다.

모발의 상태는 식사, 충분한 휴식, 많은 운동에 크게 달려 있다. 모발은 영양이 철저해야 한다는 것을 명심한다. 균형 있는 영양식은 더욱 건강한 모발을 의미한다.

(2) 모발의 색깔을 바꾸는 방법에는 여러 가지가 있다. 일시적인 염색은 머리를 감아서 물들였다가 씻어 낸다. 그것은 표백제가 없기 때문에, 모발의 색을 바래지 않으면서도 강한 강조를 줄 수 있다. 반영구적인 염색은 머리를 감아 물들이고 3~4회 감아서 씻어 낼 때까지 지속된다. 염색이 몇 분간 남아 있기 때문에, 색감이 머리카락 속에 스며든다. 과산화수소가 없기 때문에 모발은 바래지 않는다. 그러나 모발의 자연 색조를 밝게 한다. 영구적인 모발 염색은 여러 가지 색조로 머릿결을 바래게 할 수 있는 과산화수소를 포함하고 있다. 그것은 또 머릿결을 검게 할 수도 있다. 영구적인 모발 염색은 머리카락 속에 침투하기 때문에 씻겨 나가지 않는다. 대신, 머리카락이 자라 나와야 한다.

강조와 탈색, 염색은 모발에 강조를 더해 준다. 이렇게 하려면 머리 전체보다는 오히려 몇 가닥만 표백하면 된다. 잘만 하면 햇빛이 그렇게 만든 것처럼 보인다.

8. 현대적 난방 시스템은 편안함, 안전, 연료의 경제성 등을 주기 위해 자동 조절 장치가 되어 있다. 보일러와 난로는 지나치게 뜨거워지는 것을 막아 주는 장치를 가지고 있다. 전기히터는 일반적으로 내부 퓨즈가 있어서 너무 뜨거워지는 것을 방지해 준다. 물 순환 난방 시스

템은 건물의 다른 곳에 각기 다른 온도를 제공하기 위해 '구역'이 나누어진다. 전기 난방 시스템은 모든 방에 온도 조절 장치를 가지고 있다.

최근에 조절 장치의 혁신은 난방이 필요할 때까지 버너를 완전히 꺼두는 2단계 실내 온도 조절 장치가 있다. 또, 실내외 장치가 실외 온도의 변화에 따라 난방 시스템의 작동을 조정한다. 또 다른 인기 있는 조절 장치는 온도 조절 시계 장치인데, 하루의 각기 다른 시간마다 실내 온도를 자동적으로 올리고 내린다.

가정에서는 열을 보존하고 연료비를 줄이는 다른 많은 방법이 있다. 적절한 단열, 단단히 밀봉된 창과 문, 사용하지 않는 방의 난방 줄이기, 실내 난방기와 난로의 사용 등이 취할 수 있는 몇 가지 조처이다.

9. 하이파이 시스템은 소리를 재생하도록 설계된 전자 장비로 구성되어 있다. 이 시스템은 가능한 원음에 가장 충실한 정도로 재생한다. 이 시스템이 일반적으로 입체(두 채널)음향을 전달하기 때문에 흔히 스테레오라고 한다.

그래도 바로 그 최고의 고충실도 시스템이 실황 공연과 같은 사운드를 내지는 않는다. 이것은 어떤 기계적 또는 전기적 부품이 아무리 정교하다 해도 그 일을 완벽하게 할 수는 없다. 각기 뒤틀림과 소음을 더할 뿐이다. 충실도는 그 시스템이 본래 공연의 사운드를 얼마나 정확하게 재생하느냐에 따라 결정된다.

모든 하이파이 시스템은 세 가지 형태의 오디오 요소 또는 부분으로 구성되어 있다. CD 플레이어, 테이프리코더, 튜너 등, 공급원 요소들은 미약한 전기 부호를 생산한다. 그 다음 이 부호들은 증폭기(앰프)로 보내지고, 증폭기는 그 부호들을 증폭시켜 확성기(스피커)로 보낸다. 그곳에서 그 부호들은 음파로 변환되어 공기를 타고 우리 귀에까지 이동한다.

사운드는 자기테이프 같은 물질로 저장되거나, 라디오 방송처럼 공중파로 오기도 한다.

10. 북미에서는 도보여행 길이 수천 개나 있다. 초보자들이 선택할 수 있는 곳들로는 수많은 국립 공원과 산림 외에도 지역이나 지방 · 주립의 공원, 산림 · 야생동물 보호구역 등이 있다. 그리고 또 조지아주와 메인주 사이를 달리는 애팔래치아 행로, 또는 멕시코-캘리포니아 국경에서 계속 북쪽으로 워싱턴-브리티시 컬럼비아(캐나다 남서부의 주) 국경까지 달리는 장대한 태평양 정상행로 등, 유명한 먼길들이 있다. 도보여행 길에 대한 최고의 정보 출처는 지역의 스포츠 용품점이나 여행클럽, 도서관 등이다.

도보여행과 배낭여행은 일단 시도하고 보면 좋아하게 되고 싫증나지 않는다는 점에서 다른 스포츠와 비슷하다. 산간 오지에서의 반복되는 경험들과 함께, 배낭 꾸리는 법, 불을 피우는 법, 야영지 고르는 법 등, 많은 기술을 배울 수 있을 것이다. 이런 기술을 배우면 도보여행과 배낭여행의 즐거움을 한층 더해 줄 것이다.

11. 여러분이 만일 즐겨했던 취미를 가진 적이 있다면, 그것이 여러분에게 줄 수 있는 흥미와 즐거움을 알 것이다. 그런데 취미는 또 다른 이점이 있다. 취미란 여러분에게 어떤 일을 오로지 혼자서 시작하고 수행하는 만족감을 줄 수 있다. 여러분이 만든 벤치나 뜨개질한 스카프 등, 자신의 작업이 완성된 것을 보면 여러분에게 특별한 긍지를 준다. 또 열중하게 되는 어떤 취미를 가질 때, 여러분은 아주 행복하게 혼자서 시간을 보낼 수 있다는 것을 발견할 것이다.

흔히 취미는 의식하지도 못하는 사이에 여러분에게 많은 것을 가르쳐 준다. 예를 들어, 앨범에 우표들을 넣을 때, 여러분은 특정 국가의 지리와 역사에 대해 어떤 것을 알게 된다. 그리고 수집된 돌을 분류할 때, 여러분은 지질학과 지구 역사에 대한 어떤 것을 배우게 된다.

12. 집은 사람들이 요리하고, 식사하고, 잠자고, 아이들을 기르는 곳이다. 집은 곤충, 야생 동물, 기타 위험뿐 아니라, 추위, 비, 바람, 뜨거운 햇빛 등, 거친 날씨로부터 사람들을 보호한다.

어떤 사람들은 나무나 기둥 위 높은 곳에 지은 초가에서 산다. 다른 어떤 사람들은 높이 솟은 아파트 건물에서 산다. 어떤 사람들에게는 집이 동물 가죽으로 만든 천막이요, 짚으로 이은 초가 지붕의 오두막이며, 벼랑 쪽의 동굴이기도 하다. 사람들은 보트나 트레일러, 소박한 농가나, 장중한 저택에서 살기도 한다. 철재, 유리, 콘크리트, 목재, 석재, 벽돌, 진흙, 눈, 풀잎, 흙, 나뭇잎 등으로 지은 집들이 있다.

사람들이 오래 전에 지은 집의 종류는 거의 완전히

그들이 살고 있는 기후의 종류, 가까운 데서 손쉽게 구할 수 있는 건축 재료, 그리고 그들이 일상생활에서 접하는 위험 등에 달려 있었다. 이것들은 여전히 중요하다. 하지만, 현대적 기계와 새로운 건축 방법이 그 중요성을 줄여 주었다. 주택은 여전히 기후의 영향을 고려하여 지어진다. 그러나 난방과 에어컨은 주택을 어떤 기후에서도 편안하게 해준다. 가까운 데서 손쉽게 구할 수 있는 재료로 집을 지으면 값싸고 쉽다. 그러나 오늘날은 먼 데서 건축 재료들을 수송해 오는 것이 가능하다.

13. 가정학은 지식과 직업의 한 분야이다. 이 분야의 목적은 개인과 가족의 일상 생활의 질을 향상시키는 일이다. 주제는 음식, 주거, 의복, 관리, 성장과 발전 과정, 그리고 서로 관계를 맺는 과정 등, 사람들, 특히 가족들이 매일 부딪치는 것들이다. 가정학은 이런 분야들을 따로따로 취급할 수도 있다. 그러나 가정학은 일상생활을 향상시키기 위해 그 분야들이 서로 어우러지는 과정을 강조하였다.

가정학은 대부분의 프로그램을 학문 분야로서 설명하는 데 사용되는 명칭이다. 그러나 다른 명칭들도 가끔 사용된다. 그중 일부는 소비자 가정교육, 소비자학, 가족학, 인간 발달, 인간 생태학, 인간 자원 등이다. 대체로 이 분야를 공부하는 사람들은 가정학자라고 하는데, 간혹 다른 명칭으로 알려져 있기도 하다.

14. (1) 장식가들은 많은 분야에서 일을 한다. 부동산 개발업자들이 장식가들과 일을 한다. 많은 가구업체들은 소비자들에게 자문을 해주기 위해 장식가들을 중역으로 데리고 있다. 또, 장식가들은 주택 외에도 사무실, 식당, 학교, 병원 등을 설계하는 것을 도와준다. 사실은 상업 인테리어는 실내장식의 모든 작업의 절반 정도에 해당할 뿐이다.

대부분의 성공한 장식가들은 자기 직업을 준비하기 위해 어떤 공식적인 공부를 하였다. 색상, 직물, 벽지 등을 사용하는 기본 기술을 가르치는 6개월 과정이 있다. 그러나 실내디자인 직업에 대해 진지하게 생각하고 있는 사람이라면, 4년의 교육과정을 제공하는 대학들이 많이 있다. 이 학교들은 도면 작성 방법, 실내를 측량하고 축적 도면을 작성하는 방법, 어떤 공간에 어떤 장식이 적당할지를 결정하는 방법, 구조 변경 설계 방법 등을 가르친다. 그 과정은 실내장식의 역사뿐 아니라 주택과 기업체의 디자인도 포함한다.

(2) 자기 방을 연구한다. 어떤 모양인가? 높이와 너비, 그리고 길이는? 자기 방을 정확히 잰 다음, 그래프 용지에 축적 도면을 작성한다. 창과, 출입문, 라디에이터의 위치를 포함하는 것을 명심한다. 창으로부터 들어오는 자연광을 이용하고 싶을 것이다. 출입문은 어떤 것에도 부딪쳐서는 안 되고, 가구도 라디에이터를 차단해서는 안 된다. 또 다른 용지에는 침대와 기타 가구들의 모양을 축적으로 그려서 잘라 낸다. 이제 그 가구 모양들을 도면 위에 놓아 보면, 가구를 정돈하는 길을 알려준다. 가구 모양 조각들을 이리저리 움직여서 보기 좋은 위치가 될 때까지 정돈하는 실험을 한다.

자기 방에서 하게 될 활동을 다시 생각하고, 어떤 가구가 그런 활동을 가능케 할 것인지를 생각한다. 숙제를 하는 데는 튼튼한 의자와 조명이 좋은 실용적인 책상이 중요하다. 프로젝트용 작업 테이블을 사용할 수 있을까? 공간이 충분하다면, 방을 취침과 작업, 놀이 공간으로 나누고 싶을 것이다. 어떤 가구는 두 가지 용도로 쓸 수 있다. 벽에 붙은 침대는 적절한 쿠션들만 준비하면 침대 겸용 소파로도 이용될 수 있다.

이제 누군가의 도움을 받아서, 실제로 가구를 정돈해 본다. 정돈한 것이 실용적이고 마음에 드는가? 제대로 되었는가? 그렇다면, 훌륭하게 작업을 한 것이다. 그렇지 않다면, 용지에다 재편하여 다시 시작한다.

15. 보물은 매우 다양한 형태로, 수많은 종류의 물질로 만들어진다. 귀한 보물은 가장 드물고, 가장 아름다운 금속과 보석으로 만들어진다. 귀하지 않은 보물은 구하기 쉽고, 비싸지 않은 물질로 만든다.

옛날 사람들은 조약돌, 조개 껍질, 과일 열매, 새의 깃털 등으로 자신들을 장식하였다. 돌 조각과 동물의 뿔이나 이빨로 목걸이를 만들었다. 고대 미국의 인디언들은 조가비 염주(반짝이는 조개 껍질의 염주), 뼈, 금속으로 목걸이를 만들어 걸었다. 세계 여러 지역의 원시인들은 여전히 비슷한 장식을 하고 있다.

16. 반대되는 두 힘이 연에 작용한다. 하나는 공기의 상승하는 힘이다. 다른 하나는 땅으로 잡아당기는 연줄

이다. 이 두 힘이 균형을 이루거나 거의 똑 같을 때, 연이 공중에 떠 있다.

공기의 상승하는 힘은 비행기가 나는 것을 가능하게도 한다. 출발 위치에서 연을 잡고 있을 때, 연에 마주치는 공기는 두 기류로 나뉜다. 한 기류는 연의 상단 부분으로 지나가고, 하나는 아래 부분을 지나간다.

연의 상단 부분을 지나가는 기류는 하단 부분을 지나는 기류보다 이동 경로가 더 길다. 이것은 바로 연의 모양과 각도 때문이다. 그러나 상단 기류는 하단 기류와 같은 시간에 더 긴 경로를 이동해야 한다. 이것은 상단 기류가 하단 기류보다 더 빨리 이동한다는 사실을 의미한다. 그 결과, 상단 기류의 공기가 더 엷다. 하단 기류의 기압이 더 크고, 그래서 연이 날아오른다.

17. 뜨개질바늘은 매우 다양한 크기와 모양으로 나온다. 바늘들은 흔히 대부분 금속, 플라스틱, 나무로 만들어진다. 미국에서는 0번에서 50번까지 바늘에 번호를 매겨 크기를 표시한다. 번호가 높을수록, 바늘이 굵다. 뜨개질바늘의 모양은 3가지가 있다. 쌍침형, 원형, 곧은 형이다. 쌍침형 바늘은 4개가 세트로 나오는데, 주로 양말이나 장갑 같은 작은 튜브형 제품을 짜는 데 사용된다. 원형 바늘은 양쪽 끝에 금속이나 플라스틱 침을 달아 유연성이 있다. 스커트나 스웨터 몸통같이 주로 커다란 튜브형 제품을 만드는 데 사용된다. 가장 흔한 형태의 바늘이 곧은 바늘이다. 이것들은 항상 쌍으로 나오며, 길이가 보통 10~14인치이다. 초보자는 가장 사용하기 쉬운 10인치짜리 바늘을 찾을 것이다. 왜냐하면 이것이 적당한 길이이고, 잘 구부려지지도 않기 때문이다.

18. 현대의 유람선은 물 위에 떠 있는 호텔과 같다. 많은 승객들이 잠을 자는 객실과 접견실 외에도 라운지, 식당, 부엌, 휴게실, 상점, 수영장, 체육관, 극장, 병원, 차고, 그리고 애완견의 집까지 있다. 엘리베이터는 승객들을 이 갑판 저 갑판으로 실어다 준다.

여러 날 동안 수천 명을 먹이기 위해서는 엄청난 양의 음식이 필요하다. 큰 여객선은 육류와 닭고기, 생선, 채소, 달걀, 그리고 기타 식품들을 몇 톤씩 싣고 다닌다.

큰 배는 배를 운행하고 승객들을 보호할 승무원들이 수백 명 필요하다. 객실 승무원들은 객실을 청소하고, 승객들에게 개별적인 시중을 들어준다. 식당 승무원들은 테이블을 시중든다. 갑판 승무원들은 갑판 의자들을 설치하고, 갑판에 있는 승객들에게 음식과 음료를 접대한다.

배의 선원들은 배의 운항을 책임지고 있고, 모든 사람의 안전을 책임지고 있다. 우두머리는 선장이다. 그는 선원들과 승무원, 승객들에 대해 권한을 가진 배의 주인이다. 폭풍이나 심각한 사고 같은 위급한 상황에서 어떤 조치를 취할 것인가를 결정하는 것은 선장이다.

여객선이 출항한 직후에는 모든 승객들이 구명정 훈련에 참석해야 한다. 여객선은 모든 승객들에게 구명조끼를 지급한다. 훈련을 하는 동안, 승객들은 구명조끼를 입어야 하고, 배정된 구명정 보관소에 가서 보고해야 한다.

19. 가끔 테마 공원이라고 하는 놀이 공원은 탈것, 게임, 오락 등으로 특화하고 있다. 공공 공원과는 달리 이런 공원들은 기업 또는 개인들이 소유하고 있다. 그들은 입장료를 받고, 공원 내의 모든 시설과 서비스에 대해 돈을 받는다.

아직 운영되고 있는 가장 오래된 놀이 공원은 덴마크 코펜하겐에 있는 '바켄 놀이 공원'이다. 개장한 지 400년이 넘었다. 그런데 코펜하겐에는 유명한 공원이 하나 더 있다. 도시 한가운데 있는 '티볼리 가든'이다. 이 공원은 탈것과 게임들을 극장, 콘서트홀, 식당, 예쁜 정원들과 조화를 시켜 놓았다.

미국 최초의 놀이 공원은 1850년대 중반에 전차 회사들에 의해 건설되었다. 그때는 자동차가 없었다. 그래서 부자들만이 마차를 가지고 있었다. 일반 사람들이 어디를 가고 싶다면, 그들은 걷거나 전차를 타야 했다.

20. (1) 향수는 기분 좋은 향기이다. 그것은 비 온 뒤의 숲, 꽃이 핀 사과나무, 금방 딴 오렌지, 또는 향수병의 액체 등에서 난다. 자연 재료의 향기는 그 안에 있는 기름이 원인이 된다.

이런 기름은 액체로든 고체로든 향수를 만드는 데 사용된다. 액체 향수는 일반적으로 향수병이나 에어로졸 스프레이, 목욕 오일 등으로 볼 수 있다. 액체 향수는 비누, 핸드 크림, 화장실 탈취제 등에 기분 좋은 냄새를 첨가할 때도 사용된다. 향수 지팡이, 분향, 향 양초 등이 고체 형태로 된 향수의 예들이다.

우리는 보통 향수를 사람이나 방의 냄새를 좋게 하는 데 사용하는 꽃이나 과일 향의 물질들로 생각한다. 그러나 팝콘이나 새 자동차, 바닷가 같은 냄새가 나는 향을 만드는 것도 가능하다.

(2) 콜로뉴는 목욕을 할 때나 한 뒤에 피부 청결제로 사용되는 향수 액이다. 대체로 알코올이다. 전통적으로 콜로뉴는 밀감류의 향기를 바탕으로 하였으므로, 이 향기가 화장수와 콜로뉴를 구별해 주었다. 그러나 오늘날은 전통적인 방식으로 화장수와 콜로뉴를 만드는 회사가 거의 없다. 이제 '콜로뉴' 나 '화장수' 라는 말은 향수 오일의 각기 다른 농도를 가리킨다. 일반적으로 화장수가 둘 중에서 더 강하다. 둘 다 몸이나 머릿결에 자유로이 뿌리도록 되어 있다. 화장수와 콜로뉴는 알코올을 많이 함유하고 있어서, 향수보다 훨씬 싸다. 이것들은 농도가 연하기 때문에, 그 향기가 향수의 향기만큼 오래가지 않는다.

21. 우편공사는 우편물을 담당하는 정부 기관이다. 우편 업무는 편지나 소포를 전세계의 사람들과 기업들에 전달하는 일이다. 그 목표는 목적지에 가능한 빨리 우편물이 도착하는 것을 보는 것이다. 사람들은 중요한 편지나 귀중품까지 제시간에 임자에게 전달하는 것을 우편공사에 의존하고 있다.

세계의 많은 기업들이 우편공사에 의존하고 있다. 그것은 대부분의 국가들이 우편 업무에 밀접하게 협조하기 때문이다. 우편물은 언제나 '통과' 이다. 남미의 홍수나 아시아의 지진이 연착시킬 수는 있으나, 신속히 새로운 길이 찾아지는 대로 우편은 전달된다. 북미의 알래스카에서 부친 편지는 아프리카의 케냐까지 배, 비행기, 기차, 트럭, 심지어 말을 타고 여행하기도 한다.

22. 롤러스케이팅은 평평하고 꽤 매끄러운 표면이 필요하다. 쉽게 굴러서 스케이트 지치는 사람을 멀리까지 가게 하기 때문에 지역이 아주 넓고 한적한 곳이라야 한다. 실외 링크는 언제나 부드러운 콘크리트 표면의 스케이트장을 가지고 있다. 실내 링크는 플라스틱으로 코팅된 압착된 목재인 합판 마루 바닥을 가지고 있다.

스케이트를 지칠 때는, 걸을 때와 달리 균형을 잘 잡아야 한다. 롤러스케이팅은 발끝이 발뒤꿈치를 따라간다기보다는 오히려 발을 평평하게 놓는다는 점이 걷기와 다르다. 균형을 잘 잡기 위해서, 스텝을 밟을 때마다 무릎을 구부리고 몸을 머리와 바닥에서 떨어져 있는 발 사이에 두려고 한다.

롤러스케이팅은 훌륭한 근육운동이 된다. 격렬한 움직임이 필요 없기 때문에, 롤러스케이팅은 모든 연령, 다양한 육체적 조건의 사람들에게 알맞다.

23. 스케이트보드는 1960년대 초반에 미국에서 캘리포니아의 10대들이 롤러스케이트를 나무판에 붙여 길거리에서 '서핑' 을 연습하면서 시작하였다. 그렇게 타는 것이 결코 완벽하지는 않았다. 울퉁불퉁한 도로와 자갈들이 작은 스케이트 바퀴를 가로막았다. 이것이 거리의 서핑족들을 넘어지게 하였다.

1970년대에는 제작자들이 향상된 바퀴와 보드를 사용해 이 유행에 부응하였다. 폴리우레탄으로 만들어진 새로운 플라스틱 바퀴는 스케이트 바퀴보다 더 크고 부드러웠다. 이 플라스틱 바퀴는 매끄럽게 나가고 뛰어난 마찰력을 주었다. 바퀴는 기동성이 더 나은 보드로 만들어진 차대라고 부르는 특수 완충 장치 위에 얹혔다. 여러 가지 모델의 향상된 보드가 나왔다. 플라스틱, 섬유 유리, 알루미늄뿐 아니라 다양한 목재로도 만들어졌다. 새로운 장비로, 그 스포츠는 빠르게 인기를 얻었고, 오늘날 전세계 2천만 명 이상이 스케이트보드를 타고 있다. 심지어 그중 일부는 주문 제품을 쓰고 있다.

24. 잠의 깊이는 잠자는 시간 내내 똑같다. 잠의 깊이는 자는 이를 깨우는 데 필요한 소리의 양으로 잴 수 있다. 잠의 첫째 주기는 약 1시간 30분 정도 간다. 이 주기 동안에 깊은 잠은 더 옅은 잠으로 대체된다. 이런 1시간 30분의 주기는 밤 사이 계속된다. 밤이 끝나 가면서 깊은 잠이 줄고, 잠이 점점 옅어진다.

최근의 연구는 잠에는 꿈을 꾸는 잠과 꿈을 꾸지 않는 잠, 2가지가 있는 것으로 나타났다. 비록 깨어났을 때 그 꿈을 기억하지 못하는 사람이 있지만, 잠을 자는 동안 누구나 꿈을 꾼다. 꿈꾸는 능력은 깨어났을 때 그 사람을 상쾌하고 편안하게 하는 데 어떤 역할을 하는 것으로 보인다.

사람이 필요한 잠의 양은 개인마다 다르다. 성인들은

대체로 하루에 7~9시간 필요하다. 두 살이 된 아기들은 밤에 12시간, 낮에 1~2시간의 잠을 필요로 한다. 6~9살 사이에는 밤잠이 11시간으로 줄어든다. 12살이 되면 하룻밤에 10시간으로도 충분하다. 하지만 이것들은 평균치이다.

25. 태피스트리는 손으로 짠 직물이다. 일반적으로 몇 가지 색상의 굵은 실로 만들어진다. 대부분의 태피스트리는 벽이나 천장에 걸린다.

손으로 직물을 짜기는 시간이 많이 들고 대단한 기술도 필요하다. 그 직조공은 다른 예술가들이 좀처럼 만나지 않는 문제점들로 제한을 받는다. 그는 그림을 그릴 캔버스가 없고, 모형을 만들 점토도 없고, 조각할 목재도 석재도 없다. 오로지 색색의 실만을 가지고, 그는 자신의 직물을 제조하고 동시에 장식을 해야 한다. 끈기와 기획력, 직조 기술이 있는 예술가들은 언제나 드물고, 그래서 태피스트리는 전통적으로 아주 비싸고 귀하다.

교회와 위대한 왕가들이 세계를 지배할 당시에는 태피스트리가 부(富)의 상징이었다. 연극과 공식 행사, 공식 축전이 열릴 때마다, 태피스트리는 그 행사에 미(美)와 부를 더해 주었다. 종교적인 행렬은 태피스트리로 표시된 길을 따라갔다.

26. 일을 잘 해치우는 어떤 바쁜 사람에게 어떻게 스케줄이 아주 빡빡한 여러 일들을 수행하는 것이 가능한지 물어 보라. 다음과 같은 대답이 나올 것이다. "해야 할 일들의 목록을 작성하고, 그 일들을 할 때마다 지우는 것이죠."

해야 할 일들의 목록을 작성하는 것은 자신의 시간을 관리하는 최선의 길이다. 우선 순위에 따라 항목을 작성한다. 즉, 어떤 일이 얼마나 중요한지 그리고 언제 마쳐야 하는지를 결정한다. 예를 들어, 자신의 과학 과제가 이번 금요일까지이고 독서 숙제는 다음주까지라면, 과학 과제를 첫 번째로 놓는다. 이 두 가지 일을 자기 방 정리 같은 덜 중요한 일보다 앞에 둔다.

매우 스케줄이 바쁘다면, 일주일 또는 하루를 시작할 때 새 목록을 작성한다. 각각의 일을 마칠 때까지 성실하게 일하고, 즉각 목록에 있는 다음 일로 옮긴다. 일들을 미루거나 시간을 낭비하는 것은 유쾌하지 않은 일을 연장할 뿐이고, 홀가분하지도 않다. 목록의 마지막 일을 지운 다음에는, 자신이 정말 좋아하는 것을 하여 자신에게 보상을 한다.

27. 게임 기술의 발전이 많이 연구되고 완벽해지고 있다. 언젠가 비디오 게임 플레이어는 뇌파를 이용해 작동을 통제할 수도 있을 것이다. 아주 가까운 장래에는 플레이어들이 음성 명령을 사용해 게임 과정을 통제할 것이다. 그런 게임에서는 컴퓨터가 어떤 말들을 인식하고 거기에 반응한다.

비디오 게임은 대부분 어떤 스토리나 일련의 이벤트를 연기하는 만화 캐릭터들이나 컴퓨터 주인공들의 이미지를 사용한다. 그러나 새로운 비디오 기술은 사람들에게 실제 연기자들을 등장시키는 게임들을 하는 것을 가능케 한다. 이 게임들은 컴퓨터 지시와 비디오 디스크에 녹화된 영상 이미지들을 조화시킨 것이다. 컴퓨터는 플레이어가 무엇을 하느냐에 따라, 비디오 디스크의 여러 부분들과 스크린 변화에 등장하는 액션을 이용한다.

다중 이용자 게임도 개발중이다. 이것들은 많은 사람들, 예를 들어, 50개의 서로 다른 도시에 있는 50명의 플레이어들이 같은 게임을 동시에 할 수 있도록 전화선을 이용하여 정보를 전송할 것이다. 이중 어떤 게임들은 어떤 목표를 이루기 위해 서로 협조하는 플레이어들을 필요로 할 것이다. 다른 어떤 게임들은 대규모 경연대회에서 플레이어들을 서로 겨루게 할 것이다.

비디오 게임은 아직 발전 초기 단계이다. 미래에는 분명히 좀 더 복잡하게 되어 더욱 도전적인 것이 될 것이다.

제 2장

1 ①	**2** (1) ④ (2) ③ (3) ② (4) ④	**3** ⑤	**4** ①	**5** 1. ② 2. ③ 3. ②	**6** 1. ⑤
2. ④ 3. ③	**7** ③	**8** 1. ④ 2. ③ 3. ④ 4. ③ 5. ④ 6. ③ 7. ⑤ 8. ②		**9** ②	**10** 1. (1)
④ (2) ④ 2. ⑤	**11** 1. ② 2. ③	**12** ④	**13** ⑤	**14** (1) ③ (2) ④	**15** ⑤

1. 과학자들은 새로운 항생제를 찾고, 박테리아가 이 약들을 어떻게 퇴치하는지를 이해하기 위해 적극적으로 연구하고 있다. 과학자들은 어떤 약이 세균에 작용을 할 것 같은지를 보기 위해 컴퓨터를 이용해서 모델을 연구할 수 있다. 새로운 자연 제품들이 동식물에서 발견되고 있다. 상어와 개구리들이 디펜신이라고 하는 작은 단백질 분자를 함유하고 있는데, 과학자들은 그것을 항생제로 개발하기를 원하고 있다.

일부 과학자들은 박테리아를 죽이기보다 확산을 멈추게 하는 새로운 분자들을 실험하고 있다. 이 분자들은 박테리아가 세포에 달라붙어서 감염을 시작하는 것을 막아 준다. 그러나 항생제가 박테리아의 확산을 멈추든지 죽이든지, 항생제 연구의 목표는 세균 질병을 제거하는 것이다. 많은 사람들의 생명이 그것에 달려 있다.

2. 맥주는 수천 년을 마셔 온 알코올 음료이다. 맥주의 제조 또는 양조는 세계 여러 지역에서 매우 일찍부터 시작된 것으로 보인다. 기원전 약 6천년에 메소포타미아에서 맥주 같은 음료가 만들어졌다. 또 이집트, 그리스, 로마에서도 양조되었다.

중세에는 대부분의 맥주를 수사(修士)들이 양조하였고, 거의 모든 수도원이 양조장을 가지고 있었다. 나중에는 다른 데서 이 임무를 넘겨받았고, 양조는 양조자들의 조직, 길드를 갖춘 하나의 산업으로 성장하였다. 중세의 맥주는 오늘날의 맥주보다 알코올 농도가 훨씬 높은 진하고 독한 음료였다. 음료수와 같은, 거의 식품인, 이 진하고 영양가 높은 음료는 사람들의 일상적인 식사에 중요한 식단이었다.

중세 영국에서는 흔히 맥주(비어 또는 에일)가 축제나 경축일의 주요 음료였다. 축제를 의미하기도 하는 단어 '에일'은 이 술잔치의 아주 중요한 부분이었다. 램-에일(양 축제)은 양털 깎는 시기에 개최되는 축일이었다. 칼리지-에일(대학 축제)은 학생들이 자신들이 양조한 에일(맥주)을 마신 파티였다. 브라이들(결혼 피로연)이라는 말은 결혼 잔치였던 브라이드-에일(결혼 축제)에서 온 말이다.

맥주를 양조하는 지식은 초기의 식민지인들에 의해 신세계에 전파되었다. 처음에는 맥주가 작은 가내 양조장들에서 양조되었다. 그러나 식민지가 성장하면서, 양조는 하나의 산업으로 형성되었다. 최초의 양조장 가운데 하나는 1683년 펜실바니아주 펜스베리에 세워졌다. 100년만에 양조 산업은 국가 경제활동의 중요한 부분이 되었다.

3. 캔디 형태로 된 초콜릿은 온스(30ml)당 약 145칼로리 또는 평균적인 초콜릿 바에 약 220칼로리가 있다. 단백질, 비타민 B2, 칼슘에 대한 미국 일일 권장 허용기준의 약 5% 이상을 $1\frac{1}{2}$온스(43g)짜리 초콜릿 바가 차지하고 있다. 밀크 초콜릿은 지방이 35%이고, 탄수화물이 50%이다. 초콜릿은 카페인이 들어 있긴 하지만, 커피 한 잔의 카페인 양과 같으려면 초콜릿을 1파운드 이상 섭취해야 한다.

초콜릿이 처음 유럽에 소개되었을 때, 결코 증명되지 않은 건강상 많은 유익한 것들이 있다고 여겨졌다. 최근에는 여드름과 충치를 일으키는 것으로 생각되었다. 그러나 연구 결과 초콜릿은 여드름을 유발하지 않고, 다른 많은 캔디들보다 오히려 충치를 덜 유발하는 것으로 나타났다.

1인당 연평균 10파운드(4.5kg)를 소비하는 미국에서는 초콜릿이 캔디, 쿠키, 아이스크림, 기타 과자들에 최고의 맛을 낸다. 그러나 미국은 세계의 초콜릿 소비에 겨우 11번째이다. 선두는 1인당 연평균 소비량이 22파운드(9.5kg)나 되는 스위스이다.

4. 사람들이 언제부터 요리를 하기 시작하였는지 아무도 모른다. 석기 시대 사람들이 불에다 음식을 요리한 증거가 있다. 사람들이 곡식을 재배하고 토기를 만들 줄 알게 되면서 요리가 발전하였다. 고대 이집트인들이 최초로 발효된 빵을 만든 것으로 생각되는데, 그들은 불로 가열한 토기 솥에다 빵을 구웠다. 고대 로마인들은 큰 연회를 즐겼는데, 정교하게 준비한 음식들이 나왔다.

석탄 난로가 발명된 1800년대로 오면서 불은 요리에 열을 가하는 기본 원천이었다. 오늘날 대부분 선진국 가정의 부엌에는 전자 렌지, 가스 렌지, 전자 오븐 같은 여러 현대적 기구들이 있다. 요리는 더 쉽고 신속해졌다. 그러나 음식을 준비하고 요리하는 여러 기본적인 단계는 수백 년 동안 변하지 않았다.

5. (1) 오늘날 대부분의 버터는 기계적인 교유(攪乳) 장치로 만들어진다. 지방이 크림에서 분리되어 따로 모일 때까지 크림을 앞뒤로 계속 흔든다. 버터가 만들어진 뒤에 남는 부분을 버터 밀크라고 한다. 탈지우유와 거의 똑같은 구성을 가지고 있다.

버터를 만들다가 나온 버터 밀크는 주로 다른 식품을 만드는 데 사용된다. 마시는 용도로 파는 버터 밀크는 특수 박테리아 활동으로 생산되는 배양된 버터 밀크이다.

버터는 물로 씻어서 부드러워질 때까지 반죽한다. 흔히 소금이 첨가된다. 어떤 때는 부풀어 오른 가벼운 버터를 만들기 위해 공기를 버터 속으로 불어넣는다. 버터는 흔히 색깔 때문에 또 우유에서 가장 풍부하고 가장 비싼 부분인 크림으로 만든다고 해서 '황금 선물'이라고 한다.

(2) 요구르트는 많이 이용되는 음식이다. 단백질, 칼슘, 비타민 B군, 무기물 등의 훌륭한 원천이다. 그 영양학적 가치 때문에 많은 사람들이 일상적인 식사의 보조 식품으로 또는 식사 사이에 먹는 간식으로 요구르트를 먹는다. 요구르트는 그냥 먹어도 되고 애플소스나 땅콩버터, 마른 곡물 등 다른 음식과 섞어 먹어도 된다. 많은 요리사들이 샐러드 드레싱, 소스, 수프, 주식, 디저트 등의 조리에 요구르트를 사용한다.

요구르트는 세계 여러 지역에서 인기 있는 식품이다. 인도, 발칸반도, 중동 등지에서는 요구르트가 여러 주식의 재료로 사용된다.

(3) 치즈를 만들기 위해서는 우유가 먼저 응결되어야 한다. 수백 년 간 '레닛'이라는 응유 효소를 우유에 넣어 응결시켰다. 레닛은 일부 초식동물의 위 속에 있는 소화즙 또는 효소이다. 오늘날에는 레닛을 어린 송아지의 위에서 채취한다. 그러나 오늘날 대부분의 상업용 치즈 제조자들은 우유를 시게 만드는 유익하고 해가 없는 박테리아를 특별히 배양하여 첨가한다. 어떤 때는 산(酸)으로 우유를 응결시킨다.

치즈를 만드는 두 번째 단계에서는 응결된 우유에서 '훼이'라는 유장(乳漿)을 대부분 제거한다. 응결된 우유 또는 응유(凝乳)를 작은 조각들로 자름으로써 보다 신속하게 떼어 낼 수 있다. 이 작업은 응유 칼이라고 하는 하프같이 생긴 기구로 한다.

6. (1) 약품을 분류하는 가장 기본적인 방법 가운데 하나는 구매 방법과 관련되어 있다. 어떤 약품은 의사의 지시 또는 처방 없이 살 수 있다. 이것들을 '계산대 약품'이라고 한다. 약국이나 식품점, 심지어 주유소에서도 계산대 약품들을 판다. 일반적인 계산대 약품으로는 복통에 먹는 제산제, 발열과 두통에 먹는 아스피린, 옻독에 바르는 칼라민 연고 등이 있다. 계산대 약품 광고에 연간 수백만 달러가 소비된다.

의사가 질병이나 질환을 진단한 뒤에만 특정한 사람에게 안전하고 효과적으로 생각되는 약품은 처방약이라고 한다. 흔히 약국에서 구입한다. 의사가 종이에 쓰고 서명하는 소위 처방을 의사가 요청한 약품을 사람들에게 팔도록 교육받고 면허를 받은 사람인 약사에게 가져간다. 처방은 환자에게 무슨 약을 얼마나 조제하여 투약할 지를 지시하고 있다. 적절하게 복용하라는 지시도 있다. 미국에서는 약봉지에 다음과 같은 글을 적은 라벨을 붙여야 한다. "주의: 연방 법률은 처방 없는 조제를 금하고 있습니다."

(2) 약리학은 약의 특성과 약이 인체의 특정 기관이나 세포에 작용하는 방식을 연구하는 학문이다.

약은 인체에 들어가 다양한 방법으로 작용한다. 알약과 물약, 당의정은 모두 삼켜 먹는다. 이것들은 위장과 소장에서 소화된 다음 혈관으로 들어간다. 어떤 약은 근육질이나 신체 구멍으로 직접 주사하여 주입된다. 크림과 연고, 안약 같은 물약들은 인체 표면에 직접 바른다. 마취 가스 같은 다른 약들은 흡입한다. 약이 인체에 효과를 나타내는 방식을 작용의 메커니즘이라고 한다. 여러 약의 작용 메커니즘은 세포에 화학작용의 속도를 변화시키는 것이다. 약은 이 불균형을 시정하고, 질병이나 질환을 치료하거나 그것이 인체에 퍼지는 것을 방지할 수 있다.

약이 언제나 건강한 세포와 병든 세포를 구별할 수는 없기 때문에, 어떤 약도 완전히 안전할 수는 없다. 약은 건강한 세포나 기관에 영향을 미칠 경우, 때때로 바람직하지 않은 부작용을 낳을 수 있다. 이런 이유 때문에 약은 반드시 의사의 지시에 따라 사용되는 것이 중요하다. 여러분은 어떤 약이 부작용을 일으키는지를 의사에게 말해야 한다. 그래야 복용 분량을 조절하거나 다른 약을 조제할 수가 있다.

(3) 가장 오래된 약의 원천은 식물과 동물이다. 예를 들어, 디기탈리스는 심장마비 치료에 쓰이는 약인 디고센의 원천이다. 양귀비 식물은 통증을 완화시키는 모르핀을 제공한다. 동물의 분비샘은 여전히 당뇨병 치료제인 인슐린과 왜소 발육증에 쓰는 성장 호르몬을 제공한다.

살아 있는 생물체인 박테리아와 곰팡이는 항생물질의 원천이다. 박테리아와 곰팡이의 각 세포는 다른 박테리아나 버섯균을 죽일 수 있는 소량의 화학 물질을 가지고 있다. 약품 제조업체들은 이 세포들을 수십 억 개씩 발효조라고 하는 큰 탱크에서 기른다.

비록 많은 약이 본래 식물과 동물에서 왔지만, 오늘날 대부분의 약은 약제 화학자들의 실험실에서 합성으로 만들어지고 있다. 더 크고 더 복잡한 분자를 생산하기 위해 일련의 화학작용으로 단순한 분자들을 조합하여 만든 것들이 합성 약품이다. 많은 가능한 분자 조합들은 합성 약품을 새로운 약품을 위한 중요 원천으로 만들어 준다.

7. (1) 패스트푸드는 한정된 메뉴와 신속한 서비스를 제공하는 식당에서 이용되는 값싼 식품이다. 대부분의 패스트푸드는, 적어도 일부는 중앙에서 준비된 다음 각 식당으로 배달된다. 프라이팬, 그릴, 전자 오븐과, 어떤 것은 컴퓨터화된 기타 장비들이 음식을 팔기 전에 요리를 마무리하는 데 사용된다. 패스트푸드 식당에서 인기 있는 품목으로는 햄버그, 프라이드 치킨, 밀크쉐이크, 프렌치 프라이드 포테이토, 샐러드 등이 있다. 1950년대에 최초로 맥도널드 식당이 문을 연 이래, 패스트푸드 체인점들이 수십 억 달러짜리 산업으로 성장하였다.

8. (1) 프랑스처럼 요리의 예술에 많은 것을 첨가한 나라는 거의 없다. 세계의 주요 식당들은 '고도의 예술적인 요리 스타일'이라는 뜻의 '오트 퀴진'이라고 하는 전통 프랑스식 요리를 특징으로 하고 있다. '누벨 퀴진' 역시 프랑스에서 비롯되었다. 그것은 음식을 준비할 때 양념을 많이 쓰거나 버터의 남용을 피하는 담백한 요리 방식이다.

프랑스 요리사들은 상상력을 동원하여 허브, 양념, 와인을 잘 섞는 것으로 유명하다. 육류와 닭고기, 생선을 위한 훌륭한 소스들이 그 결과이다. 프랑스는 과자와 빵으로 유명하다. 프랑스 와인과 치즈는 세계 최고에 속한다.

토마스 제퍼슨은 주프랑스 미국 공사로 파리에 사는 동안 아이스크림을 만드는 것을 알았다. 그는 조리법을 직접 적어서 미국으로 가지고 돌아왔다. 그는 공식 만찬에서 디저트로 아이스크림을 최초로 내놓은 사람이었다.

(2) 거의 모든 사람들이 여러 가지 소스로 양념을 한 스파게티, 국수, 마카로니, 라비올리 등의 형태로 말린 가루 반죽인 이탈리아식 파스타를 즐겨 먹는다. 피자리아라고 하는 작은 식당들은 전통 이탈리아식 피자를 특징으로 한다. 이것은 둥근 가루 반죽 위에 토마토 소스, 녹인 치즈, 버섯, 안초비(멸치류), 약간의 쇠고기와 소스 등을 얹은 다음 구운 것이다.

이탈리아의 한정된 육류와 낙농 제품 공급으로는 많은 훌륭한 이탈리아 요리사들이 많은 훌륭한 요리를 만들게 할 수 없었다. 그들은 육류의 적은 양을 파스타, 쌀, 콘밀, 소스, 치즈 등으로 입지를 넓혔고, 허브로 요리에 활력을 넣었다. 얇게 썬 송아지 고기를 버터나 올리브 기름에 요리하여 소스를 입힌 스캘러피니는 인기 있는 요리이다. 이탈리아 와인과 치즈, 과자는 세계 여러 지역으로 나간다.

(3) 어떤 식품은 다른 식품들 보다 쉽게 상하지 않는다. 오렌지는 껍질이 두꺼워서 미생물의 접근을 막기

때문에 부패를 방지한다. 내부 섬유질의 높은 산성도와 신맛 역시 부패를 늦춘다. 오렌지 내부와 같은 강한 산성의 환경에서는 박테리아가 거의 자랄 수 없다.

반면에, 신선한 우유와 육류는 쉽게 상한다. 오렌지와 같은 보호막이 없어서 제조 과정에서 공중 박테리아에 감염될 수 있다. 이런 제품들은 또 그것을 얻는 동물에 서식하는 박테리아를 함유할 수 있다.

식품 부패를 일으키는 이 요소들을 통제하고 파괴하기 위해 여러 처리과정들이 개발되었다. 이 과정들로는 건조, 냉장, 냉동, 열처리, 화학약품으로 보존하는 방법 등이 있다.

(4) 1804년에 아페르라는 프랑스의 캔디 업자이자 요리사는 미리 조리한 식품을 유리 용기에 담아 가열한 다음 단단히 밀봉함으로써 식품을 보존하는 방법을 발견하였다. 요리만으로는 식품을 보존할 수 없다. 식품이 식을 때 공기 중의 미생물들이 식품에 닿고 시간이 지나 부패를 유발하기 때문이다.

아페르의 공정은 실제로 모든 미생물을 죽이며 식품을 살균하였다. 그것은 또 공기나 새로운 미생물들이 용기에 들어가는 것을 막아 준다. 이런 방식으로 처리된 식품은 수년 간 보관되고 용기를 열었을 때도 먹기가 좋다. 유리병, 깡통, 플라스틱 용기, 비닐 봉지, 금박 포장 상자 등은 모두 살균된 식품을 포장하는 데 사용된다.

(5) 미국의 새로운 식품 설명 규정은 식품에 대해서 제기되는 잘못된 주장들로부터 소비자를 보호하기도 한다. 이제 정확한 설명이 식품 표시에 사용되는 구체적인 말로 주어진다.

또, 7가지 식품-질병 관계에만 식품 설명에 건강 문구가 허용된다. 이들 관계로는 칼슘과 골다공증, 나트륨과 고혈압, 지방과 암, 지방과 심장병, 섬유질과 암, 섬유질과 심장병, 그리고 과일, 채소와 암이 있다. 어떤 식품이 이런 건강 문제와 관련된 주장을 하기 위해서는 그 영양 함유를 고려하여 특정한 조건들을 충족해야 한다.

(6) 평균적인 미국인 가정의 수입 가운데 약 15%가 식품에 소비된다. 미리 계획을 세우는 것은 여러분의 돈을 최대한으로 이용하게 하는 데 도움이 될 것이다. 첫 번째가 며칠 또는 일주일이나 2주일 치의 식단을 준비하는 것이다. 다음, 식단의 식사를 준비하는 데 필요한 식품의 리스트를 작성한다. 쇼핑을 할 때 거의 이 리스트를 따른다. 배고플 때는 식료품 쇼핑을 피하는 것이 좋다. 그렇지 않으면, 식품 리스트에 없는 맛있어 보이는 품목들을 사게 되는 유혹을 받을 것이다.

(7) 어느 한 해에 세계의 식량 공급은 주로 그 해 생산되는 것으로 이루어진다. 어떤 식량은 다음 해로 넘어간다. 그런 예비분을 비축하기 위해서는 필요한 양보다 더 많은 식량이 생산되어야 한다. 그러나 미국을 비롯한 소수의 국가들만이 이렇게 할 수 있다. 다른 나라들은 여러 가지 이유로 자국의 수요에 충분히 생산할 수 없기 때문에 추가 공급량을 수입해야 한다.

어떤 나라들은 너무나 가난해서 식량을 수입할 수도 없고, 자립으로 재배할 수도 없다. 이런 나라들은 경제 개발이 필요하고, 경제 성장의 이익을 국민들에게 공정하게 분배하는 것이 필요하다.

(8) 새로운 기술과 향상된 유통 방법이 미래의 세계에 식량을 공급할 수 있을 것이다. 새로운 식량들이, 예를 들면 콩과 다른 단백질이 풍부한 오일 씨앗들로 만들어지고 있다. 유전 공학이 질병과 가뭄에 저항이 강한 새로운 작물들을 개발하는 데 도움을 줄 것이다. 언젠가는 바다에서도 더 많은 식량이 생산될 수 있을 것이다.

그러나 지금 가장 필요한 것은 식량이 부족한 국가들의 발전이다. 그런 국가들이 스스로 미래를 위한 기본적인 결단을 내린다 해도, 그들을 지원하려는 커다란 국제적인 노력 또한 필요할 것이다.

9. 아이스크림의 역사는 수수께끼이다. 언제 어디서 사람들이 먹기 시작하였는지 아무도 정확히 모른다. 로마 황제 네로가 노예들을 산으로 보내서 눈을 가져오게 하여 꿀과 과일로 달게 맛을 내어 먹었다는 이야기가 있다. 우리는 마르코폴로가 저 유명한 아시아 여행 중에 맛을 낸 얼음을 먹어 보았다고 알고 있는데, 1295년에 그가 이탈리아로 돌아올 때 조리법을 가져왔기 때문이었다.

맛을 낸 얼음의 조리법은 1500년대에 이탈리아에서 유럽의 다른 지역으로 퍼져 나갔다. 궁중의 요리사들은 주인들을 기쁘게 하기 위해 꾸준히 새로운 조합을 실험하였다. 어느 시점에서 크림과 버터가 조리법에 첨가되었고, 그 새로운 것을 '크림 아이스'라고 했다.

아이스크림이 미국에서 처음으로 만들어진 것이 언제인지는 정확히 알려지지 않고 있다. 아이스크림에 관해 최초로 알려진 미국의 참고문헌들 가운데 하나는 1786년 뉴욕의 어느 신문에 낸 어느 선술집의 광고에 서였다. 제임스 매디슨 대통령의 부인 돌리 매디슨이 1800년대 초에 백악관에서 아이스크림을 처음으로 내놓았다. 1800년대 내내 '아이스크림 친목회'가 친구를 접대하는 인기 있는 방식이 되었다. 오늘날도 사람들은 여전히 전기나 손으로 돌리는 아이스크림 기계로 집에서 아이스크림을 만드는 재미를 맛볼 수 있다.

10. (1) 냉장고가 광범위하게 이용되기 전에는 육류를 신선할 때 먹거나 아니면 소금절이나 훈제 과정으로 보관하였다. 소금절이 육류는 부패를 방지하기 위해 소금에 많이 절인다. 오늘날 절임 과정은 소금과 물, 때로는 설탕의 용액을 고기 속에 주입하는 것으로, 대부분 맛을 향상시키는 데 이용된다. 훈제는 장작을 태우는 연기에 고기를 노출시켜 절이는 과정으로 역시 고기에 뚜렷한 맛과 향을 준다. 훈제된 육류로는 대부분의 햄, 베이컨, 소시지 등이 있다.

다른 두 가지 육류 보관 방법은 통조림과 냉동이다. 샌드위치용 버터나 잼, 칠레고추, 비프스튜, 소금절이 쇠고기 해시 요리 등의 육류를 포함한 통조림 식품은 수년 간 개봉되지 않고 보관될 수 있다. 육류는 냉동할 수도 있지만, 제한된 기간 동안만 가능하다. 요리하지 않은 쇠고기와 양고기는 냉동실에서 6개월까지 (요리하면 3개월까지) 보관될 수 있고, 요리하지 않은 돼지고기와 송아지 고기는 4개월 간 (요리하면 2개월 간) 얼려 보관될 수 있다.

(2) 육류는 영양소가 많다. 지방, 단백질과 어느 정도의 탄수화물을 함유하고 있고, 철과 동, 칼륨, 인산 등, 무기물의 훌륭한 원천이다. 육류는 또 비타민 B1, B2, B6, 판토텐산, B12 등을 함유하고 있다.

고기를 얻으려고 도살되는 동물의 많은 부위는 먹을 수가 없다. 예를 들어, 전형적인 수송아지 무게의 절반 정도가 실제 쇠고기이다. 그러나 나머지가 버려지지는 않는다. 거의 모든 부위가 어떤 목적에 사용될 수 있다.

육류 동물의 분비샘은 펩신, 코티손, 인슐린 같은 약품을 만드는 데 사용된다. 송아지 가죽과 돼지 가죽은 의복과 운동 장비를 포함하여 가죽 제품으로 만들어진다. 돼지털은 솔과 실내 가구를 만드는 데 사용된다. 동물의 지방은 비누, 화장품, 동물의 사료가 된다. 뼈, 뿔, 발굽은 단추, 본 차이나, 젤라틴아교, 풀 등으로 만들어진다. 양털은 털실과 의복으로 변한다. 기타 못 먹는 부위들은 비료로 사용된다.

11. (1) 식품에는 여러 가지 화학 요소들이 함유되어 있지만, 일반적인 기능을 하는 식품에서 우리가 얻게 되는 영양소라고 하는 어떤 필수 요소들이 있다. 우리의 신체는 에너지와 성장을 위해 그리고 손상된 조직을 아물게 하기 위해 이 영양소들을 이용한다.

인체의 건강에 활력이 되는 주요 영양소 집단이 6가지 있다. 단백질, 탄수화물, 지방, 비타민, 무기물, 그리고 물이다. 모든 필수 영양소들이 세포를 도와 일반적인 기능을 하게 하는 반면에, 단백질, 탄수화물, 그리고 지방은 인체에 에너지를 공급하는 영양소들로 킬로칼로리로 측정된다. 1칼로리는 물 1그램의 온도를 섭씨 1도 높이는 데 필요한 열에너지의 양과 같다. 비록 식품 에너지가 기술적으로 킬로칼로리로 설명되지만, 대부분은 흔히 그냥 칼로리로 표현된다.

(2) 다른 일부 영양소와 달리, 물은 신체에 에너지를 공급하지 않는다. 그럼에도 불구하고, 물은 몇 가지 중요한, 어쩌면 무엇보다도 가장 중요한 기능을 한다. 물은 인체에서 일어나는 모든 화학 과정들을 위한 환경을 제공한다. 혈액의 한 가지 성분으로서 물은 인체의 모든 세포에 영양소를 날라다주고, 세포에서 노폐물을 배출시킨다. 이 무미건조한 액체는 신체를 냉각시키는 데 결정적으로 중요하다. 또 신체의 노폐물을 오줌으로 배설시킨다.

인체는 기능을 하기 위해 하루에 약 2.5리터의 물이 필요하다. 개인은 다른 영양소 없이는 몇 주일을 살 수 있지만, 물이 없이는 일주일 이상을 버틸 수 없다. 다행히 물은 쉽게 구할 수 있다. 우리는 물을 마시기도 하고, 또 음료수나 과일, 채소에서 물을 섭취하기도 한다. 기타 고체 식품들 또한 물을 함유하고 있다. 그러나 과일이나 채소보다는 훨씬 적은 양이다.

12. 중독 환자를 도울 수 있는 몇 가지 응급조치가 있다. 환자가 의식이 있으면서 경련이 없다면, 우유나 물을 반 컵 정도 마시게 한다. 다음, 복용한 독약의 종류를 판단한다. 독약이 약물이거나, 농약, 또는 유독 식물이라면 환자를 토하게 한다. 토제 시럽을 주는 것은 사람을 토하게 한다. 소금물이나 겨자는 토하기를 유도하는 데 사용해서는 안 된다.

그러나 석유 제품이나 가성 제품을 삼킨 사람은 토하게 해서는 안 된다. 이 두 가지 독극물은 토할 때 더 많은 문제를 일으킬 수 있다. 석유 제품은 폐에 들어갈 수도 있고, 화학적 폐렴을 일으킬 수 있다. 인체 속으로 내려 갈 때 식도나 위장에 화상을 입히는 가성 독극물은 토하는 동안 다시 올라오면서 더 많은 화상을 일으킬 수 있다.

세제액, 4염화탄소 같은 독극물을 흡입한 사람은 즉시 열린 창가로 데려간다. 이렇게 하면 그 사람이 신선한 공기를 들이마시고 4염화탄소를 내 뱉게 할 수 있다. 어떤 사람이 세제액이나 살충제 같은 독액을 피부에 쏟았을 경우에는 물로 씻어 내야 한다.

13. 쌀은 여러 가지로 쓰인다. 풍부한 식품 에너지를 제공하지만, 균형 있는 식사를 제공하기 위해서는 다른 식품들이 필요하다. 북미에서는 장곡, 중곡, 단곡 3부류의 쌀이 있다. 모두 똑 같은 식품 가치가 있다. 그러나 장곡 쌀은 밥이 건조하게 되는 경향이 있다. 중곡과 단곡 쌀은 촉촉하고 굳게 밥이 된다.

쌀은 삶거나 쪄서 또는 아침 시리얼 형태로 먹을 수 있다. 제분 제품인 쌀가루는 빵이나, 설탕, 전분, (얼굴 화장용) 분, 풀 등을 만드는 데 사용된다. 쌀을 발효하여 와인을 만들 수 있다. 그런 와인을 일본에서는 사케라 하고, 중국에서는 삼슈, 인도에서는 아락이라 한다. 쌀은 또 맥주의 성분인 맥아를 만드는 데도 사용된다.

제분된 쌀에서 나오는 껍질과 겨는 농장 동물을 먹일 수도 있다. 껍질은 또 농장이나 실험실 동물들을 위해 바닥을 깔아 주거나, 깨지기 쉬운 제품들을 포장할 때, 또는 연료로 사용되기도 한다. 아시아에서는 볏짚이 종이를 만들거나 매트, 모자, 바구니, 지붕을 이는 재료로 사용된다.

14. 좋은 차를 만들기 위해서는 신선한 물을 사용하여 완전히 끓인다. 차를 위한 주전자는 미리 데워 사용한다. 물 한 컵에 분말 차 한 스푼씩을 주전자나 주전자 안에 있는 차 여과기 안에 넣는다. 차에다 끓는 물을 붓는다. 3~5분 동안 차가 우러나게 한다. 차가 너무 오래 우러나면 쓴맛이 나게 된다.

티백으로 차를 한 잔 만들려면, 신선한 물을 사용해 완전히 끓인다. 티백을 넣기 전에 컵을 미리 데운 다음, 끓는 물을 담는다. 3~5분 정도 우려낸 다음 티백을 꺼낸다.

50% 정도 더 많은 차 잎으로 만드는 아이스 티는 얼음이 녹을 동안 놔둔다. 차는 얼음이 $\frac{2}{3}$정도 차 있는 큰 잔에 담는다. 개인의 취향에 따라 얇게 썬 레몬이 곁들여지고, 설탕이 첨가된다. 때로는 클로브, 빻은 오렌지 껍질, 또는 민트 등의 향료가 첨가되기도 한다.

15. 채소들은 수확 후에 지속되는 시간의 길이가 다르다. 채소가 수확되는 성장 단계는 선적, 처리, 저장 후의 질과 관련이 많다. 예를 들어, 흔히 토마토는 장거리로 선적될 경우 아직 푸를 때 수확된다. 덩굴이 마른 토마토는 일반적으로 맛이 아주 뛰어나서 지역 생산지나 텃밭용으로만 소비할 수 있다. 완두콩과 강낭콩은 꼬투리와 껍질 속에 있으면 아주 오랜 기간 저장된다.

흰 감자, 고구마, 양파, 당근 같은 많은 채소는 서늘한 온도에서 몇 달 간 저장될 수 있다. 건조 저장법은 원시인 시절부터 사용되었다. 옛날에는 채소가 동굴에 저장되었다. 오늘날은 특별히 지은 건물들이 각기 최적 온도와 습도에서 채소를 저장해 준다. 건물들은 흔히 냉장으로 서늘하게 된다.

오랫동안 도시 주변에는 매일 시장에 농산물을 내가는 소규모 트럭 농장들이 있었다. 나중에는 채소가 냉장된 철도 차량으로 장거리를 실려 갔다. 그러나 최근에는 많은 특화된 대형 농장들이 특정 작물을 재배하기에 최적 지역에 설립되었다. 들에서 포장하고 장거리 냉장으로 운송하여 신선한 채소를 신속하게 시장에 배달하는 것을 가능케 하였다. 어떤 경우에는 최상의 상태에서 멀리 떨어진 시장에 도착할 수 있도록 채소가 비행기로 운송되기도 한다.

제 3장

1 ① **2** ② **3** ⑤ **4** ④ **5** ⑤ **6** ⑤ **7** 1. (1) ① (2) ③ (3) ③ 2. ①
8 1. (1) ① (2) ③ 2. ⑤ **9** 1. ① 2. ② **10** 1. ④ 2. ⑤ **11** 1. ① 2. ① 3. ① 4. ② 5. ④
12 1. ⑤ 2. ③ **13** 1. ① 2. ⑤ **14** 1. ④ 2. ⑤ 3. ③ **15** 1. ④ 2. ④ **16** 1. ④
2. ① **17** ③ **18** ④ **19** ① **20** ④ **21** ⑤ **22** ③ **23** 1. ⑤ 2. ①
24 1. ③ 2. ① **25** ② **26** 1. ③ 2. ③ **27** ⑤ **28** 1. ② 2. ⑤ 3. ① **29** 1. ④
2. ④

1. 낙태는 태아가 어미 몸 밖에서 충분히 살 수 있을 정도로 발달하고 성장하기 전에 임신을 초기에 끝내는 것이다. 낙태가 임신 20주 전에 자연스럽게 생긴다면, 자연 유산 또는 조산이라고 한다. 만약 낙태가 의료 절차와 같은 인공적인 수단으로 발생된다면, 유도 낙태라고 한다. 미국에서는 유도 낙태의 윤리적 법률적 측면에 대한 논쟁이 만연하다. 낙태반대운동 회원들은 낙태가 도덕적으로 나쁘고 규제되거나 금지되어야 한다고 믿고 있다. 자신들을 낙태 합법화 지지자라고 하는 다른 사람들은 여성들이 낙태를 할 것인가 말 것인가를 스스로 선택할 권리를 가져야 한다고 믿고 있다. 1973년 로우-웨이드 사건에 미국 연방 대법원은 여성이 임신 3개월 동안 낙태를 금지당해서는 안 된다고 판결을 하였다. 그 후, 법원은 낙태에 대해 여러 규제를 허용하였다. 예를 들면, 부모가 알 권리나 24시간 대기 기간을 주 정부에서 요구할 수 있다.

2. 늙음에 대한 또 다른 연구는 동물의 나이와 성장률에 관한 사실들을 수집하는 것이다. 동물의 생명을 유지해 주고 죽을 때를 기록하여 동물 사망의 원인을 연구하기란 매우 힘들다. 이유는 많은 동물들이 우리 자신들이 사는 수명의 절반밖에 살지 못하기 때문이다.

우리가 알아봐야 할 것은 혼합된 동물 집단에서 각기 다른 나이로 사망하는 원인이다. 이것은 우리가 각각의 나이를 알아야 한다는 것을 뜻한다. 그런데 야생 동물은 출생증명서가 없다. 비록 기록이 결코 완전하지 않다 해도, 우리는 대부분 연구 기록에 의존해야만 한다. 그러나 드문 경우, 규칙적으로 성장하는 동물 신체의 일부 조직을 통해 동물의 나이를 알 수 있다. 어떤 동물의 껍질, 뼈, 이빨은 매년 고정된 수의 반점이나 테를 그린다. 우리가 테를 세어 보고서 나무의 나이를 알 듯이 우리는 이 동물들의 나이를 알 수 있다.

3. 에이즈의 이해에는 커다란 진전이 있었다. 그 질병을 일으키는 바이러스는 1983년에 HIV(인체 면역결핍 바이러스)로 확인되었다. 과학자들은 사람들이 감염되었는지를 확인하기 위한 혈액검사를 발전시켰다. 이런 검사는 바이러스와 싸우기 위한 노력으로 신체가 생산하는 물질인 에이즈 항체를 찾고 있다.

그러나 연구원들이 에이즈 치료제를 찾기까지는 여전히 멀다. 병의 진전을 늦추는 약품은 발견되었다. 그러나 그것들은 치료제가 아니고, 심각한 부작용을 일으킬 수도 있다. 사람들을 에이즈로부터 보호하는 백신도 아직은 없다. 그것이 발견되기까지는, 최선의 방어가 그 병을 확산시키는 행동들을 하지 않도록 사람들을 가르치는 데에 있다.

4. 알코올 중독의 정확한 원인은 알 수 없지만, 이 병과 관련된 문제들은 치유될 수 있다. 알코올 중독자에게는 어떤 형태로든 알코올의 사용을 영원히 피해야 한다.

이 목표를 달성하기 위해서, '알코올중독자 자주(自主)치료 협회' (Al-Anon) 같은 단체들은 환자들에게 안내와 지원, 희망을 준다. 의사, 심리학자, 훈련 받은 상담원들은 환자를 도와 회복 계획에 들어가도록 동기를 부여한다. 사설 재활 센터들이 중독자를 도와 회복하도록 설립되었다. 많은 대기업들 역시 알코올 중독인 직원들을 돕는 프로그램들을 수립하였다.

알코올중독자 가족들이 환자들의 문제점을 잘 이해

하도록 도와주는 여러 프로그램들이 수립되었다. Al-Anon은 알코올 중독자의 가족과 친구들을 위한 것이다. Al-Anon의 한 부서인 Alateen은 알코올 중독 가족 속에 살고 있는 12살에서 20살까지의 청소년들을 위한 것이다. ACOA는 알코올 중독자 부모와 함께 성장하였기 때문에 문제를 가지고 있는 성인들을 도와준다. 치료나 예방법의 연구는 이 중요한 건강 문제를 해결하는 데 도움을 줄 것이다.

5. 모든 마취제는 이점과 해가 있다. 다목적용 단일 마취제는 없다. 의사들은 환자와 수술의 종류에 따라 가장 적절해 보이는 것을 선택한다. 그들은 어느 특정한 하나의 마취제를 선택할 수도 있고, 아니면 여러 가지를 함께 사용할 수도 있다.

좋은 마취제는 환자에게서 통증을 없애 주고, 안전하고 믿을 수 있어야 한다. 대부분의 경우에, 수술이 성공적으로 진행되도록 근육이 이완되어야 한다.

이상적으로는, 마취제는 복용하기 좋아야 하고, 환자를 신속히 잠들게 하고, 심장과 폐에 가능하면 가장 적은 영향을 주어야 하고, 아무런 불쾌한 후유증을 남기지 않고 금방 사라져야 한다.

환자가 마취를 준비하도록 도움을 주기 위해 마취전 약이 주어진다. 그 약은 마취제가 부드럽게 작용하고, 특히 어린이들에게서 화를 삭이게 해준다. 전마취제로 가장 흔하게 쓰이는 약은 환자를 졸리게 하는 데머롤과 세코날, 환자를 이완시키는 발리움이 있다. 이 약들은 또 메스꺼움 같은 마취의 후유증을 줄이는 데에 도움을 주기도 한다.

6. 최초의 성공적인 수혈은 500년 전에 남미의 잉카인들에 의해 행해졌다. 한 잉카인이 다쳐서 많은 피를 쏟은 고통을 겪었을 때, 환자는 건강한 다른 사람에게서 피를 받았다. 잉카 의사들은 튜브를 사용해 다친 사람과 혈액 기증자를 연결하였다.

세계의 다른 여러 지역의 의사들도 수혈을 해보려고 시도하였으나, 수혈을 하였을 때, 흔히 수혈자들이 사망하였다. 의료 전문가들은 잉카인들이 모두 같은 혈액형을 가졌을 가능성이 높기 때문에 수혈이 성공하였다고 생각하고 있다. 같은 혈액형을 가진다는 것은 그들끼리 위험한 수혈 반응이 일어날 부담 없이 혈액을 주고받을 수 있다는 것을 의미할 것이다.

7. (1) 인체에는 수백 종 이상의 다른 세포들이 있다. 각기 해야 하는 특별한 임무가 있고, 그 임무에 적합한 특별한 형태를 가지고 있다. 같은 종류의 세포들이 모여 흔히 조직을 만든다. 혈액 세포들은 예외이다. 그것들은 모이지 않는다. 그것들은 혈관을 통해서 홀로 이동한다.

조직이란 같은 종류의 세포들의 섬유질이다. 예를 들어, 근육은 근육세포들로 구성된 조직이고, 신경조직은 신경세포들로 구성되어 있다. 4가지의 주요 조직이 있다. 신체의 표면을 덮고 있는 상피조직, 신체의 각 부분을 지원하고 연결을 도와주는 연결조직, 신체 운동을 가능케 하는 근육조직, 온 신체로 신경 부호들을 운반하는 신경조직 등이다.

각기 다른 종류의 조직이 신체의 기관들로 결합된다. 하나의 기관은 신체의 다른 부위들을 위한 한 가지 이상의 특별한 임무들을 수행하는 하나의 신체 부위이다. 심장, 폐, 위, 두뇌, 피부 등이 모두 기관이다.

함께 작용하는 기관들의 집단을 체계라고 한다. 예를 들어, 심장, 혈액과 혈관을 순환계라고 한다. 코, 식도, 기도, 폐는 호흡계를 형성한다. 신장(콩팥)과 방광은 비뇨계를 구성한다. 신체의 체계들은 한 팀의 구성원들과 같다. 각기 특정 임무를 가지고 있으나, 그것들은 함께 신체가 일하고, 놀고, 성장하고, 다른 여러 기능들을 수행하는 것을 가능케 한다.

(2) 여러분이 알고 있는 대로, 인체는 복잡한 화학적 기계이다. 단순한 화학 물질들이 복잡한 고분자들로 만들어진다. 일부 고분자들은 세포를 형성하는 다양한 조직으로 엮어진다. 그 세포 내부에는 수백 가지의 화학반응들이 진행되고 있고, 효소라는 다른 고분자들이 이 반응들에 촉매작용을 한다. 이 화학반응들은 새로운 세포를 만드는 에너지를 제공하고, 신체의 여러 기능들 곧, 근육을 움직이고, 생각하는 기능 등을 수행한다. 각 세포는 독자적인 단위이지만, 그러나 신체 기계를 부드럽고 효율적으로 작동하기 위해 다른 세포들과 협력한다.

8. (1) 우리가 기억이라고 부르는 정보를 두뇌는 어떻게 어디에 저장을 할까? 그것은 물어 보기는 쉽지만,

대답하기는 어려운 질문이다. 인간의 두뇌에서는 피질 영역이 관련된 것으로 보인다. 이 영역들이 약한 전류에 자극을 받을 때, 그 사람은 과거의 경험들을 '되살린다.' 겉으로는 이런 전기 자극이 두뇌로 하여금 과거부터 그 안에 저장되어 있는 경험을 재생하게 한다. 어떤 영역이 손상되면 결국 기억을 잃어버리게 된다는 것 또한 알려진 사실이다.

그러나 이것은 이 영역들이 두뇌 속에 정보가 저장되어 있는 자리임을 뜻하지는 않는다. 정보가 저장되는 방법에 관한 어떤 것도 말해 주지 않는다. 어떤 과학자들은 기억 저장이 실제는 화학적이라고 생각한다. 즉, 각 신경세포들이 그 속에 화학적으로 부호화된 정보를 가지고 있다고 생각한다. 다른 과학자들은 기억을 신경 구조 속에서 생기는 어떤 영구적인 변화의 결과라고 믿고 있다.

(2) 오늘날 여러 나라의 과학자들은 사람과 다른 동물의 뇌를 연구하고 있다. 최근에는 전기 장비가 발달하여 과학자들로 하여금 신경세포가 생성하는 작은 전기 신호들을 관찰하게 하고 있다. 이 신호들은 뇌의 작용에 관한 아주 중요한 정보를 제공한다. 다른 기구들은 뇌의 어떤 부분의 활동을 자극하거나 방지하기 위해 실험자들에게 소량의 전기 사용을 가능케 한다. 이런 방법들은 두뇌 속의 경로들을 추적하고, 세포들의 연결을 발견하고, 그리고 신호들이 어떻게 한 곳에서 다른 곳으로 보내지는지를 보기 위해 사용되어 왔다. 이 실험들은 또한 두뇌의 다른 영역들이 어떤 기능들을 제공하는지 말해 주기도 한다.

그럼에도 불구하고, 우리는 두뇌 내부에서 진행되고 있는 기본 과정들을 찾아내기 시작하였다. 우리가 더 많은 것을 알게 되면서, 여러 새로운 의문들이 생긴다. 두뇌는 모든 기관 중에서 가장 복잡한 것이다. 그리고 사람들이 계속해서 살아 있는 신체의 작동에 대해 의문을 가지는 한, 과학자들에게 그것은 하나의 도전일 것이다.

9. (1) 영양의 무질서, 호르몬의 불균형, 어떤 바이러스의 감염, 면역 체계의 무질서 등 모두가 암의 발전에 기여할 수 있는 요소들로 확인되었다. 예를 들어, 인체 면역결핍 바이러스에 의해 생기는 에이즈는 림프종과 육종이 발생할 위험성을 증가시킨다. 유전적 변종도 암을 유발시킬 수 있다. 이런 변종들이 유전된다면, 온 가족이 특정한 종류의 암을 일으킬 높은 위험성을 안고 있을 수 있다.

발암 물질이라는 어떤 물질들은 건강한 세포를 암세포로 바꿀 수 있다. 이 물질들은 세포 내의 유전적 변종들과 상호작용을 함으로써 그렇게 한다. 발암 물질의 예는 벤젠 같은 화학 물질, 석면 같은 섬유질, 자외선 햇빛, X선, 방사능 요소 같은 다양한 원천의 복사가 있다. 담배와 담배 연기 같은 일부 물질은 많은 다양한 발암 물질을 가지고 있다. 연구원들은 발암 물질이 서로 상호작용을 하여 발암의 위험성을 크게 증가시킬 수 있다는 사실을 발견하였다. 예를 들어, 폐암의 알려진 최고의 위험성은 우라늄 광부로 일하는 흡연자에게 있다.

(2) 어떤 눈에 띄는 증상들이 나타나기 전에도 여러 가지 암을 찾아내기 위한 특별한 검사들이 시행될 수 있다. 그 예로는 너무 작아서 느낄 수 없는 유방암을 찾아낼 수 있는 X선인 유방암 사진이 있고, 대변의 혈액을 검사하여 대장암을 알려줄 수 있는 실험실 검사가 있다. 정기적으로 시행할 때, 이와 같은 절차들이 초기 진단으로 도움이 된다. 이것들은 암의 발생률을 줄였고, 암에 걸린 사람들이 치료될 수 있는 기회를 증가시켰다.

종양이 암이라고 생각되면, 한 조각의 종양 조직을 떼어내 현미경으로 검사를 하는 조직 검사라는 절차를 한다. 종양 세포의 외형은 종양이 양성인지 또는 악성인지를 드러내고, 또 그 질병의 과정을 예측하게 도와준다.

평가는 암이 확산된 정도를 판단하는 데 이용된다. 이 정보는 효과적인 치료 과정을 계획하기 위해서 필수적이다.

10. (1) 옛날에는 우리가 치아가 아프면 어머니께서 입 안에 정향(丁香)을 넣어 주시고는 그 매운 맛이 통증을 막아 주기를 바랬었다. 치통이 계속되면, 어머니는 우리를 동네 대장장이나 이발사에게 데려가셨고, 운이 좋으면 의사에게 데려가셨다.

당시에는 치아를 치료하고 보존해 주는 치과의가 없었다. 대장장이나 이발사는 멋지고 강한 집게로 힘세게 잡아당겼다. 그런 식의 구강 치료로 생긴 문제는 대부분의 사람들이 중년이 될 때에는 치아가 거의 남아 있지 않았다는 것이다.

오늘날 치의학은 현대 보건의 중요한 부분이다. 치과의사들은 전문직으로서, 그 주된 임무가 치아와 구강을 보호하는 것이다. 그들은 치아, 잇몸, 볼, 입술, 혀, 입천장, 아래 · 윗니의 맞물림 등과 관련된 보건 분야에서 교육을 받는다.

(2) 인간의 치아는 젖니와 영구치로 두 번 자란다. 태어날 때는 일반적으로 치아가 보이지 않는다. 그러나 잇몸 아래에 20개의 젖니와 32개의 영구치가 형성하기 시작한다.

젖니는 아기가 태어난 지 6개월에서 1년 사이에 나오기 시작한다. 아기가 3년이 될 때까지는 윗니 10개와 아랫니 10개인, 20개의 젖니 1세트를 가지게 된다.

6살쯤 되면, 입 안쪽의 마지막 젖니 뒤에서 영구치가 나기 시작한다. 비슷한 나이에 입 앞쪽에서는 젖니가 흔들리기 시작한다. 나중에는 모든 젖니가 흔들려서 빠져 버린다. 젖니가 하나씩 빠질 때마다 영구치로 교체된다. 대부분의 어린이들이 11살이 될 때까지는 모든 젖니가 영구치로 교체된다.

입 안에서 나오는 마지막 영구치는 세 번째 어금니이다. 세 번째 어금니는 흔히 '지혜의 치아' (우리는 '사랑니' 라고 함)라고 한다. 왜냐하면 그 치아는 어릴 때의 젖니가 교체된 지 한참 뒤인 10대 후반에서 20대 초반에 나오기 때문이다.

11. (1) 상한 음식을 먹은 뒤의 구토와 같이 갑자기 찾아오는 질환은 급성으로 여긴다. 반면에, 만성적인 상태에서는 증상이 계속되거나, 몇 개월 또는 몇 년을 두고 이따금씩 돌아온다. 어떤 질병은 만성이었다가 급성으로 되기도 한다. 예를 들면, 당뇨병은 만성 질병으로 신체가 당분을 적절히 이용하거나 저장하지를 못한다. 당뇨 환자들은 흔히 특정한 음식을 먹거나, 어떤 약을 복용하거나, 호르몬 인슐린을 주사함으로써, 증상을 완화시켜 비교적 정상적인 생활을 영위할 수 있다. 그러나 당분을 너무 많이 섭취하거나 인슐린을 너무 많이 주사하는 당뇨 환자는 갑자기 급성 증세를 보여 의식을 잃게 될 수도 있다.

(2) 1940년대까지는 전염병이 세계 여러 지역에서 사망의 주원인이었다. 박테리아와 바이러스가 전염병을 일으킬 수 있는 주요 세균 집단이다. 박테리아는 독소라고 하는 독을 생산하여 신체를 손상시키고, 바이러스는 그것들이 감염시킨 세포를 죽일 수 있다. 식물 같은 버섯균, 미세한 동물 같은 원생동물, 수많은 벌레 등 다양한 기생 생물(숙주의 신체에 기생하는 작은 생물)들이 인간에게는 발병의 원인이 될 수 있다.

(3) 호르몬은 내분비선이라고 하는 조직에서 생산되는 화학적 메신저이다. 호르몬은 성장과 생식 외에도 여러 가지 중요한 신체 기능의 관리를 도와준다. 특정 호르몬을 너무 많이 또는 적게 생산하는 결과를 가져오는 내분비선의 장애는 심각한 질병을 일으킬 수 있다. 예를 들어, 뇌하수체의 장애는 왜소 발육증(성장 호르몬이 너무 적음)이나 거인증(성장 호르몬이 너무 많음)을 낳는다. 갑상선 호르몬은 신체의 화학적 반응이 얼마나 빨리 발생하는지 그 판단을 도와준다. 이런 호르몬이 너무 적으면, 사람이 둔하고 뚱뚱해지고, 너무 많으면 사람을 긴장하게 만들어 신경과민, 체중 감소, 불면증으로 고통을 겪게 한다.

여러 가지 내분비 호르몬은 여러 가지 복잡한 방법으로 상호 작용한다. 예를 들면, 일반적인 성(性) 발육은 생식 기관(여성의 난소와 남성의 고환)에서 생산되는 성호르몬뿐만 아니라 뇌하수체와 부신에서 분비되는 호르몬에 의해서도 영향을 받는다.

(4) 알츠하이머병은 치매의 한 형태로서, 마음이 제 기능을 하지 못하게 되는 상태이다. 이 질병은 새로운 기억을 습득하고 오래된 기억을 상기시키는 정보처리에 필요한 뇌의 여러 곳에 있는 신경세포를 변질시킨다. 이 장애를 가진 사람들은 또렷하게 기억하고 생각하는 능력을 점차 상실한다. 병이 진행되면서 알츠하이머병을 가진 사람들은 스스로를 돌볼 수 없게 된다. 그들은 혼동이 되고 식사하는 일도 잊어 버리게 되고, 집을 나와 방황하며 길을 잃을 수도 있다. 알츠하이머병의 발병 위험도는 나이와 함께 증가한다. 80세가 넘은 사람들의 약 20%가 장애를 일으킨다.

과학자들은 이 병의 원인과 치료법을 찾기 위해 연구하고 있다. 현재의 연구는 환경 요인과 함께 유전적인 요인도 발병에 어떤 역할을 한다고 지적하고 있다.

(5) 볼거리는 침샘을 붓게 하는 바이러스성 질병이다. 이것들은 입 안의 습기인 침을 만드는 분비샘이다. 분비샘은 혀 밑 턱뼈와 귀 앞에 있다. 귀 앞에 있는 것은 귀밑샘(이하선)이라고 한다. 이것들은 볼거리에서 가장 흔히 부어오르는 것들이다. 이것들이 부어오를 때는 씹거나 삼키기가 아프다. 두통이 볼거리의 또 다른 증상이다.

볼거리는 특히 어른이 걸렸을 때는 췌장이나 고환 같은 다른 분비샘을 붓게도 한다.

그러나 볼거리는 주로 5~15세 어린이들의 질병이다. 바이러스는 공기나 오염된 물체를 통해 이 사람에게서 저 사람에게로 퍼진다. 어떤 사람이 바이러스에 노출된 다음 볼거리가 발병하기까지는 2~3주일 걸린다. 흔히 사람들은 한 번씩 볼거리에 걸린다. 대부분의 어린이들은 생후 15개월쯤 되었을 때 볼거리 면역 주사를 맞는다.

12. (1) 과거에 질병에 대한 의학적 지식이 부족하였다는 것은 사람이 어떤 질환에서 나을 기회가 적었다는 것을 의미한다. 사람이 아플 때 흔히 의사들은 질환을 정확하게 확인할 수 없었고, 그 원인을 진단할 수도 없었다. 치료 역시 주로 위로와 휴식, 단순한 가정 치료로 이루어졌다. 그 결과 인간의 수명은 아주 짧았다.

대부분의 인류역사를 통해 존재하는 이런 상황은 20세기에 극적으로 바뀌었다. 의학 지식의 폭발은 의사들이 많은 질환을 아주 정확하게 진단하고 성공적으로 치료하는 것을 가능케 하였다. 진단과 치료의 향상은 오늘날 사람들을 더 건강하고 오래 살게 해주었다.

(2) 대개 우리의 신체는 스스로 '치료' 한다. 많은 질병의 징후나 증상들은 실제로 우리의 신체가 특정한 질병과 어떻게 싸우는지 증거를 보여준다. 열은 비록 몸을 불편하게 만들지만 우리를 아프게 하는 병원균을 억제하거나 죽이는 것을 돕는다. 감염된 상처에 있는 고름은 종기를 일으키는 박테리아를 섭취하거나 죽이는 백혈구 세포에서 온 것이다. 임파선은 감염과 싸우는 항생제를 생산할 때 확대된다. 우연히 독극물을 삼켰을 때도, 우리는 위에서 그 물질을 토하거나 배출해 냄으로써 반작용을 하기도 한다. 또는 그 물질은 설사를 통해서 신체에서 배출된다.

질병 치료의 첫째 규칙들 가운데 하나는 신체 자체의 방어 능력을 도와주라는 것이다. 예를 들어, 후두염에 걸렸다면, 약하고 더운 소금물로 양치질을 함으로써 감염의 일부분을 씻어낼 수 있다. 설사나 구토로 고생을 할 때, 신체는 많은 양의 물과 염분을 잃으므로, 물을 마셔서 보충해 줄 필요가 있다. 그리고 치료 방법으로 휴식을 잊지 말아야 한다. 휴식은 신체가 모든 에너지를 질환과 싸우는 데 이용하도록 도와주는 것이다.

13. (1) 신체는 침입하는 미생물들을 방어하는 여러 가지 방법을 가지고 있다. 신체를 덮고 있는 피부와 입, 코, 기타 구멍에 입힌 점막은 대부분의 세균을 쫓아내는 장벽의 역할을 한다. 미생물이 가까스로 혈류나 체세포 속에 들어올 때는 몇 가지 방어 작전에 들어간다. 침입 미생물에 손상된 세포들이 화학적 메신저들을 파견한다. 일부 메신저들은 혈관을 누출시켜, 혈액은 조직 속에 누적되고 부어오른다. 다른 화학적 메신저들은 두뇌 속의 특수 관제 센터에 도착하여 발열이라고 하는 체온의 상승을 일으킨다.

조직을 감시하는 백혈구는 화학적 구조 신호를 포착하여 감염 지역으로 이동한다. 그곳에서 그것들은 미생물들을 먹어 치운다. 말 그대로 그것들을 먹어서 소화시켜 버린다. 다른 종류의 백혈구는 질병 미생물 같은 외부 요소들을 인식하고, 신체 자체의 물질과 그것들을 구별해 낸다. 여전히 다른 백혈구는 특정 세균을 공격하는 매우 특수한 방어 물질인 항생제를 생산한다.

이런 방어 물질은 각기 질병을 방지하는 데에 중요하지만, 그 어느 것도 모든 질환에 효과적이지는 않다.

(2) 건강을 보호하기 위해서는 여러분이 할 수 있는 모든 것을 하는 것이 중요하다. 건강한 사람은 나약하고 쇠약한 사람보다는 질병 세균을 훨씬 더 잘 이겨낼 수 있다. 젊었을 때 건강을 유지하는 사람은 역시 노년에도 좋은 건강을 지속할 수 있는 더 좋은 기회를 가지고 있다.

건강을 보호하는 최선의 길은 균형 있는 식사(생선, 육류, 우유, 녹색과 황색 채소, 과일 등을 포함)를 하고, 매일 어떤 종류의 운동을 하며, 매일 밤 8~10시간의 수면을 취하고, 몸을 청결히 하고, 정기적으로 의사의 검진을 받는 일 등이다.

질병을 피하기 위해서는, 전염될 수 있는 질환을 가지고 있는 사람들을 여러분이 알고 있다면, 그 사람들 가까이 가기를 피하는 것이 현명할 것이다. 칼에 베이거나 긁힐 경우, 감염을 막기 위해 비누와 물로 상처를 씻거나 국부 소독제를 사용함으로써, 패혈증 같은 질병을 피할 수 있다.

아프게 되더라도, 여러분은 악화되거나 더 심각한 질병에 합병되는 것을 막기 위한 조치를 취할 수 있다. 이렇게 하는 최선의 길은 휴식을 취하고, 식사를 적당히 하고, 약을 복용하라는 의사의 지시를 따르는 것이다.

14. (1) 의료 윤리는 의사들에게 환자들을 보살필 때 어떻게 행동해야 하는지를 말해주는 규칙이다. 예를 들어, 의사들은 환자들의 프라이버시를 존중해야 한다. 환자가 의사에게 말하는 어떤 정보나 어떤 진찰 결과도 환자의 동의 없이는 누구에게도 말해서는 안 된다.

현대 의료 기술이 중환자의 생명을 연장시킬 수 있기 때문에, 오늘날 의사들은 때때로 심각한 의료 윤리의 문제들과 마주치게 된다. 예를 들어, 환자가 영원히 의식을 잃거나, 회복의 희망이 없을 때, 의사와 환자의 가족은 질환을 언제 치료하고, 얼마 동안 치료할 것이며, 언제 치료를 그만 둘 것인지를 결정해야 한다. 이것들은 매우 내리기 어려운 결정들이다. 어떤 사람들은 치료를 그만두는 것이 안락사의 한 형태라고 믿고 있다. 그런 행위의 윤리성은 격렬한 논쟁과 의견이 일치되지 않는 문제이다. 의사들은 이 문제들을 숙고해야 하고 동시에 환자들의 권리와 의사를 존중해야 한다.

(2) 의사와 환자가 만날 때는, 일반적으로 많은 것들이 일어난다. 첫째, 의사는 환자와 이야기를 하고, 환자의 문제나 관심사에 대해 많은 질문을 한다. 이런 질문들은 환자의 건강 이력(뼈를 다쳤거나 심하게 아팠던 병력), 가족, 습관(흡연 등), 일상(식사와 수면 시간 등) 등에 관한 정보를 포함한다. 이 모든 것이 환자의 의료 기록이라고 한다.

다음, 의사는 신체적 검사를 한다. 이것은 신체의 정밀 검사로서, 환자의 건강에 관한 추가적인 정보를 의사에게 제공한다. 때때로 의사는 신체의 작동을 들여다보고 들어보기 위해 특별한 전등이나 도구들을 사용한다.

건강 기록과 신체검사가 끝난 뒤에도, 의사는 더 많은 정보가 필요할 수가 있다. 이 경우 체액(혈액이나 소변)의 실험실 검사와 X선이나 다른 특별한 과정을 통해 얻는다. 이 모든 정보를 가지고 의사는 환자에 대한 결론 또는 진단을 내린다. 그리고 환자는 의사로부터 치료를 받거나 권유를 받는다. 이것들은 약을 먹거나, 수술을 받거나, 특별한 식이요법이나, 운동 프로그램을 시작하는 것을 포함한다.

(3) 현대 의료와 의사들이 당면한 문제들이 끊임없이 변하고 있어서, 의과대학은 그 내용과 스타일을 시대에 따라 맞추어야만 한다. 오늘날 학교에서 학생들은 해부학, 생화학, 생리학에서 소아과학, 외과학, 정신의학에 이르는 의학 과목들을 공부한다. 그들의 학습은 병원과 의원뿐만 아니라 강의실에서도 이루어진다. 의료 윤리의 문제들도 토론을 한다. 그들은 똑같이 중요한 문제인, 사려 있고 유익한 방식으로 환자들과 관계를 맺는 방법을 배운다.

일반 대학 4년과 의과대학 4년을 마친 뒤에 학생은 의사 학위를 받는다. 그리고 선택한 분야에서 전문의가 되기 위해 병원에서 수련의 교육과정에 들어간다. 이것을 의과대학원 교육이라고 하고, 2년에서 10년 이상까지 지속된다. 그것은 신임 의사에게 환자 진료에서의 부가적인 경험을 제공한다.

의과대학이나 수련의 과정 기간에, 학생은 특별한 시험을 마친다. 이 시험은 의학박사 학위를 주게 되고, 수련의 교육은 의사에게 자신의 주에서 환자들을 돌볼 수 있는 면허를 얻게 한다. 미국에서는 면허가 없이 어떤 의사도 진료를 할 수 없다. 의사의 사무실 벽에서 그것을 찾아 보라.

15. 열이나 어떤 화학 물질, 전기 또는 방사능에 노출되는 것은 화상이라고 알려진 일종의 피부 손상을 일으킨다. 화상은 정도에 따라 분류된다. 1도 화상은 빨갛고 통증이 있으며, 피부의 최상층부만 해당된다. 2도 화상은 빨갛게 붓고 물집이 생긴다. 그것은 피부의 둘째 층으로까지 확대된다. 3도 화상은 검은 색 또는 갈색이 되거나, 때로는 하얗게 반점이 생긴다. 그것은 피부 아래 조직에까지 확장되고 생명이 위험하기도 하다.

화상의 치료 방법은 그 원인에 달려 있다. 열 화상과

햇볕 화상은 찬물에 담그거나 젖은 천으로 싼다. 일단 화상 부위가 시원해진 다음 살균 밴드로 느슨하게 싼다. 화학적 화상은 흐르는 찬물에 담가야 한다. 전기 화상의 응급치료는 현장이 안전하고, 화상을 일으킨 전기가 단절되었을 경우에만 해야 한다. CPR(심폐기능소생술)이 필요 없다면, 화상을 마른 살균 밴드로 싸 주어야 한다.

16. (1) 병원에는 종류가 많다. 어떤 병원은 정신적인 질환, 만성 질병, 암 등으로 고생하는 환자들만을 치료한다. 다른 병원은 어린이나 노인들 같은 특정 연령 집단의 환자들만의 치료를 전문으로 한다. 그러나 미국에서 가장 많은 병원은 단기치료 종합병원이다. 이 병원들은 30일 이상의 입원을 요하지 않는 모든 종류의 질환이나 상처를 가진 환자들을 치료한다.

미국에는 약 6,800개의 병원이 있다. 이 병원들은 25명 미만의 환자를 수용하는 병상을 가진 작은 시골 의료시설에서부터 3,000병상 이상을 가진 대형 도시 병원에 이르기까지 크기가 다양하다.

(2) 대부분의 병원은 지역사회에서 눈에 띄는 중요한 부분이 되기 위해 열심히 일한다. 병원이 제공하는 모든 서비스를 대중에게 알리는 것을 임무로 하는 홍보 전문가를 고용한다.

대부분의 병원은 많은 환자 교육과정을 무료로 또는 적은 비용으로 제공한다. 이 프로그램에는 예비 부모들, 체중 관리, 금연 클리닉, 특정한 질병으로 고생하는 지역사회의 주민들을 위한 집단 모임 등을 위한 강좌가 포함된다. 많은 병원에서 CPR(심폐기능소생술)도 가르친다. 무료 혈압 검사를 해주기도 하고, 알코올과 약물남용 치료과정을 운영하기도 한다.

17. 어떤 사람들은 신장을 하나만 가지고 태어난다. 다른 사람들은 어떤 질병으로 인해 신장을 하나 잃을 수가 있다. 연약한 신장이 비록 두꺼운 지방층으로 보호받고 있지만, 신체에 강한 타격을 받아 손상을 입을 수가 있다. 그것이 권투에서 신장을 가격하는 것이 규정에 어긋나는 이유이다. 그러나 신장이 어떤 식으로 손상을 입든지, 하나만 가지고도 정상적이고 건강한 삶을 사는 것이 가능하다.

두 개의 신장은 신체의 노폐물과 독소를 제거하고, 체액의 균형을 조절하며, 적절한 혈압 범위를 유지해 주는 똑같은 임무를 정확히 수행한다. 일생 동안 이 놀라운 기관들은 작은 호수를 채우기에 충분한 1백만 갤런이 넘는 액체를 정화한다. 그러나 한 개의 신장이 이 엄청난 임무를 담당할 수 있다. 사실은, 신장 하나가 제거되면, 남은 신장이 전체 임무를 감당하기 위해 두 달 안에 50%까지 크기가 증대된다.

18. 정신적으로 건강한 사람들은 살아 있는 것이 즐겁고 자신에 대해서도 만족스럽다. 이것은 그들이 언제나 완전히 행복하고 만족한다는 뜻이 아니다. 그들도 성공과 실패, 오르막과 내리막이 있다. 그러나 그들은 일반적으로 미래에 대해 희망적이다. 그리고 그들은 삶의 일상적인 문제들을 대처함에 있어 합리적으로 성공한다.

훌륭한 정신 건강을 가지는 것은 다른 사람들과 같아지는 것을 의미하는 것은 아니다. 당신은 많은 시간을 혼자서 보내기를 좋아하는 조용한 사람일 수도 있고, 또는 매우 사교적이고 개방적일 수도 있다. 여러분은 다른 사람들과 다른 느낌과 생각, 관심을 가질 수 있다.

중요한 것은 여러분이 현실 속에서 살 수 있다는 사실이다. 여러분은 자신의 재능과 능력을 이용하고 다른 사람과의 관계를 즐기는 방식으로 삶의 도전들을 대처할 수 있다.

정신적으로 건강한 사람들은 자신들을 알고 있다. 자신들의 한계를 인식하고 있지만, 자신을 좋아하고, 자신의 가치를 느끼고 있다. 그들은 자신들이 인간이고 완전하지 않다는 사실을 받아들인다. 그들은 여전히 성장하고 변화하려고 노력한다. 분노, 공포, 좌절, 질투 등 여러 감정을 가지는 것이 정상이라는 점을 그들은 알고 있다. 그러나 그들은 또 이런 감정들에 대해 자신들을 통제하는 것도 알고 있다.

19. 많은 신체적 질병과는 달리 대부분의 정신 질환은 알 수 있는 한 가지 원인을 가진 경우가 없다. 다른 많은 것들이 사람을 정신적으로 혼란하게 한다. 그러나 어떤 정신 질환은 신체적 원인을 분명하게 알 수 있었다. 감염으로 인해 고열을 느끼는 사람들은 너무나 정신이 없어서 자신들이 누구이며 어디에 있는지를 알지

못한다. 이 상태를 정신착란이라고 한다. 그 증상은 감염이 없어질 때 사라진다. 어떤 사람들은 오랫동안 제대로 음식을 먹지 못했을 때 정신 질환을 갖게 된다. 그들은 식사가 제대로 주어질 때 회복된다. 노인들은 또렷하게 생각하는 능력을 상실할 수가 있다. 이것은 행동을 통제하는 뇌세포에 해를 입히는 노인병인 뇌동맥 경화가 원인일 수 있다.

어떤 사람들이 정신 질환을 얻은 이유에 대한 단순한 해답은 없다. 그 중 많은 사람들은 자신감을 쌓을 수 없는 불행한 조건에서 살아왔다. 어떤 사람들은 다른 사람들의 일행에서 이탈하여 홀로 살아왔을 수도 있을 것이다. 그들은 쓸모 없거나 사랑받지 못한다고 느끼게 되었을 것이다. 그들은 자신들의 성취에 대해 가족들로부터 인정을 받지 못했을 수도 있다. 그들은 자신들이 어쩌지 못하는 외모나 태도의 어떤 것 때문에 조롱을 받았을 수도 있다. 이들이 사랑받고 인정받는 가정에서 자란 사람들보다 더욱 정신 질환을 일으키기 쉽다.

20. 삶의 모든 순간에, 심지어 잠을 잘 때에도, 인체의 일부 근육은 작용을 한다. 이 글을 읽을 때도, 미세한 근육이 여러분의 눈동자를 앞뒤로 움직이게 하고, 단어들이 잘 보이도록 도와준다. 책장을 넘길 때는 팔과 손에 있는 근육이 작용한다. 비록 여러분이 가만히 앉아 있어도 등에 있는 근육은 몸을 구부정하게 되지 않도록 작용하고 있다. 동시에 신체 내부의 다른 근육은 여러분이 호흡을 하고, 가장 최근에 섭취한 음식물을 소화하도록 도와준다.

650개가 넘는 근육이 인체의 근육계를 구성하고 있다. 정상적인 성인 체중의 거의 절반에 해당하는 이 강하고 탄력 있는 조직은 모든 신체의 움직임을 책임지고 있다. 걷기, 달리기, 뛰기 같은 움직임은 쉽게 보인다. 그러나 근육은 눈동자를 떴다 감았다 하고, 음식물을 장 속으로 넣고, 혈액이 신체를 통해 흐르게 하는 등의 다른 움직임도 책임지고 있다.

21. 모든 진통제는 신체에 효과를 낸다. 거의 모든 신체 체계에 작용하지만, 가장 강하고 가장 두드러진 효과는 신경계에서다. 진통제는 뇌와 척수로 구성된 중앙 신경계의 활동을 완화시킨다. 그 결과는 모든 행동이 완화되고, 과민성과 노여움이 약화되며, 졸음이 온다. 아주 소량의 진통제라도 의식을 들게 하고 나가게 할 수 있다.

아프거나 심한 통증이 있는 사람에게는, 진통제가 생산하는 효과가 많은 필요한 위안을 준다. 사실, 통증을 제거하는 진통제의 능력은 그 약의 가장 중요한 의학적 적용이다.

진통제의 다른 효과로는 눈동자의 동공을 축소시키고, 현기증, 메스꺼움, 구토, 가려움, 혈압 저하 등의 증세들이 있다. 특정한 개인에 대한 정확한 효과는 진통제의 종류, 복용의 양, 복용 방법, 복용 빈도 등에 달려 있다.

22. 1854년에 크림 전쟁이 발발하였다. 뉴스는 곧 러시아 크림에 있는 병원의 끔찍한 상황을 런던에 전했다. 플로렌스 나이팅게일은 자신의 병원이 아주 성공을 거두어서 영국 정부의 전시 장관인 시드니 허버트는 그녀에게 전쟁 지역에 가서 간호 부대를 지휘할 것을 요청한다. 그녀는 그것을 수락하고, 1854년 10월 21일에 38명의 간호사를 데리고 크림으로 배를 타고 떠났다. 그곳에서 그녀는 소위 병원이라는 곳에 5,000명이 넘는 부상자와 환자들이 있는 것을 발견하였다. 그곳은 의료는 물론이고 심지어 평범한 청결 상태를 유지하는 시설도 없는 벌거벗은 건물이었다.

한번에 20시간을 밤낮으로 일하면서 플로렌스 나이팅게일은 몸소 매일 모든 병동을 검열하였다. 그녀는 장교들과 의료진들의 질시로 곤란을 겪기도 했지만, 그녀는 이겨냈다. 그녀는 병원에 장비를 갖췄고, 위생적으로 만들었다. 군대가 그녀를 존경하였기 때문에, 그녀는 병사들의 치료에 혁명을 일으킬 수 있었다.

23. (1) 사람들을 돕는 것은 간호의 일이다. 간호사는 삶과 죽음의 상황을 다루기 때문에, 그들은 정확하고, 방심하지 않고, 훌륭한 판단력을 가져야 한다. 그들은 실제로 사람들을 보살피고 도와주기를 원해야 한다. 그들 스스로 신체적으로나 정신적으로 건강해야 한다.

그리고 간호는 간호 보조사에게 필요한 능력에서부터 간호학자에게 요구되는 능력에 이르기까지 광범위한 능력을 가진 사람들에게 건강 관리에서의 만족스러운 직업을 제공한다. 사람은 교육과정을 선택하기 전에 자신의 학구적인 능력과 직업 목표를 고려해야 한다.

직업 선택권은 많고 다양하다. 그것은 초기에 주의 깊은 계획을 세워야 바라는 목표를 충족시키는 데 시간과 돈을 절약할 수 있기 때문이다.

전세계적으로 간호사가 많이 필요하다. 그러나 어떤 나라에서는 그 필요가 절실하다. 간호사가 크게 부족한 곳에서는 전문 간호사들의 감독 아래 간호보조 요원이나 기타 보조 요원들이 실제로 환자들을 간호하는 많은 일을 하기도 한다. 전문 간호사들은 가르치고, 감독하고, 가장 고도로 숙련된 간호에 필요하다.

(2) 많은 환자들이 자신들을 낫게 하는 데 도움을 줄 간호사들을 필요로 한다. 병원에는 환자들을 돌보는 간호사들이 있어서 치료를 하고 투약을 한다. 그러나 때로는 환자가 집에서 간호를 받을 수도 있다. 그때 가정 간호사가 필요하다.

집안 운영을 책임지는 사람들이 흔히 가정 간호의 임무를 수행한다. 의사의 감독에 따라 그들은 일반적인 간호를 한다. 사람들이 심하게 아파서 고도의 숙련된 간호를 받아야 할 때는, 전문 간호사의 근무가 필요할 것이다.

가정 간호사로서 일하는 사람의 첫째 임무는 가정 의사(주치의)에게 자문을 해주고, 질환의 징후를 설명해 준다. 의사는 그때 환자를 진찰하고, 간호와 치료에 관한 완전한 지시를 남긴다. 의사는 약과 특별한 식단을 처방할 수도 있다.

24. (1) 사람들은 언제나 식량을 구하고, 기후로부터 자신들을 보호할 수 있는 의복과 은신처를 만들고, 삶을 보다 편안하게 만들어 주는 여러 가지를 생산해야 했다. 간단히 말해, 사람들은 살기 위해 일해야 한다. 그리고 일하면서, 사람들은 생명과 건강을 위협하는 많은 위험에 노출된다.

직업적인 건강과 안전의 분야는 이런 위험성을 줄이는 것과 관계된다. 이 분야에서 일하는 사람들로는 화학자와 안전 기술자 외에도 의사, 간호사, 기타 건강 관리 전문직이 있다. 그들은 어떤 특정한 작업에 흔한 사고와 질병들을 줄이고 제거하는 길을 찾으려고 노력한다.

(2) 가장 쉬운 일 조차도 수행하기가 어려운 신체 장애를 가진 사람들이 많이 있다. 출생 때 나타나는 어떤 장애들은 영구적이다. 사고나 질병의 결과로 생긴 장애는 일시적일 수 있다. 장애자들은 전신 마비, 신체 불구, 시각 장애, 또는 청각 장애가 있다. 그들은 팔이나 다리 하나, 또는 어떤 근육을 움직이는 능력을 잃었을 수도 있다.

이런 신체적인 문제점들은 흔히 정서적인 문제로 이어진다. 자신들이 한때 했던 일이나 친구들이나 가족들이 할 수 있는 일을 자신들이 할 수 없기 때문에 장애자들은 자주 우울증에 걸린다. 때때로 정서적인 문제들은 신체적인 문제들만큼이나 치료하기 힘들다.

작업 요법은 장애자들이 행복한 삶을 영위하도록 도와주는 치료의 한 가지 형태이다. 잘 계획된 프로그램을 통해서 작업 치료사들은 장애자들이 스스로 하기, 학습, 작업, 레저 등, 여러 활동들을 수행할 수 있도록 가르쳐 준다.

25. 오랫동안, 대부분의 사람들은 신체 건강이 얼마나 중요한지를 깨닫지 못했다. 하지만, 오늘날 우리는 양호한 신체 조건을 유지하는 것이 삶을 보다 즐겁게 할 뿐만 아니라 더 오래 살게 도와주기까지 한다는 것을 알고 있다. 그것이 바로 오늘날 수백만의 사람들이 매주 여러 차례 어떤 종류의 운동에 열심히 참가하는 이유이다.

신체 건강에는 네 가지 기본이 있다. 첫째, 좋은 영양 원칙에 따라 현명한 방식으로 식사를 해야 한다. 둘째, 많은 휴식과 수면을 취해야 한다. 이것이 성장기에는 절대 필요하고, 그리고 평생을 두고 중요하다. 셋째, 훌륭한 위생과 건강 습관을 실천해야 하고, 담배나 진통제 같은 해로운 물질들을 피한다. 넷째, 운동을 많이 해야 한다. 운동은 근육과 심장, 폐 등을 좋은 기능 상태로 유지해 준다. 운동에는 여러 가지가 있으나, 세 가지 기본 종류가 신체 건강에 필요하다. 유산소 운동, 탄력 운동, 근육강화 운동 등이 그것들이다.

26. (1) 공중 보건은 사람들이 질병을 관리하고 예방하기 위해 전문화된 과학적 방법과 기술, 신뢰 등을 이용하여 지역사회의 보건을 측정하고 개선하며 유지하는 일이다. 공중 보건 프로그램은 흔히 정부 기관으로부터 재정과 행정의 관리를 받는다. 이 기관들은 노인, 만성 질환자, 장애자, 중독자, 가난한 사람들 같이 발병

위험성이 높은 사람들을 위한 특별 프로그램들을 개발한다.

의사가 환자를 진단하고 치료하는 방법과 비슷한 방식으로 공중 보건 기관도 지역사회를 진단하고 치료한다. 첫째, 기관은 특정 질병에 감염되었을 가능성이 있는 사람들을 면밀하게 진찰하여 진단을 내린다. 어떤 사람들이나 집단이 위험하다고 판단되면, 기관은 질병이나 장애의 실제적인 위험성이 얼마나 될지 평가를 내린다. 기관은 각기 독특한 지역사회에 맞춘 예방책들을 계획하고 이행하기 위해 이 정보를 이용한다. 예를 들어, 전염병이 발병하는 동안, 공중 보건 기관은 그 질병의 원인과 더 확대될 가능성을 조사하여 대응한다. 그 다음 전염되지 않은 사람들을 보호할 뿐만 아니라 모든 전염자들을 치료하기 위한 프로그램을 개발하고 조정한다. 위급한 상황이 끝난 뒤에, 기관은 미래의 발병을 예방하기 위한 어떤 계획을 공식화한다.

(2) 많은 사람들은 공중 보건 서비스의 성과가 흔히 드러나지 않기 때문에 그 중요성과 범위를 깨닫지 못하고 있다. 공중 보건 서비스는 전염병, 식수 오염, 불량 식품 등의 주요 재난을 예방한다. 건강의 중요성을 무시하면 대가를 치른다. 매독과 결핵의 재등장이 그런 것처럼, 에이즈 전염병은 1980년대에 모든 사람들에게 주요한 공중 보건의 위협으로 등장하였다.

건강은 의사, 치과의사, 간호사, 공중 보건 종사자들을 포함하는, 열심히 일하고 헌신하는 전문가들의 조직인 공중 보건 체제만의 책임이 아니다. 건강은 모든 개인의 책임이다. 공중 보건 권고 사항들을 명심함으로써, 사람들은 이제 전보다 더 자신의 건강과 지역사회에 있는 다른 사람들의 건강을 보호할 수 있다.

27. 지난 100년 동안 적십자는 전시(戰時) 봉사만 하는 프로그램을 가진 조직에서 항상 봉사를 하는 조직으로 변화를 하였다. 몇몇 유럽 국가에서는 적십자가 간호사 교육 센터의 역할을 하는 병원과 의원을 소유하고 운영하고 있다. 또한 지역사회 공중 보건 종사자들의 교육을 돕는다. 아프리카 신생국들과 아시아 국가들에서 적십자사들의 일상 업무는 사람들에게 건강과 위생의 좋은 습관을 교육하는 것이다. 캐나다에서는 적십자사가 수질 안전, 응급 처치, 일반 건강을 포함하는 아동과 성인용 프로그램을 가지고 있다.

많은 적십자사들은 헌혈 프로그램을 가지고 있거나 참가하고 있다. 자원자들에게서 헌혈을 받아 보존 처리하여 민간이나 군대 병원과 의사들에게 나누어준다. 대부분의 적십자사들은 적십자 하급 지사들과 재난 구조 프로그램을 가지고 있다. 재난 구조 프로그램은 광범위한 것으로, 지역사회 대비 태세, 긴급구조 활동, 재난 희생자들이 스스로 재활할 수 있을 때까지 보살피는 일들을 망라하고 있다. 어떤 나라들은 적십자 구급단을 훈련시켰다.

모든 적십자사들은 전쟁이나 기타 재난으로 서로 헤어지거나 잃어버린 가족들을 찾아 주기 위해 국제적인 탐색에 참가하고 있다.

28. (1) 백신이 작용을 하는 것은 그것들이 감염에 대해 방어를 하기 위해 신체를 자극하기 때문이다. 이런 방어는 신체의 면역 체계의 일부이다. 면역 체계의 임무는 감염이나 질환으로부터 신체를 보호하는 것이다.

박테리아와 바이러스같이 질병을 일으키는 조직체(병원균)들이 신체에 들어갈 때, 면역 체계의 어떤 세포들은 항생제를 만들기 시작한다. 항생제는 질병 조직체들이 대량 감염을 일으키는 것을 막을 수 있는 화학물질이다. 면역 체계 세포들은 각 형태의 질병 조직체에 대해 특수 항생제를 만든다. 다른 세포들은 그 조직체들을 직접 공격하여 신체에서 그것들을 제거하는 작업을 한다.

사람이 어떤 전염병에서 회복한 후에, 그 특정 질병에 대한 일부 항생제와 방어 세포들은 신체 안에 남는다. 만약 같은 질병 조직체들이 또 다시 신체 속으로 들어오면, 그 방어 물질은 질환의 예방을 도울 준비가 되어 있다. 이것이 우리가 홍역이나 풍진 같은 어떤 전염성 질병들이 재발하는 경험을 좀처럼 하지 않는 까닭이다. 신체의 방어 물질이 어떤 질병의 감염을 막을 때, 그 사람은 그 질병에 대한 면역을 가지고 있다고 한다.

(2) 면역은 신체가 침입 병원균으로부터 자신을 방어하도록 도와준다. 병원균의 공격을 받을 때, 신체는 항생제라고 하는 물질을 만든다. 항생제는 병원균과 병원균이 생산하는 독소와 싸운다.

어떤 질병은 일부러 그 병원균 또는 독소를 신체 안

에 넣어서 예방할 수 있다. 이것을 백신 또는 예방 접종이라 하고, 그 물질을 백신이라고 한다. 어떤 종류의 백신에서는 병원균이나 독소가 약화되어서 무해하게 된다. 다른 백신에서는 병원균이 죽었다. 하지만 약하고 죽은 병원균이나 독소라 할지라도 신체로 하여금 항생제를 만들게 한다. 나중에 신체가 이런 질병을 일으키는 병원균의 침략을 받게 되더라도, 신체는 그 질병과 싸우는 데 필요한 항생제의 보호를 받는다.

대부분의 백신은 주사로 투입된다. 면역 절차는 소아마비, 디프테리아, 파상풍, 홍역, 볼거리, 백일해, 폐렴의 일종 등, 매우 다양한 질병에 대항하여 보호를 해줄 수 있다.

태어난 첫 해에 아기는 흔히 많은 질병에 대한 백신을 맞는다. 좀 더 크면 두 번째 예방주사를 맞는다. 두 번째 예방주사는 처음의 백신에 의해 생산된 면역을 강화해 준다.

(3) 때때로 질환이나 사고가 신체 조직에 너무 심한 손상을 입혀서 더 이상 정상적인 기능을 할 수 없을 때가 있다. 그때 손상된 부분을 교체하기 위해 조직 접합 또는 이식이라고 하는 수술을 실시할 수 있다. 피부같이 건강한 조직을 신체의 한 부위에서 떼어내 다른 부위에 접합시킬 수 있다. 신체는 그것이 동일한 유전 지표를 가지고 있기 때문에 이식된 조직을 받아들인다. 문제는 어떤 사람의 조직 또는 기관을 떼어내 다른 사람에게 이식할 때 발생한다. 그때 면역 체계는 그 이식 부분을 외래의 것으로 인식하고 공격을 개시한다. 이런 일이 발생할 때는 면역 체계의 공격을 완화시키기 위해 특별한 약을 사용한다.

신체가 다른 유전 지표를 가지고 있는 세포들을 공격하더라도, 어떤 유전 지표들은 화학적으로 다른 것들보다 좀더 비슷해서 면역 반응을 적게 일으킨다. 유전 지표는 각기 부모에게서 물려받은 유전자에 의해 암호화되기 때문에 형제자매들은 똑 같지는 않더라도 비슷한 유전 지표를 가지게 될 확률이 높다. 같은 유전 지표를 가지게 될 유일한 사람들은 일란성 쌍둥이일 것이다. 왜냐하면 그들은 같은 유전자를 공유하기 때문이다.

29. (1) 바이러스가 증식하기 위해서는 어떤 종류의 세포를 필요로 한다. 식물 바이러스는 식물 세포에서만 증식하고, 동물 바이러스는 동물 세포에서만 증식한다. 어떤 바이러스는 동물에 있는 어떤 종류의 세포를 감염시키기만 하는 동물 바이러스처럼 아주 특이하다.

숙주 세포를 감염시킨 후에는, 한 개의 바이러스가 수백 또는 수천 개의 비슷한 바이러스를 생산할 수 있다. 바이러스는 유전자 속에 생의 주기를 알 수 있는 필수 정보를 가지고 있는 한편, 숙주 세포는 바이러스가 살고 증식하는 데 필요한 에너지, 조직, 서식 공간, 생산 효소를 제공한다. 새로운 바이러스들은 질서 있게 단계적인 과정으로 만들어진다. 모든 바이러스가 이용하는 단계는 1) 흡착 2) 입장 3) 바이러스 부위의 합성 4) 조합 5) 방출이다.

(2) 그것은 모든 시대 최대의 살인자 중에 하나로 기억될 것이다. 파라오 람세스 5세가 최초의 희생자가 된 기원전 1157년 이후, 천연두는 수백만의 사람들을 죽이거나 눈멀게 하고, 얼굴을 추하게 만들면서 세계의 모든 나라를 휩쓸었다.

그 치명적인 바이러스를 박멸하는 첫걸음이 영국인 의사 에드워드 제너가 천연두 백신을 개발한 1796년에 있었다. 백신이 천연두를 예방하였지만, 그 질병에 걸린 사람들을 위한 치료는 없었다. 세월이 흐르면서 천연두와 싸우기 위해서는 세계적인 백신 프로그램이 필요하다는 사실이 명백해졌다.

1967년, 세계보건기구는 강력한 백신 프로그램을 시작하였다. 수백 명의 보건 요원들이 감염 국가에 가서 천연두에 걸린 사람들을 격리시키고, 걸리지 않은 사람들에게 백신을 주사하였다. 캠페인은 성공적이었다. 1980년에 WHO는 세계에 천연두가 없어졌음을 선언하였다. 인간이 정복한 최초의 질병이었다.

제 4 장

1 1. ③ 2. ④	**2** ③	**3** 1. ④ 2. ③ 3. ①	**4** ①	**5** ①	**6** 1. ⑤ 2. ③	
7 1. ⑤ 2. ① 3. ⑤	**8** ③	**9** 1. ② 2. ① 3. ① 4. ③		**10** ③	**11** ②	**12** ③
13 ①	**14** ④	**15** 1. ① 2. ①	**16** ③	**17** 1. ④ 2. ④	**18** ③	

1. (1) 예를 들어, 산업 공장이나 자동차 엔진에서 석유, 석탄, 가스 등 화석 연료가 연소할 때, 아황산가스와 산화질소가 공기 중에 배출된다. 오염 통제 장치가 없는 산업용 굴뚝 하나가 매일 아황산가스를 500톤이나 배출한다.

일부 대도시에는 자동차가 배출하는 산화질소와 탄산가스가 너무나 많아서 공기가 그것들로 채색되었다. 산화질소는 또 농업용 비료가 분해되면서 공기 중에 들어온다. 기타 산성 화학 물질은 소량으로도 발생한다. 염산은 흔히 굴뚝에서 직접 나온다. 일산화탄소와 이산화탄소는 자동차에서 배출된다.

(2) 매년 미국과 캐나다에서는 수백만 톤의 산성이 비로 내린다. 이 산성의 농도는 아주 약해서 화상을 일으키지는 못한다. 그러나 다른 덜 심한 영향을 준다.

산성비가 금속 물체에 떨어지면, 그 물체는 바람직하지 못한 식으로 변화를 시작할 수 있다. 만약 그 과정이 몇 년 간 지속될 경우, 반짝이는 물체들은 흐릿하게 되고, 금속 물체들은 부식하여 강도를 잃거나 부서진다. 산성비는 석상이나 석재 또는 벽돌 건축물들의 표면에도 영향을 준다.

산성비가 알루미늄에 작용하는 방식은 또 다른 심각한 문제를 일으킨다. 알루미늄은 일반적으로 흙 속에 있다. 산성비가 토양을 산성화하면, 흙 속의 알루미늄은 물에 녹아, 식물에 흡수되고, 그것은 식물의 뿌리 세포를 손상시킬 수 있다. 동물 세포 역시 알루미늄에 매우 민감하다

인간 역시 산성비의 영향 때문에 위험에 처할 수 있다. 습한 공기 속에서는, 산성 에어로졸에서 나오는 고농도의 오염 물질들이 폐 기능에 영향을 주는 것이 실험적인 연구에서 발견되었다. 천식과 폐기종, 만성 기관지염 등으로 고생을 하는 사람들은 산성 환경에 더 민감하다. 현재 수준의 에어로졸 산도에 사람들이 영향을 받는지를 결정하기에는 부가적인 연구들이 필요하다.

2. 대기 성분의 작은 변화들이 지구 표면의 대기를 덥게 하는 원인이 될 것이라고 많은 과학자들은 생각한다. 그들은 우리 대기에 있는 이산화탄소, 메탄, 이산화질소 등 많은 양의 가스들이 증가하고 있어서 놀랐다. 이 가스들은 태양으로부터 지구에 도달하는 복사를 가두어 두는 경향이 있다. 우리가 받는 복사의 양은 불변하기 때문에, 만약 우리 대기로부터 빠져나가는 복사가 더 적다면, 대기는 더 더워질 것이다.

문제는 생각해야 할 요인들이 많기 때문에 복잡하다. 예를 들어, 지구의 표면 대기가 더워진다면, 더 많은 물이 지표에서 증발할 것이다. 이것은 구름의 형성, 바람과 비의 양과 패턴에 영향을 미칠 것이다. 이 두 가지 변화는 세계의 기온에 영향을 줄 수는 있지만, 그러나 정확히 그 영향들이 얼마나 지속될 것인지 완전히 이해되지 않는다.

과거 여러 해의 기록은 기온 상승을 보여주지만, 그 상승이 냉각기로 방해를 받았다. 지금까지 증거가 '지구 온난화'가 일어나고 있는지를 분명하게 보여주지는 못한다. 그러나 지구 온난화의 가능한 영향은, 일어난다면 아주 심각해서 연구가 세계적 규모로 진행되고 있다.

3. (1) 맑은 물은 생명에 필수적이다. 그러나 일부 유독한 폐기물의 투기 장소나 하수구로, 우리는 흔히 호수와 강, 그리고 특히 바다를 이용한다. 대부분의 물은 폐기물의 일부를 희석시키거나 재생할 수 있다. 그러나 많은 것은 과적 되었거나 오염되었다. 산업체들이 자신들의 폐기물을 청소하기 위해 취한 조처인 오물처리 공장들이 도움이 되었다. 우연히 바다에 유출된 기름으로 인한 오염은 문제를 증가시킨다. 배워서 관심이 있는

시민들이 세계의 물이 법률로 보호받아야 하고, 그 법률들이 지켜져야 한다는 데 앞장을 서야 한다.

개인들이 물을 보호하기 위해 할 수 있는 간단한 것들이 많이 있다. 양치질을 하는 동안 수도꼭지를 잠가둔다. 습기가 적게 증발하는 저녁에 잔디와 정원에 물을 준다. 그리고 물이 새는 수도꼭지를 고친다. 많은 양의 물을 이런 식으로 절약할 수 있다.

(2) 우리들의 가장 중요한 자원 가운데 하나는 흙이다. 흙의 맨 위층인 표토(表土)는 높은 수확량의 곡식을 생산하는 유일한 흙이다. 1인치 두께의 좋은 표토를 만들려면 거의 100년 간 주의 깊은 관리가 필요하다. 그러나 그것도 바람과 비, 범람 등으로 침식되어 금방 없어진다. 1930년대에는 미국 대평원의 광활한 지역에서 목초지가 지나친 방목과 열악한 농사법, 그리고 여러 해의 가뭄 때문에 황폐화되었다. 그 자리에 풀이 없어서 귀중한 표토가 날아가 버린 것이다. 풀과 나무가 심어지고, 땅에 공급할 물을 보유하는 저수지가 건설되기까지 그곳은 '황진(黃塵) 지대'로 알려져 있었다.

경사면을 따라 수평으로 경작을 하는 등고선 경작은 물에 의한 침식을 막는데 도움이 된다. 논밭 사이에 나무와 관목을 심는 것은 바람에 의한 침식을 막아 준다. 윤작은 흙 속의 자양분 소실을 늦춰 준다.

(3) 삼림, 공원, 야생 동물 관리 등 전통적인 직업 외에 자연보호에도 많은 직업이 있다. 모든 형태의 에너지 보존에 관한 전문가들에 대한 수요가 크다. 엔지니어들은 제조품을 재생하고 폐기물을 사용하는 새로운 방법들을 개발할 수 있다. 토양 보호론자들은 어떻게 하면 토양이 더욱 생산적이 될 것인가를 연구한다. 법률가들은 늘어나는 환경 보호 법규들로 도움을 준다. 도시 계획자들과 조경사들 역시 환경 보호 노력에 이바지한다.

환경 보호 직업을 위해서는 기초과학, 수학, 생태학 등의 과정이 특히 유용하다. 많은 환경 보호 문제들이 매우 복잡하고, 어느 하나의 학문 분야로 귀착되지 않기 때문에 폭넓은 교육이 필요하다.

4. 비누가 비록 좋은 세제이지만, 염분이 많이 든 물에 사용할 때는 욕조 속의 띠와 같은 퇴적물을 남기는 경향이 있다. 그래서 2차 세계대전 후에는 많은 사람들이 비누 대신에 합성 세제를 사용하기 시작하였다. 불행히도 많은 양의 합성 세제를 사용한 것이 제조업자들도 대중들도 예상하지 못한 여러 가지 환경문제를 일으켰다.

한 가지 문제는 표면 활성제를 포함한다. 어떤 박테리아는 하수에서 천연 폐기물질들을 먹고, 무해한 물질로 분해시켜 내보낸다. 비누 분자들은 이런 박테리아에게 신속하게 분해된다. 그러나 박테리아는 합성 세제에 처음 사용되었던 표면 활성제의 분자들은 분해할 수가 없었다. 본래의 모든 거품 능력을 유지하고 있어서, 표면 활성제는 하수 공장과 강이나 호수에서 많은 거품을 일으켰다. 거품 문제를 해결하기 위해서 합성 세제 제조업자들은 사용 후에 재빨리 분해되는 새로운 타입의 표면 활성제를 개발하였다. 1965년까지 새로운 표면 활성제의 대체가 완성되었다.

5. 사람들은 가뭄을 악화시키는 일들을 한다. 아프리카의 사헬 지방에서는 사람들이 나무를 많이 베어 낸다. 나무는 태양열을 일부 흡수한다. 일부 과학자들은, 나무가 없으면 북중앙 아프리카의 기온이 그곳에 숲이 있을 때 보다 더 더워질 것이라고 생각한다. 그래서 이런 경우에 나무를 베는 인간의 행동은 가뭄의 영향을 악화시킨다.

어떤 과학자들은 또 뉴욕시의 주민들이 다른 도시 주민들이 일반적으로 사용하는 것보다 훨씬 더 많은 물을 쓰기 때문에 가뭄을 더 악화시켰다고 믿고 있다. 그 도시의 급수 탱크는 매우 빨리 말라 버렸다. 드디어 시 당국자들이 사람들에게 잔디에 물 주기나 세차, 그리고 불필요한 물의 사용을 중단할 것을 지시하였다. 이런 조치가 취해지자 반쯤 차 있던 급수 탱크들에는 여름을 지낼 수 있을 만큼의 충분한 물이 차게 되었다.

물의 공급을 주의해서 보존하는 것이 사람들이 가뭄의 가능성에 대비할 수 있는 아마 최선의 방법일 것이다. 그러나 비가 충분히 오는 시기에는, 가뭄이 금방 발생하고 그리고 물 수급이 아주 신속하게 줄어들 수 있다는 사실을 사람들은 잊어버리곤 한다.

6. (1) 한때, 빙하시대의 추운 기후와 지진이나 화산이 원인이 된 지질의 변화 같은 자연의 격변으로 인해 생명체들이 우선적으로 위험에 처했다. 이제 식물과 동

물, 사람에게 닥친 가장 큰 문제들은 식물과 인간, 그리고 기타 동물들이 의존하고 있는 환경에 피해를 입히는 인간의 활동이다. 비록 많은 다른 인간 활동들이 멸종을 위협할 수 있다 해도, 가장 큰 문제들은 서식지 파괴 때문에 발생한다. 불법적인 사냥과 무역 그리고 새로운 종의 유입 역시 심각한 문제를 일으킨다.

(2) 서식지를 구하는 것이 생물의 종을 보호하는 초석이다. 그러나 서식지가 구해진다 해도, 어떤 종은 그 수효가 너무 적어 야생에 다시 서식하기가 어렵다. 이 중 다수는 동물원이나 공원으로 데려가 거기서 길러진다. 이들 사육 프로그램 안에서 종들은 새끼가 커서 야생으로 돌아가리라는 희망으로 길러진다. 법규와 자각, 실행과 결부된 이 같은 프로그램들은 모든 생명체들의 생존에 필요한 오묘한 자연의 균형을 유지하는 데 도움을 줄 것이다.

7. (1) 인간은 환경에 많은 변화를 주었다. 삼림을 베고 그곳에다 곡식을 심었다. 동물을 사냥하고, 다른 동물을 기르는 법을 배웠다. 인간의 발명은 연기와 유해한 화학 물질을 공기 중에 내놓았고, 호수와 냇물을 오염시켰고, 지구의 여러 곳을 소모하고 훼손하였다. 이런 인간이 원인인 환경문제들은 인간뿐 아니라 대부분의 다른 생물체들까지 위태롭게 하였다.

환경론자들은 그런 문제들을 염려하게 된 사람들이다. 그들은 인간이 후세를 위해 환경을 해치지 않고 살면서 번영할 수 있는 방법을 찾고 있다.

(2) 모든 환경에서, 모든 생명체를 구성하는 물질은 사용되고 계속해서 또 다시 사용된다. 예를 들어, 식물들은 햇빛이 있을 때 이산화탄소와 물을 이용하여 자신들의 식량을 만든다. 이 과정에서 식물들은 동물들이 호흡하는 데 있어야 하는 기체인 산소를 내놓는다. 동물들은 식물들에게 사용되는 이산화탄소를 내쉰다.

식물들이 자라면서 흙으로부터 무기물을 섭취한다. 어떤 식물들은 동물에게 먹힌다. 동물들이 죽을 때, 그 시체는 썩고 무기물들은 다른 식물들에게 다시 흡수될 수 있는 흙 속으로 되돌아간다.

이산화탄소, 물, 산소, 무기물 등 이런 물질들은 환경에서 자원이자 폐기물인 예들이다. 어떤 물질들이 한 생물체에게는 폐기물로 여겨지더라도 다른 생물체에게는 중요한 자원일 수 있다. 이래서 자원과 폐기물 사이에는 자연의 균형이 있다. 지상의 끊임없는 생명의 순환에서 각각은 중요하다.

인간은 또 자신들의 환경에서 자원을 이용하고, 폐기물을 배출해 낸다. 불행히도, 증가하는 인구를 위해 쓰려고 하였는데, 우리는 자원과 폐기물의 균형을 뒤엎어 버렸다. 폐기물은 이제 재활용될 수 있는 시간보다 더 빨리 배출되고 있다. 이런 폐기물은 더 이상 자원이 아니다. 대신, 그들이 환경을 파괴하고 있어서 오염 물질로 여겨진다. 그리고 우리 인구가 빨리 증가할수록, 오염 물질은 더 많이 배출된다.

(3) 상당한 양의 공기 오염이 발전소에서 연소되는 연료에서 비롯된다. 그러나 오염의 또 다른 형태는 열오염이라는 것으로 역시 발전소에서 비롯된다. 연료 연소와 핵발전소 모두 터빈에서 나오는 증기를 식히기 위해 거대한 양의 냉수를 사용한다. 그 결과로 물이 더워진다. 이 더운물이 강이나 항구로 돌아갈 때는, 해초의 성장을 자극할 수 있다. 물고기와 그 알을 죽이거나, 그들의 성장을 방해할 수도 있다.

물리학자들은 환경에 해를 덜 입히는 새로운 발전 방식을 연구하고 있다. 한편, 많은 발전소들은 오염이 덜한 물질을 방사하도록 현대화되었다. 또한 엔지니어들도 환경에 미치는 피해를 최소화하는 새로운 발전소들을 설계하고 설립하려고 노력한다.

8. (1) 불은 우리의 생활의 필수적인 부분이다. 비록 그것이 많은 유익한 용도를 가졌다 해도, 통제가 되지 않거나 환경문제에 영향을 미치게 되면 위험할 수 있다.

연소되는 동안에 일어나는 화학작용은 수증기와 이산화탄소를 생산한다. 수증기는 환경에 무해하다. 그러나 지구 표면 가까이 복사와 열을 가두어 두는 이산화탄소가 너무 많으면, 지표면과 대기를 점점 따뜻하게 하는 온실효과에 이바지할 수 있다.

불은 또 오염 물질을 대기 속으로 방출하기도 한다. 산업 과정에서 연료를 연소하면 아황산가스와 산화질소 같은 많은 양의 가스를 배출한다. 이것들이 대기 속에서 습기와 결합할 때 산성비를 만든다. 산성비는 식물과 수생 생물에 해를 입히고, 건축물이나 비석의 석재를 침식시킨다.

공기 오염은 전세계적인 관심사이다. 사람들은 연료를 연소하지 않고 에너지를 생산하는 방법들과, 불에서 오염 물질을 대기 속으로 배출하지 않고 잡아 두는 더 좋은 방법들을 많이 고안해 내야 한다. 불은 주의해서 사용하면, 그 혜택이 위험보다 가치가 있다.

9. (1) 산림 조성과 화재, 해충, 질병의 방제는 산림 관리의 중요한 부분이다. 또 하나는 산림 개선이다. 많은 산림이, 특히 미국 동부에서는 선별적인 벌목이 필요하다. 병들고 벌레 먹은 나무와 바람직하지 않은 수종들이 제거된다면, 남아 있는 나무들이 더 빨리 자랄 것이다. 좋은 나무들이 함께 자라는 곳에서는, 남은 나무들의 연간 총 성장률을 향상시키기 위해 일부가 베어진다. 어떤 곳에서는 땅에서 나무와 관목들을 제거하고, 건강하고 간격을 잘 맞춘 묘목들로 새로운 숲을 시작한다. 삼림 연구는 빨리 자라고, 키가 크고, 곧으며 질병에 저항이 강한 새로운 수종들을 개발하고 있다.

(2) 질병과 해충, 산불이 사람들이 벌목한 것과 거의 같은 수량의 나무를 희생하고 있다. 질병은 산불과 해충을 합한 것보다 더 많은 피해를 준다.

미국에서는 매년 약 10만 건의 산불이 난다. 그 대부분이 사람에 의한 것이다. 산불 감시탑의 감시원이나 항공기 순찰대가 신속하게 발견하면 대부분 산불의 규모는 줄일 수가 있다.

무서운 해충의 습격은 항공기나 지상에서 화학약품을 뿌려서 구제할 수 있다. 그러나 이런 화학약품들은 무해한 곤충도 죽일 수가 있다. 그리고 조류나 물고기도 죽일 수 있다. 산림학자들은 더 나은 해충 방제 방법을 찾고 있다.

어떤 질병은 화학약품을 사용하여 방제할 수 있다. 어떤 것은 병든 수종을 제거하고, 어떤 것은 병을 옮기는 식물을 제거하여 방제할 수도 있다. 그러나 현재의 방법들은 질병 피해를 약간만 줄이는 정도이다.

(3) 대기오염 문제는 열대 우림의 파괴로 악화된다. 매년 수천 에이커의 우림이 농사와 목축, 목재와 건축을 위해서 제거되고 있다.

우림의 울창한 식물들은 엄청난 양의 이산화탄소를 흡수한다. 우림의 나무들이 벌목되어 이 가스를 더 이상 흡수하지 못할 때는, 대기의 이산화탄소는 증가하여 온실효과라는 것을 만드는 데 영향을 주게 된다.

온실효과는 이산화탄소가 지표 가까이 있는 어떤 복사와 열을 붙잡고 있을 때 생긴다. 이것은 세계의 기온을 상승시키고, 기상 패턴을 변화시키고, 해수면을 상승시키는 등 세계 환경의 여러 심각한 변화를 낳는다.

온실효과를 되돌려 놓으려면 우림이 보호되어야 한다. 이것을 이룩하기 위해서 일부 환경보호 단체들이 넓은 지역의 우림을 구입하여 보호하고 있다. 어떤 나라에서는 우림이 관광지로 장려되고 있다. 어떤 경우에는 이것이 필수적인 자연 자원을 보호하는 동시에 농사나 목재보다 필요한 수입을 더 많이 올리는 것으로 나타났다.

(4) 어떤 산림은 실제로 산불이 필요하다. 많은 산림에서, 특히 습기가 거의 없는 미국 서부에서는 죽은 가지, 잔가지, 솔잎, 잎사귀들이 말라서 파삭파삭하다. 어쩌다 번갯불이나 사람의 부주의로 산불이 시작되면, 건조한 산림은 순식간에 화염에 휩싸일 수 있다.

맹렬한 산불의 위험을 줄이기 위해서, 산림 순찰대는 실제로 예방 산불이라는, 주의해서 통제하는 불을 지른다. 이런 방법으로 그들은 계획되지 않은 불이 번져가서 통제할 수 없이 불태우는 원인이 될 건조한 관목들을 미리 태워 버릴 수 있다. 예방 산불 또는 통제 산불로 산림을 처리한 후에는, 뜻하지 않은 산불이 일어날 때, 대부분의 큰 수목들을 완전히 태우기에 충분한 '연료'를 가지지 못하게 될 것이 가능한 것이다.

10. 납 복합물들은 인간과 여타 생물체에 유독한 것으로 현재 알려져 있다. 1980년 이전에 건설된 많은 주택에서는 벽과 천장, 장식에 사용된 페인트가 납을 함유하고 있을 것이다. 어린이들이 이 페인트 조각을 먹거나, 벗겨지고 갈라지는 페인트에서 나오는 납에 오염된 먼지를 흡입하게 되면, 납중독으로 발전할 위험에 처한다. 어린이뿐만 아니라 어른도 음료수나 흙, 여러 가지 세라믹 접시와 그릇, 일부 통조림 식품에 있는 납에 노출될 수 있다. 납을 사용하거나 납 광석을 제련하는 산업체에서 일하는 사람들 역시 염려해야 한다. 게

다가 이 공장들에서 나오는 폐기물은 환경을 손상할 수 있다.

납중독의 증후군은 두통과 식욕 상실, 복통 그리고 일시적인 기억상실 등이 있다. 비록 물리적인 증후군은 없지만, 납중독은 어린이의 두뇌 발달을 저해할 수 있다. 그래서 한 살에서 여섯 살까지의 어린이들은 매년 납중독에 대한 혈액검사를 받아야 한다.

이런 건강상의 위험에 대비하여 현행 법률은 가정용으로 생산되는 페인트는 납을 함유할 수 없고, 오늘날 쓰이는 대부분의 휘발유는 무연일 것을 요구하고 있다. 또한 가정과 직장에서 납에 노출되는 위험을 심각하게 인식해야 한다. 오래된 주택과 아파트, 사무실들은 벽이나 음료수, 배관 특히, 음료수용 송수관 등에 남아 있는 납의 양을 판단하는 점검을 자주 해야 한다. 산업 공장에서는 폐기물을 더욱 자세히 검사해야 한다.

11. 국립공원은 나라에서 가장 역사적일 뿐 아니라 가장 아름다운 곳들의 집합이다. 그곳들은 즐기기 위해 따로 마련되었지만 아울러 다음 세대들을 위해 보호되기도 한다. 전세계에서 매년 약 2억8천만명의 방문객들이 찾아오는 국립공원에는 365개의 산하 단체가 있다. 공원은 8천만 에이커가 넘는 땅을 가지고 있다. 이것은 전체 미국 땅의 4%에 가깝다. 천연 장소, 기념관, 사적지, 기타 지역들의 놀라운 집합은 미국의 가장 멋진 업적 가운데 하나이다.

국립공원의 설립과 보호는 전망과 보호, 힘든 작업에 달려 있다. 미국의 국립공원은 미국인들이 자존심으로 여기고, 다른 나라 사람들로부터는 경탄을 받는다. 사실은 100여개 나라들이 미국의 공원을 자국의 자연 및 역사적 장소의 집합을 설립하기 위한 모델로 삼았다.

12. 소음 공해로부터 완전히 벗어나는 길은 없을지라도, 소음 통제는 가능하다고 전문가들도 인정한다. 오늘날 대부분의 환경적인 소음 규정을 만들고 실행하는 책임은 지방 정부에 남아 있다. 이 규정들은 소음 통제를 마음에 두고 시의 주택과 교통 체계를 계획하는 것에서부터 버스에서 라디오 켜기를 금지하는 것까지 다양하다.

산업은 소음성 청각 장애에 영향을 미친다. 소음이 언어를 방해하고 경고 신호음을 차단할 때는, 업무상의 사고가 일어날 가능성을 향상시킨다. 청각보호 장치를 착용하고 동력 장치에 소음기를 장착하는 것은 작업자의 청각을 보호하고 안전을 향상시킬 수 있다.

연구를 통해서, 소리를 분리하고 흡수하는 반소음 전기장치와 건설 자재 같은 소음 통제에 도움이 되는 새로운 제품들이 개발되었다. 그러나 새로운 기술은 충분하지 않다. 소음 규제 조치를 실행하고 집행하기 위해서는 정부 지원이 필요하다. 기술과 효과적인 규제가 같이 더 조용하고 안전한 직장과 지역사회로 인도할 수 있다.

13. 현재는 우리 바다가 비교적 좋은 상태로 남아 있다. 우리는 바다의 자원이 남획되거나 오염되는 것을 허용할 수가 없다. 그 결과 미국을 비롯한 많은 나라들이 바다의 이용을 억제하고, 남획과 오염을 통한 해양자원의 파괴를 규제하는 법률을 가지고 있다.

기술적인 발전으로 우리는 오염의 많은 악영향을 막을 수 있게 되었다. 유독성 폐기물들이 육지에 묻히는 위험을 피해 바다의 소각선 위에서 소각될 수 있다. 새로운 지식과 특수장비가 대부분의 기름과 화학 물질의 해상 유출을 억제하는 데 도움을 주어, 흔히 해안에 입히는 피해를 줄이게 되었다.

바다에서 잡히는 바다 식품의 양을 제한함으로써 물고기나 귀중한 무척추동물들이 번식하게 하여, 고갈되어 가는 어종을 회복하게 하였다.

이런 예방 조치들과 기타 조치들은 우리 바다의 상태를 향상시키는 데 계속해서 도움을 줄 것이다. 그것들은 또 다음 세대들을 위해 풍부한 바다 자원을 보호해 줄 것이다.

14. 최근 몇 십 년 동안, 환경 법규와 조례들이 두 가지로 오염 방지를 도와주었다. 석유의 생산, 정유, 운송 그리고 저장하는 방법을 관리하고, 또 연료로서 연소되는 정유 제품의 질을 관리하는 것이다.

환경 법규는 또 석유가 더 이상 생산되지 않는 유정으로부터의 오염을 방지하는 방법과 유정들이 얼마나 멀리 떨어져 있어야 하는지를 지시하고 있다. 한때는 정유 공장들이 엄청난 양의 공기와 물을 오염시켰다. 그러나 이제는 그들도 정유 과정에서 오염 물질의 배출을 방지하거나 크게 줄여야 하는 많은 법규들을 지켜야 한다. 예를 들어, 정유 과정에 사용된 물이 수로로 흘러나오기 전에 정화되어야 하고 냉각되어야 한다. 만약 석유가 유조선에서 바다로 유출된다면 심각한 환경문제들이 생길 수 있다.

석유 유출은 물고기와 해양 동물, 수상 조류들을 해치거나 죽일 수 있다. 그것은 해변을 오염시키고, 해양 분지에 살고 있는 미세한 생물들을 해친다. 석유 유출은 환경뿐 아니라, 바다에 의존하고 있는 어로, 관광 등의 산업에도 영향을 미칠 수 있다.

석유 제품의 연소 역시 오염을 일으킬 수 있기 때문에, 연료의 질도 규제를 받는다. 예를 들어, 환경 법규들은 스모그와 다른 공기 오염을 방지하기 위해 휘발유가 여름에는 좀더 서서히 기화되기를 요구하고 있다. 다른 석유 제품들도 더 엄격한 환경기준을 만나게 된다. 예를 들어, 많은 법규들이 석유 제품이 함유할 수 있는 황산의 양을 제한하고 있다.

15. (1) 현재 일어나고 있는 급속한 인구 증가는 가끔 인구 폭발이라고 한다. 많은 사람들은 인구가 모든 사람들을 부양하는 데 필요한 식량, 연료, 주택 같은 자원들보다 더 빨리 성장할 것이라고 염려하고 있다. 만약 이런 일이 일어난다면, 그 첫 번째 결과는 생활 수준의 저하일 것이다. 그리고 생활 수준이 가장 가난한 사람들이 살 수 있는 최저 수준으로 떨어지면서 사망률은 상승할 것이다. 만약 생활 수준이 위험한 질병이 관리되지 못할 수준으로 떨어진다면, 사망률은 가난한 사람들뿐만 아니라 부자들 가운데도 상승할 것이다.

인구과잉의 염려는 새로운 것이 아니다. 거의 200년 전에 영국의 경제학자 맬서스는 인구 증가가 결국 생활 수준에서 만들어진 모든 소득을 앗아갈 것이라고 주장하였다. 그는 산업화 시대 초기에 글을 썼다. 그는 산업이 생산한 물질적 부(富)의 증가와 출산력을 통제할 수 있도록 개발된 안전하고도 믿을 만한 방법들을 예견하지 못했다.

(2) 세계를 한정된 자원을 가진 곳으로 보는 맬서스의 세계관에 진실은 있는가? 이것은 중요한 문제로 남아 있다. 맬서스가 옳다면, 인구의 증가가 언젠가는 멈추어야 한다. 유일한 문제는 '어떻게,' '언제'이다. 낮은 출생률로 또는 과거 산업화 이전의 높은 사망률로 돌아감으로써 인구 증가가 멈춰질 것인가? 이것이 곧 일어날 것인가 아니면 몇 십 년 동안도 일어나지 않을 것인가?

그런 문제에 대한 해답은 특정 국가에게만 줄 수 있다. 서유럽 몇 나라에서는 출생과 사망률이 균형을 이루어, 인구가 벌써 성장을 멈추었다. 그러나 이런 나라들이 필요한 모든 자원을 가지고 있는 것은 아니다. 그들은 세계의 다른 지역에서 금속 광물이나 연료, 식량을 수입해야 한다. 사실, 아주 소수의 국가들만이 현재 인구를 부양하기에 알맞은 자원을 가지고 있을 뿐이고, 인구가 두세 배되는 경우는 말할 나위도 없다. 세계의 저개발 지역에서는 상황이 훨씬 더 험악하다

16. 비는 흔히 한쪽에 수직의 계수가 있는 속 빈 튜브인 우량계로 측정된다. 튜브의 크기와 수직 계수의 길이는 변할 수 있어서, 광범위하게 달라지는 비의 양을 측정할 수가 있다. 많은 우량계는 부분적인 뚜껑이 있어서 비가 내리는 시간과 측정 시간 사이에 생길 수 있는 증발의 양을 줄이는 데에 도움을 준다.

눈은 자를 사용하여 눈 속으로 땅바닥에 닿을 때까지 찔러 넣어 측정할 수 있다. 그러나 바람이 눈을 날려보내 깊이를 다르게 하기 때문에, 이 방법으로 정확한 측정을 하기란 어렵다. 한 지역에서 몇 가지 측정을 한 다음, 그 숫자의 평균을 낸다.

눈의 액체 등가물은 우량계를 눈으로 채워서 판단할 수 있다. 계기 안에 있는 눈 기둥이 녹을 때, 물의 양이 측정된다. 액체에 대한 눈의 비율은 눈의 밀도에 따라 다르다. 전형적으로, 눈 10인치는 물 1인치와 대략 같다. 그러나 건조하고 가루 같은 눈은 약 12인치가 물 1인치와 같다. 눈의 물기가 많을수록, 눈-액체의 비율은 낮아진다.

17. (1) 물 부족에 대한 가장 실제적인 접근은 물을 보존하는 것이다. 이것은 적게 쓰는 것이다. 공장들은 냉각용으로 사용한 물을 다시 사용할 수 있다. 뉴욕이나 시카고 같은 오래된 도시들은 물이 새는 급수관만을 수리해도 엄청난 양의 물을 절약할 수 있다. 그리고 사람들은 각 가정에서 물을 덜 사용할 수 있다.

농민들은 물을 덜 쓰는 관개 방식으로 바꿀 수 있다. 급수 통로들을 플라스틱이나 콘크리트로 배선하여 물

이 땅 속으로 새어 나가지 않도록 할 것이다. 물 부족으로 고생을 자주 겪는 지역에서는 물이 적게 드는 작물들을 재배할 수도 있다. 물에 염분이 있는 곳에서는 특별한 작물이 자란다. 염분이 있는 물에 잘 견디는 담배, 귀리, 밀 같은 것들이 있다.

어떤 사람들은 낭비를 줄이는 최선의 길은 물 값을 올리는 것이라고 생각한다. 대부분의 지역에서는 물이 현재 너무 싸서, 많은 사람들이 아낄 필요성을 느끼지 못한다. 만약 사람들이 물 값으로 더 많은 돈을 지불한다면, 물을 어떻게 써야 할 지 더욱 신경을 쓸 것이다.

아주 많은 물이 호수와 저수지에서 증발하여 떠난다. 이 손실을 멈출 수 있는 쉬운 방법을 찾을 수 없다. 찾아본 몇 가지 해결책들로는 지하 저수지에 물을 저장하는 것, 증발을 막기 위해 수면에 피막을 형성하는 화학 물질을 넣는 것, 또 태양과 바람을 피할 수 있는 저수지를 건설하는 것 등이 있다.

(2) 물은 깨끗해 보이지만, 많은 물질들이 들어가서 안전하지 못하게 할 수 있다. 그때 물이 오염되었다고 한다. 위험한 물질들은 냇물, 호수, 바다, 심지어 가정으로 들어오는 물까지, 어떤 수원(水源)이든 오염시킬 수 있다. 오늘날 이 세계에는 수천 가지의 위험한 물질들이 결국 우리의 물 속에 들어온다. 이 물질들은 물에 서식하는 수상 생물, 물 가까이 살고 있는 야생 동물, 그 물을 마시거나 오염된 물고기를 먹는 사람들의 건강에는 위험하다. 거의 모든 오염은 사람들에 의한 것이다.

세계의 인구가 적었을 때는, 냇물과 강들이 사람들이 버리는 쓰레기와 오물을 처리할 수가 있었다. 자연의 정화 체계가 물을 다시 깨끗하게 만드는 것을 도왔다. 바다나 호수, 강 심지어 육지의 물이 수증기로 올라가며 뒤에 불순물을 남긴다. 물은 다시 깨끗한 비나 눈으로 떨어진다. 이 순환은 여전히 작용한다. 하지만 현재 뒤에 남은 그 불순물은 너무도 많고 위험하다. 과거에는 대부분의 오염 물질들이 미생물에 분해되는 것들이었다. 즉, 물과 흙 속의 박테리아가 폐기물을 덜 해로운 물질로 분해할 수 있었다. 오늘날은 많은 오염 물질들이 미생물에 분해될 수 없다. 이런 오염 물질들은 박테리아에 의해 소화되지도, 햇빛에 분해되지도, 어떤 물질적 과정에도 단순화되지 않는 화학 물질이다. 예를 들어, 플라스틱은 수백 년 동안 변하지 않고 남아 있다. 자연은 그것들을 처분할 길이 없다.

18. 습지는 물을 품고 있기 때문에 비와 녹은 눈에 의한 범람을 통제할 수가 있다. 그것들은 많은 양의 물을 저장하고 서서히 방류한다. 그렇지 않으면 그 물은 피해를 입히거나, 자양분이 풍부한 흙을 싣고 바다로 얼른 흘러가 버린다.

습지의 울창한 식물들은 농지와 오폐수의 유실물 속에 있는 것들인 흙과 자양분을 붙들고 있다. 많은 곳에서 사람들은 습지를 자연의 폐수 공장으로 이용한다. 오폐수가 습지를 통해 흘러갈 때, 식물들은 인산염과 기타 오염 물질들을 제거한다.

오랫동안 사람들은 습지를 육지 개발에 장애가 되는 모기나 득실대는 황무지로 생각하였다. 사람들은 습지를 주택이나 농지, 공장용 땅으로 전환하기 위해 물을 빼내고, 흙으로 매웠다. 수로를 준설하여 선박의 통로를 만들면서 물가 식물들은 파괴되었다. 사람들은 습지를 오수와 기타 폐기물을 버리는 쓰레기 투기장으로 이용하였다. 물이 인간의 용도로 전환되면서 습지들이 추가로 없어지고, 댐이 건설되거나, 강줄기가 바뀌었다. 전문가들은 시간이 지나면서 세계 습지의 약 50%가 없어졌다고 진단하였다.

최근에는 사람들이 습지의 중요성을 인식하게 되면서 습지의 파괴가 완화되었다. 물고기와 농작물 같은 습지의 생산물들이 귀중하게 여겨질 뿐 아니라, 수질 정화나 범람 억제 같은 그들의 보이지 않는 서비스도 역시 귀중하게 여겨진다.